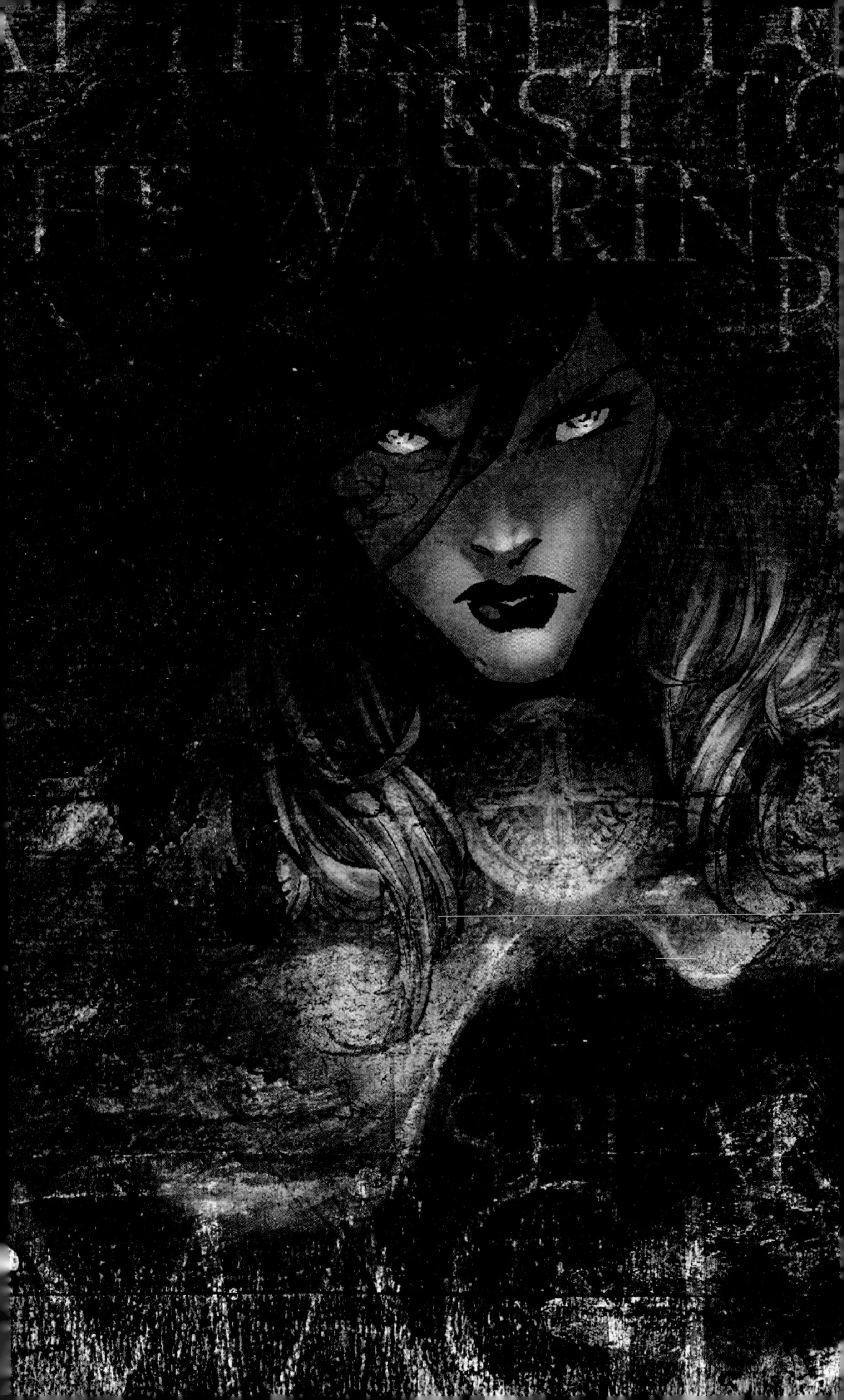

At the feet of Christ the first took her vow.

The Warring Sister,

Protector of the Faith,

Avenger of the Holy See,

By blood and honor the bearer of the spear of destiny—

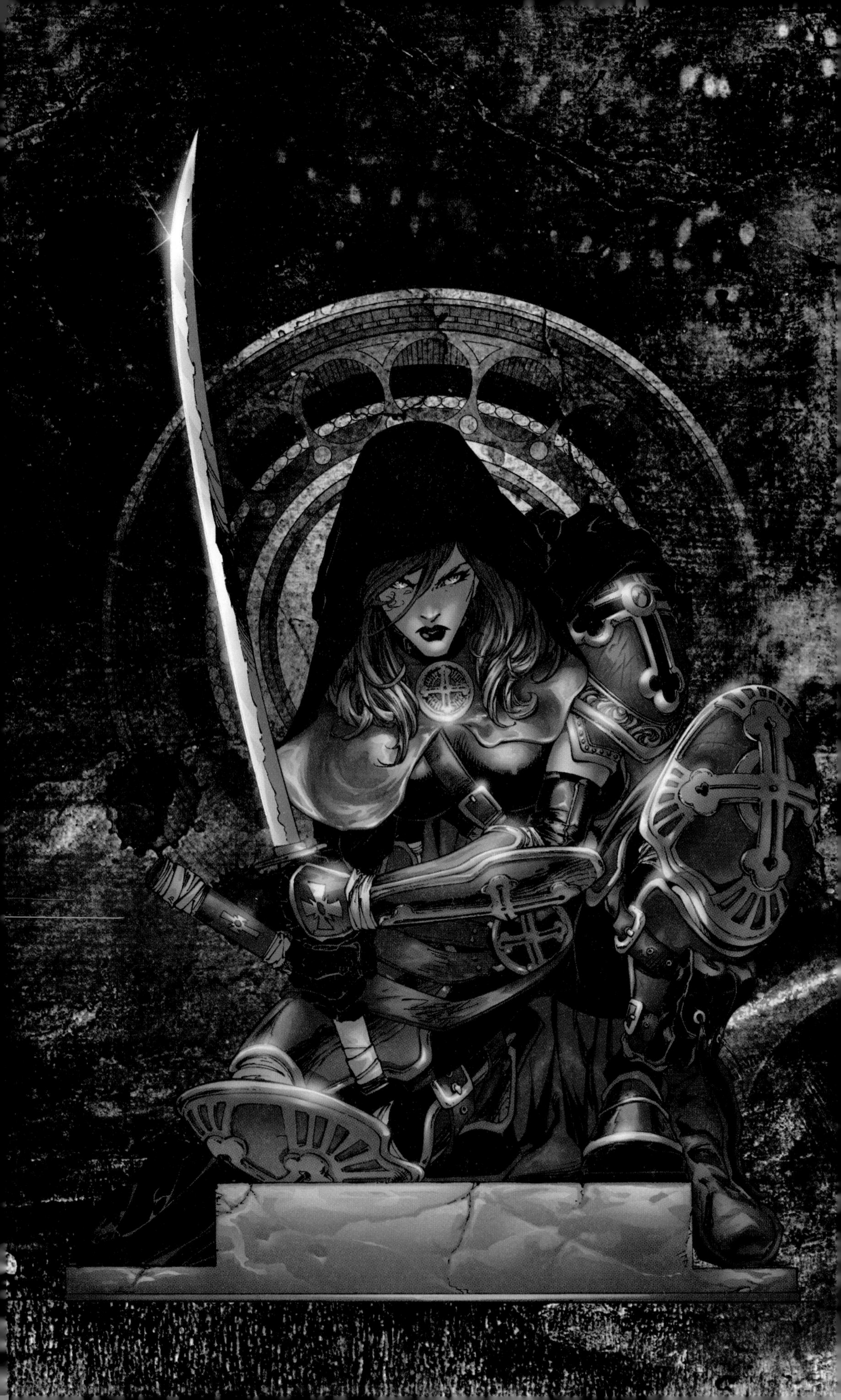

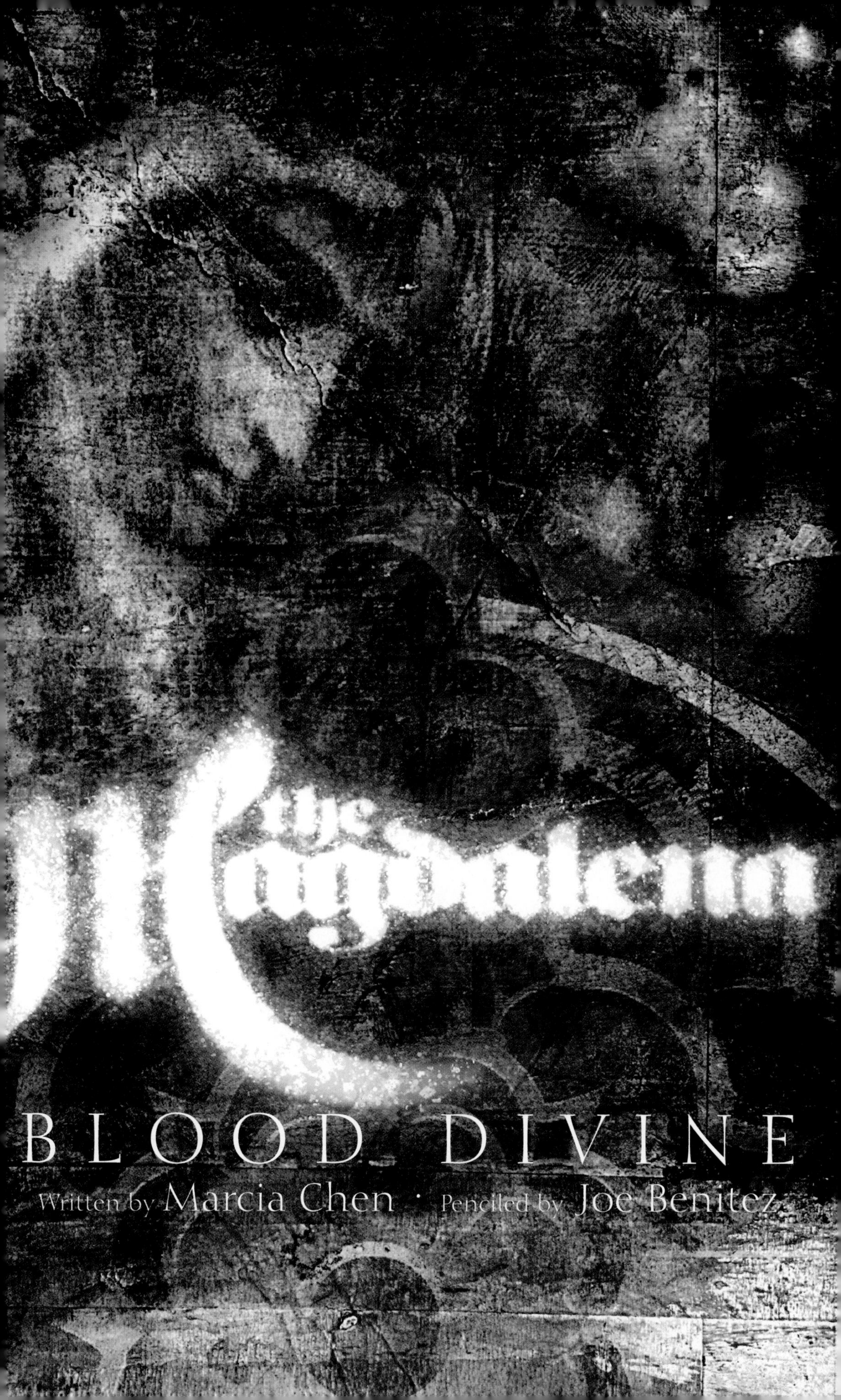
BLOOD DIVINE
Written by Marcia Chen · Penciled by Joe Benitez

ISBN: 1-58240-215-9

Published by Image Comics
MAGDALENA: BLOOD DIVINE, Vol. 1, 2002. FIRST PRINTING.
Office of Publication: 1071 North Batavia Street Suite A Orange, California 92867.
Magdalena™ it's logo, all related characters and their likenesses are ™ & © 2002 Top Cow Productions Inc.
ALL RIGHTS RESERVED. The entire contents of this book are © 2002 Top Cow Productions Inc. Any similarities to persons living or dead is purely coincidental. With the exception of artwork used for review purposes, none of the contents of this book may be reprinted in any form without the express written consent of Marc Silvestri or Top Cow Productions Inc.

PRINTED IN CANADA

To order by telephone call 1-888-TOPCOW1 (1-888-867-2691) or go to a comics shop near you.
To find the comics shop nearest you call 1-888-COMICBOOK (1-888-266-4226)

What did you think of this book? We love to hear from our readers.
Please email us at: fanmail@topcow.com.

or write to us at:
MAGDALENA c/o Top Cow Productions Inc.
10390 Santa Monica Blvd. Suite 110
Los Angeles, CA. 90025

for this edition
Book Design/Collected Editions Editor—Peter Steigerwald
Cover Art—Joe Benitez, Victor Llamas and Jonathan D. Smith
Cover Design—Peter Steigerwald
Managing Editor—Renae Geerlings
Editor In Chief—David Wohl
Editorial Assistants—Sina Grace, CJ Wilson and Joshua Reed
Production—Alvin Coats and Chaz Riggs

for Top Cow Productions Inc.
Marc Silvestri—chief executive officer
Matt Hawkins—president / chief operating officer
David Wohl—president of creative affairs / editor in chief
Peter Steigerwald—vp of publishing and design / art director
Renae Geerlings—managing editor
Frank Mastromauro—director of sales and marketing
Alvin Coats—special projects coordinator

for Image Comics
Jim Valentino—publisher
Brent Braun—director of production

INDIVIDUAL ILLUSTRATION CREDITS

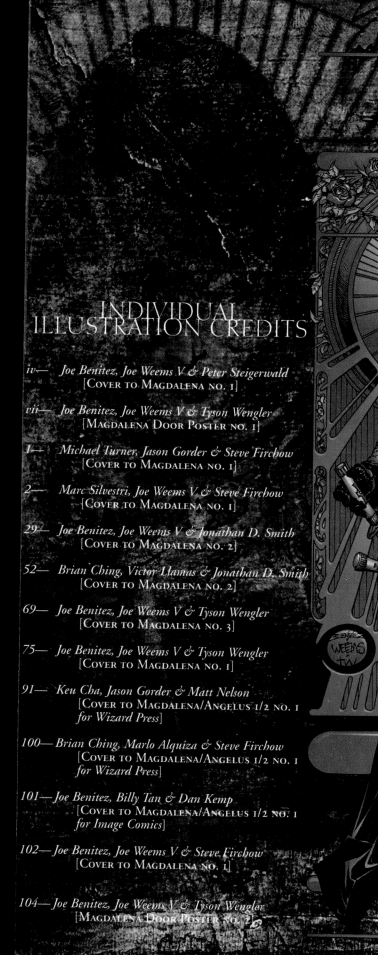

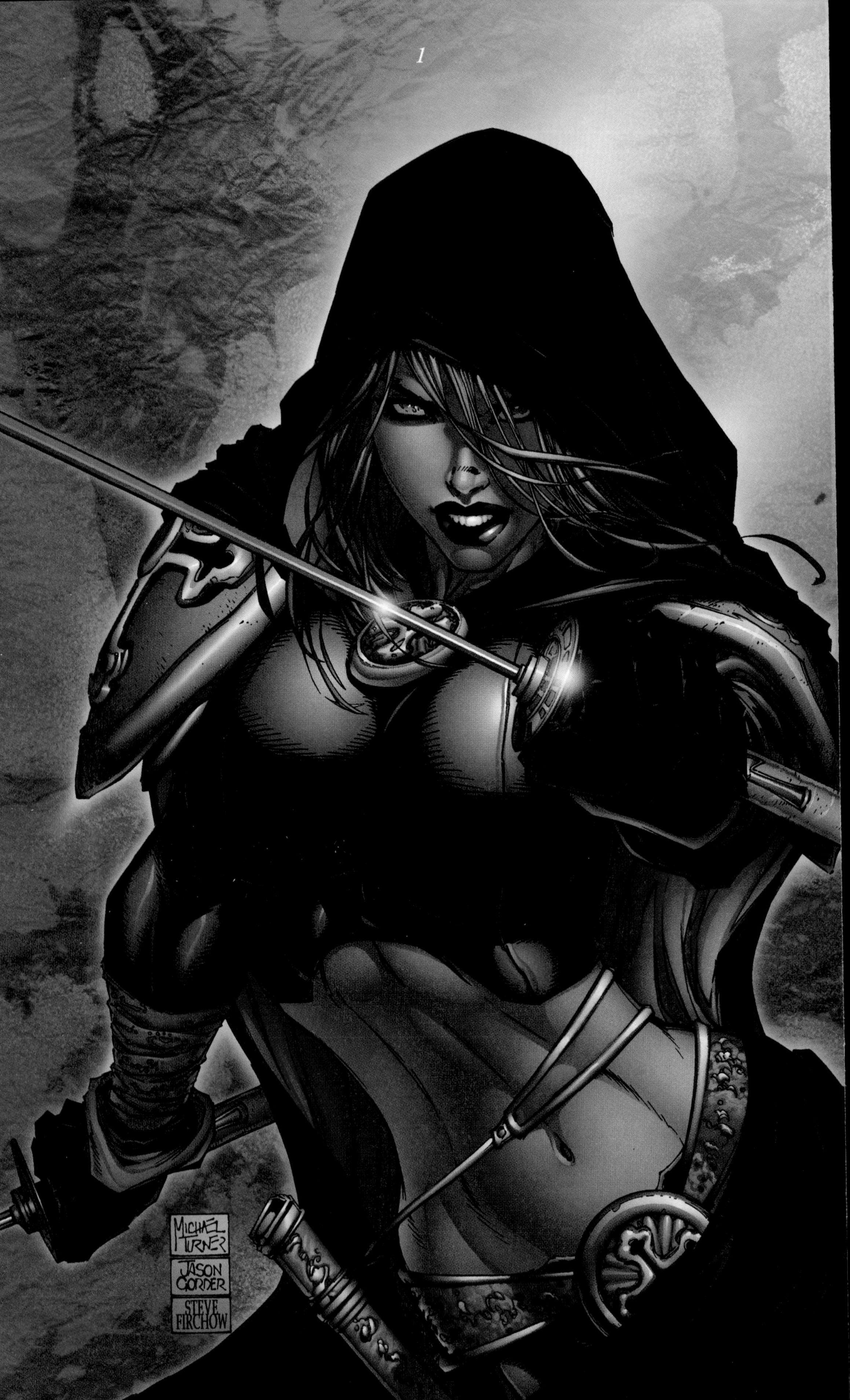
MICHAEL TURNER
JASON GORDER
STEVE FIRCHOW

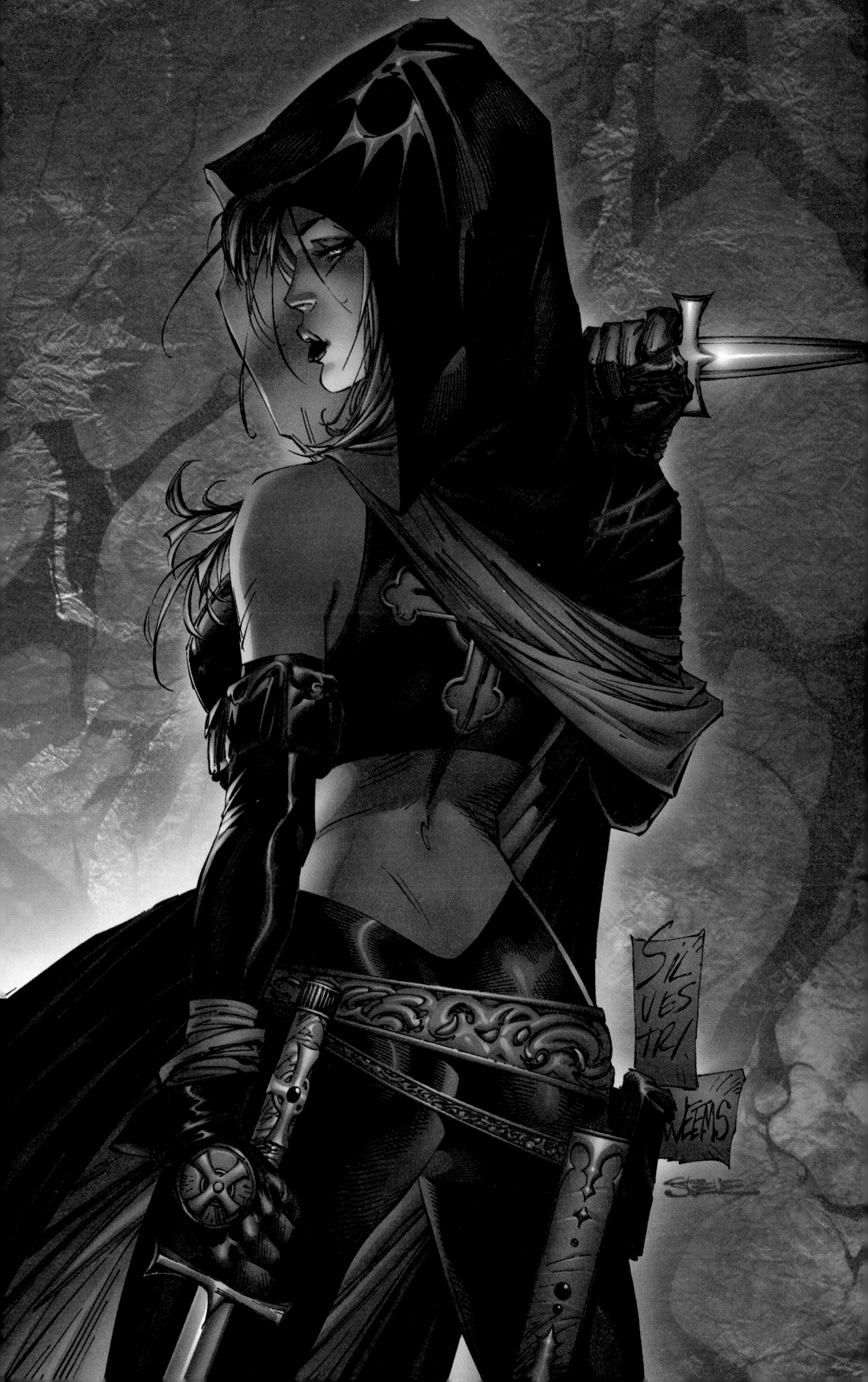
SILVESTRI
WEEMS

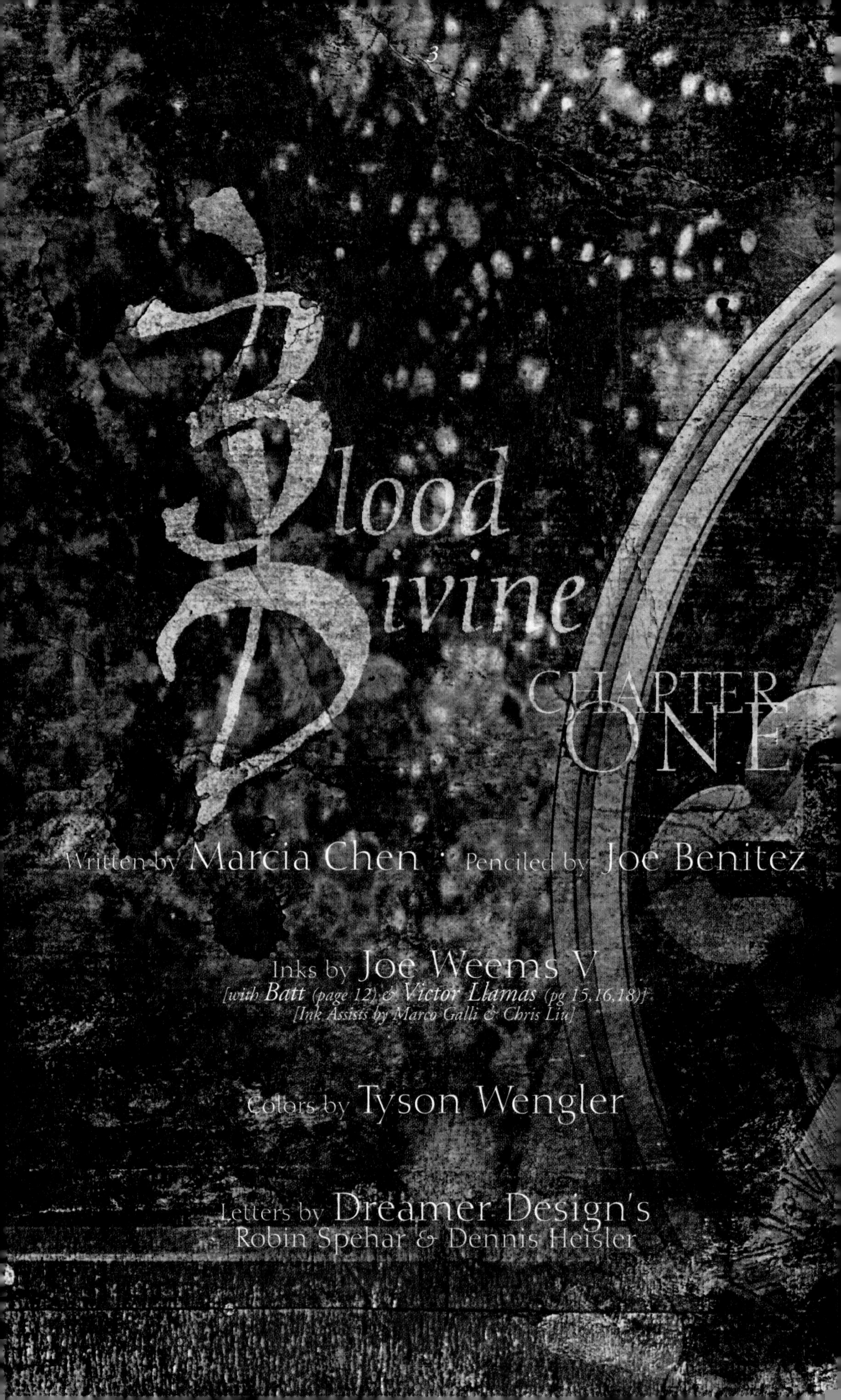

Blood Divine

Chapter One

Written by Marcia Chen · Penciled by Joe Benitez

Inks by Joe Weems V
[with Batt (page 12) & Victor Llamas (pg 15,16,18)]
[Ink Assists by Marco Galli & Chris Liu]

Colors by Tyson Wengler

Letters by Dreamer Design's
Robin Spehar & Dennis Heisler

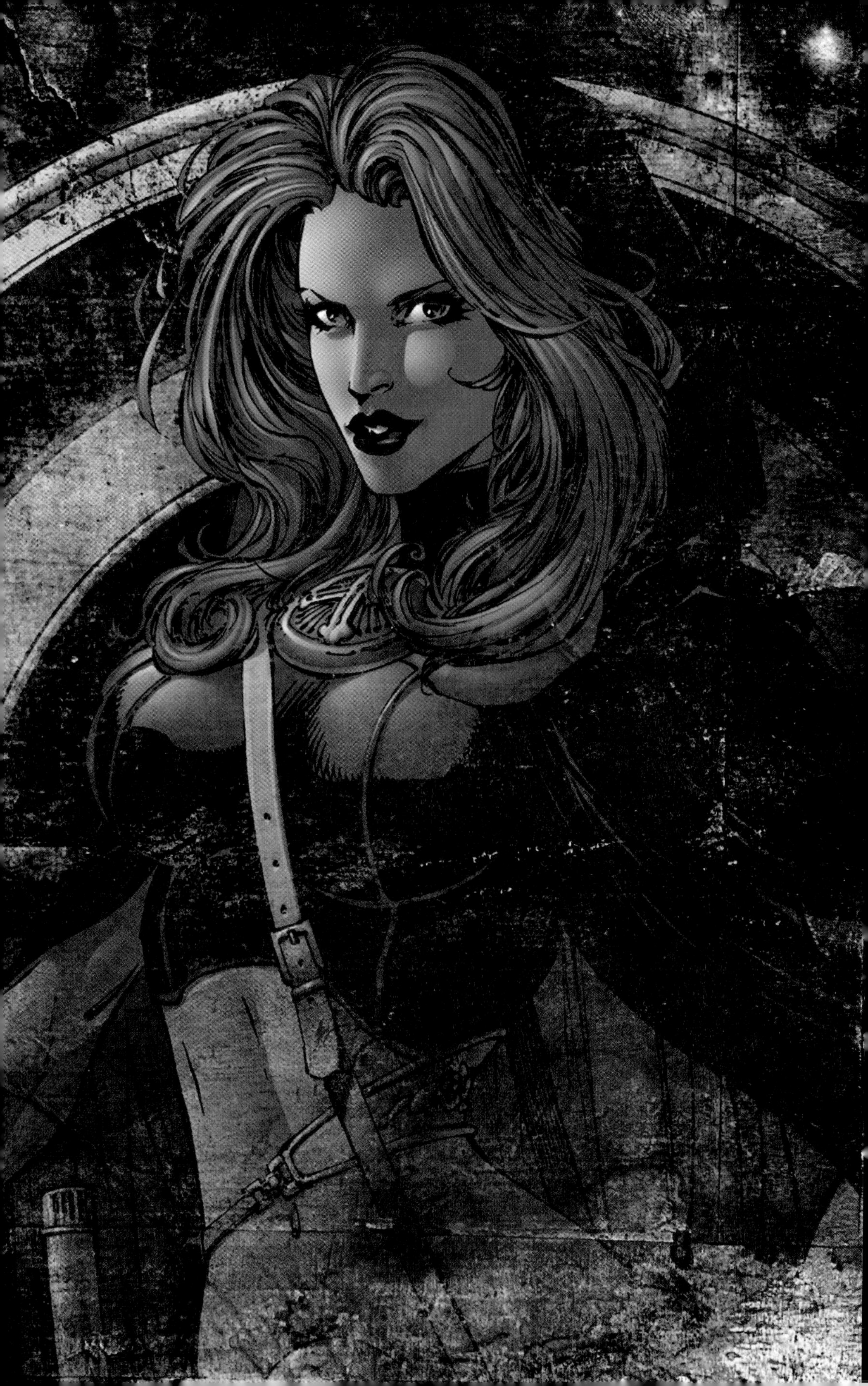

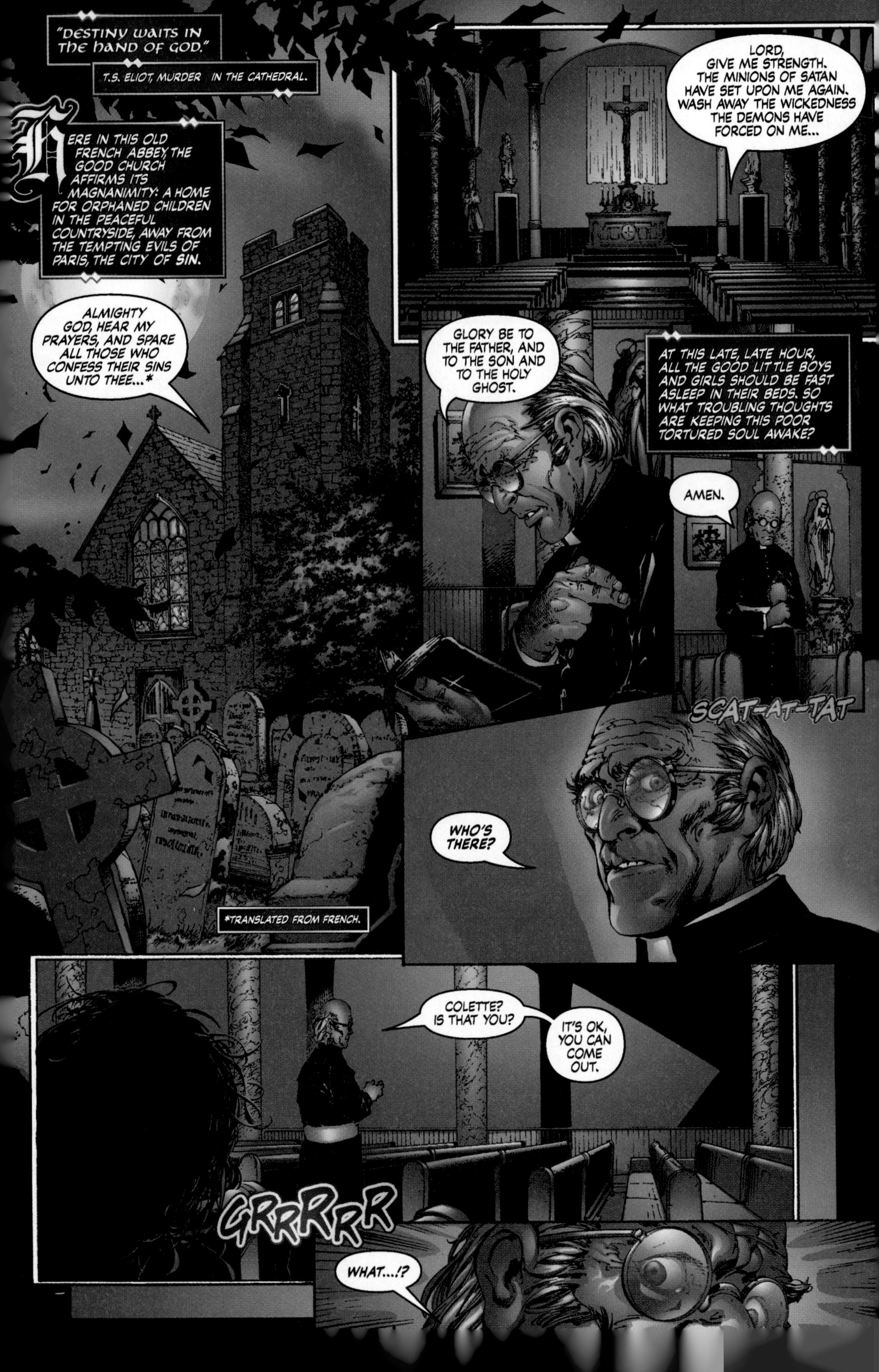
"DESTINY WAITS IN THE HAND OF GOD."
T.S. ELIOT, MURDER IN THE CATHEDRAL.
HERE IN THIS OLD FRENCH ABBEY, THE GOOD CHURCH AFFIRMS ITS MAGNANIMITY: A HOME FOR ORPHANED CHILDREN IN THE PEACEFUL COUNTRYSIDE, AWAY FROM THE TEMPTING EVILS OF PARIS, THE CITY OF SIN.
ALMIGHTY GOD, HEAR MY PRAYERS, AND SPARE ALL THOSE WHO CONFESS THEIR SINS UNTO THEE...*
*TRANSLATED FROM FRENCH.
LORD, GIVE ME STRENGTH. THE MINIONS OF SATAN HAVE SET UPON ME AGAIN. WASH AWAY THE WICKEDNESS THE DEMONS HAVE FORCED ON ME...
GLORY BE TO THE FATHER, AND TO THE SON AND TO THE HOLY GHOST.
AT THIS LATE, LATE HOUR, ALL THE GOOD LITTLE BOYS AND GIRLS SHOULD BE FAST ASLEEP IN THEIR BEDS. SO WHAT TROUBLING THOUGHTS ARE KEEPING THIS POOR TORTURED SOUL AWAKE?
AMEN.
SCAT-AT-TAT
WHO'S THERE?
COLETTE? IS THAT YOU?
IT'S OK, YOU CAN COME OUT.
GRRRRR
WHAT...!?

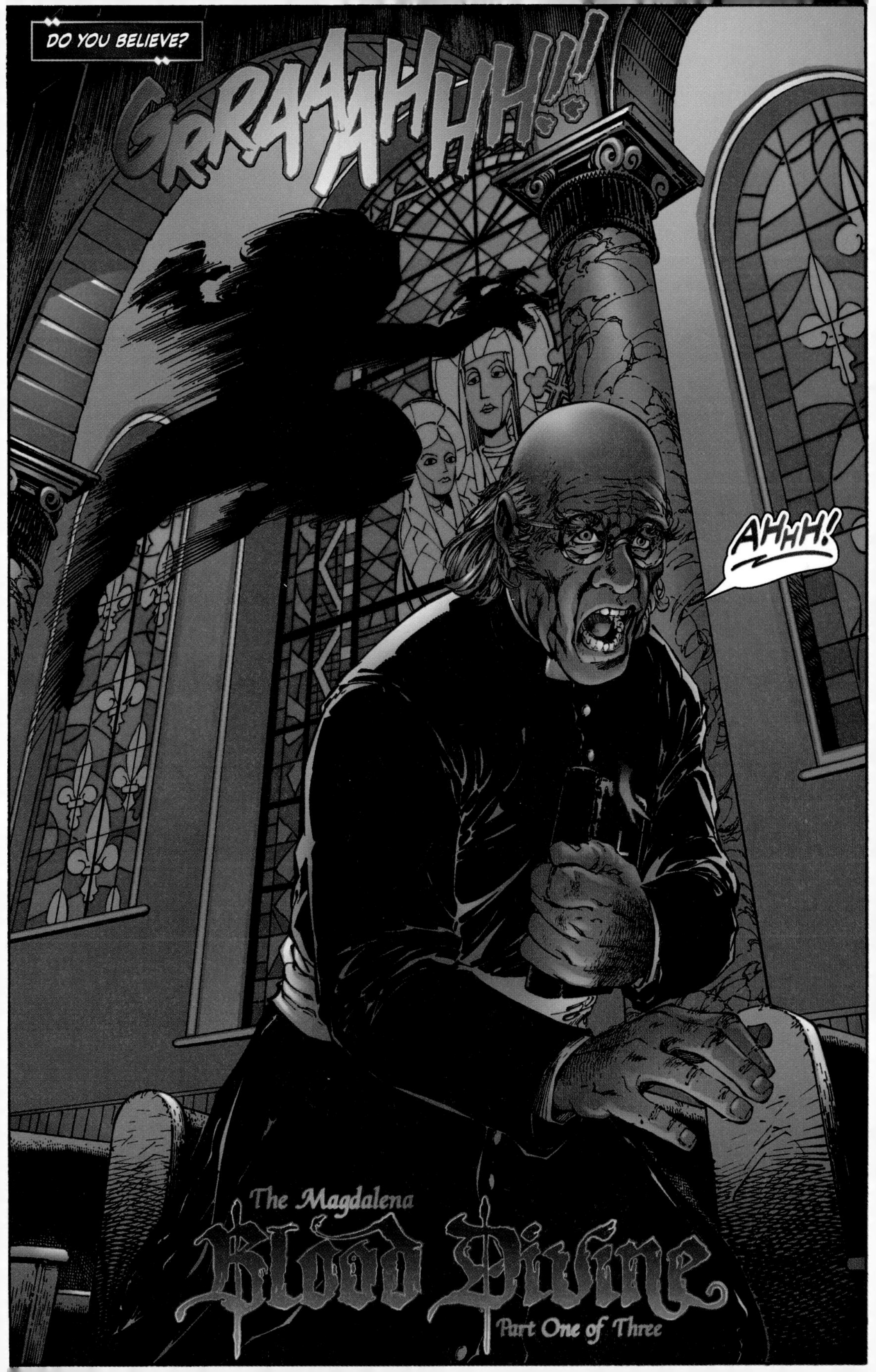
DO YOU BELIEVE?
GRRAAAHHH!!!
AHHH!
The Magdalena
Blood Divine
Part One of Three

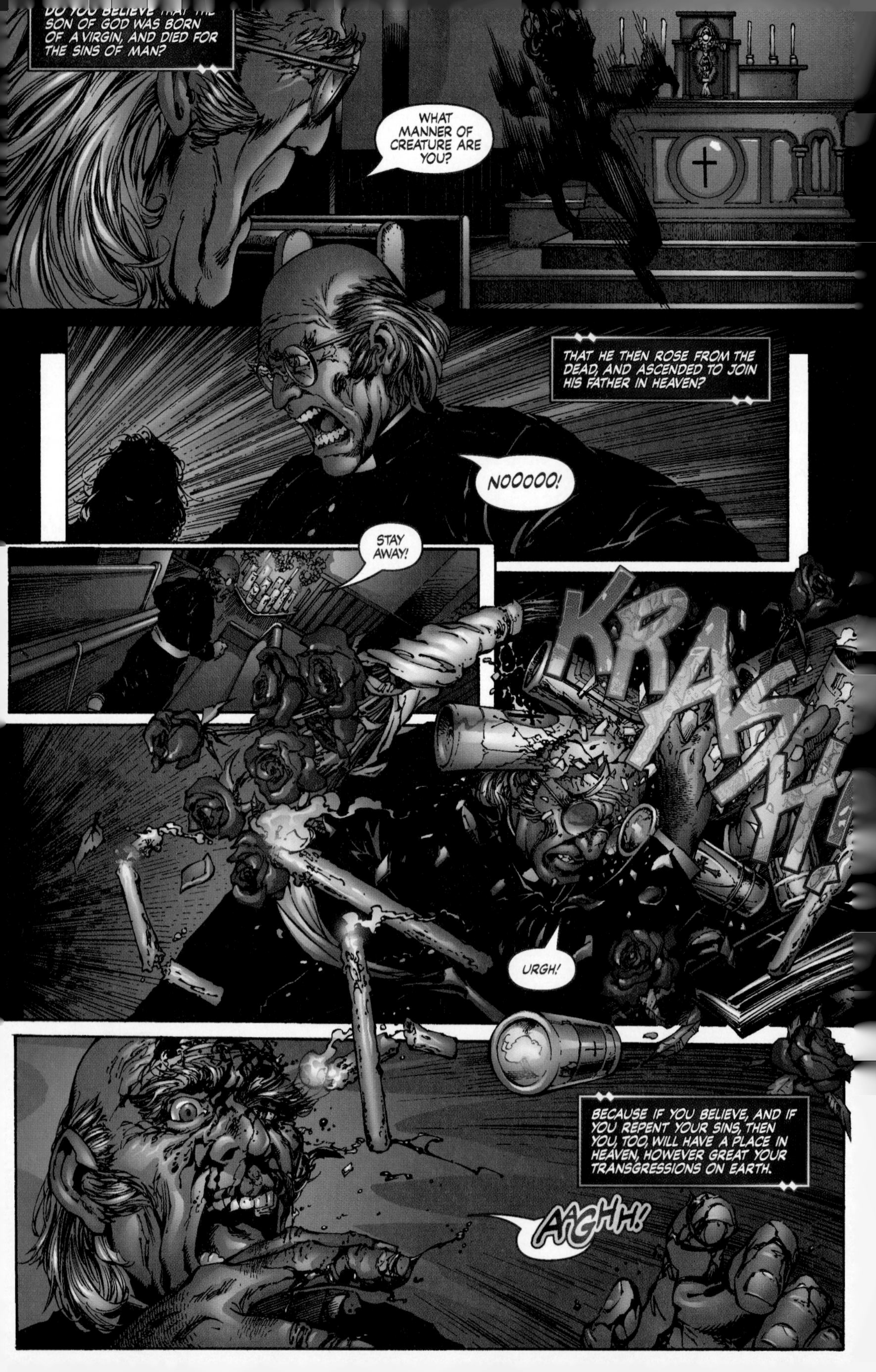
DO YOU BELIEVE THAT THE SON OF GOD WAS BORN OF A VIRGIN, AND DIED FOR THE SINS OF MAN?
WHAT MANNER OF CREATURE ARE YOU?
THAT HE THEN ROSE FROM THE DEAD, AND ASCENDED TO JOIN HIS FATHER IN HEAVEN?
NOOOOO!
STAY AWAY!
KRASH
URGH!
BECAUSE IF YOU BELIEVE, AND IF YOU REPENT YOUR SINS, THEN YOU, TOO, WILL HAVE A PLACE IN HEAVEN, HOWEVER GREAT YOUR TRANSGRESSIONS ON EARTH.
AAGHH!

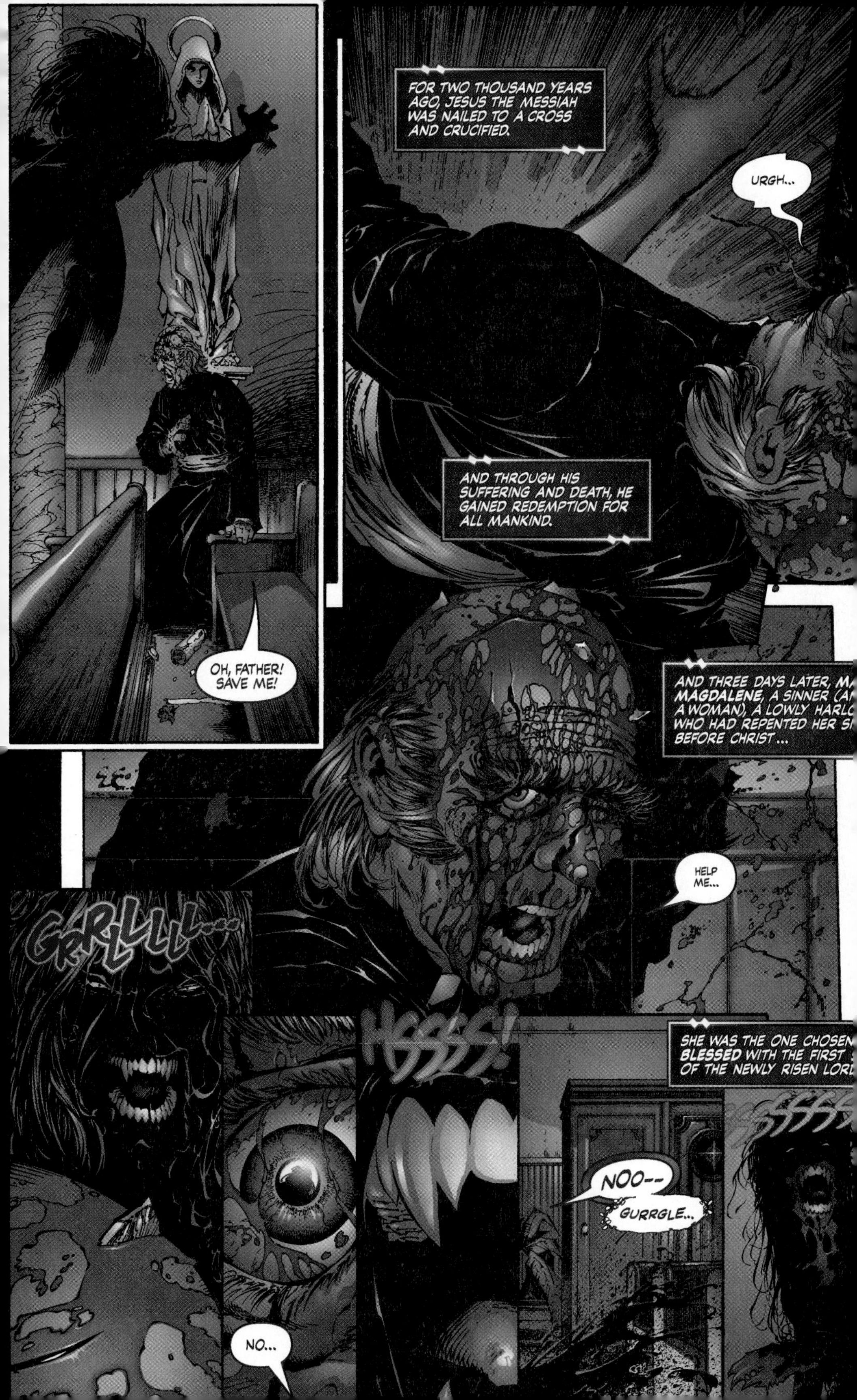
OH, FATHER! SAVE ME!
FOR TWO THOUSAND YEARS AGO, JESUS THE MESSIAH WAS NAILED TO A CROSS AND CRUCIFIED.
URGH...
AND THROUGH HIS SUFFERING AND DEATH, HE GAINED REDEMPTION FOR ALL MANKIND.
AND THREE DAYS LATER, MA MAGDALENE, A SINNER (AN A WOMAN), A LOWLY HARLO WHO HAD REPENTED HER SI BEFORE CHRIST...
HELP ME...
GRRLLLL...
SHE WAS THE ONE CHOSEN BLESSED WITH THE FIRST OF THE NEWLY RISEN LORD
HSSSS!
NOO--
GURRGLE...
NO...

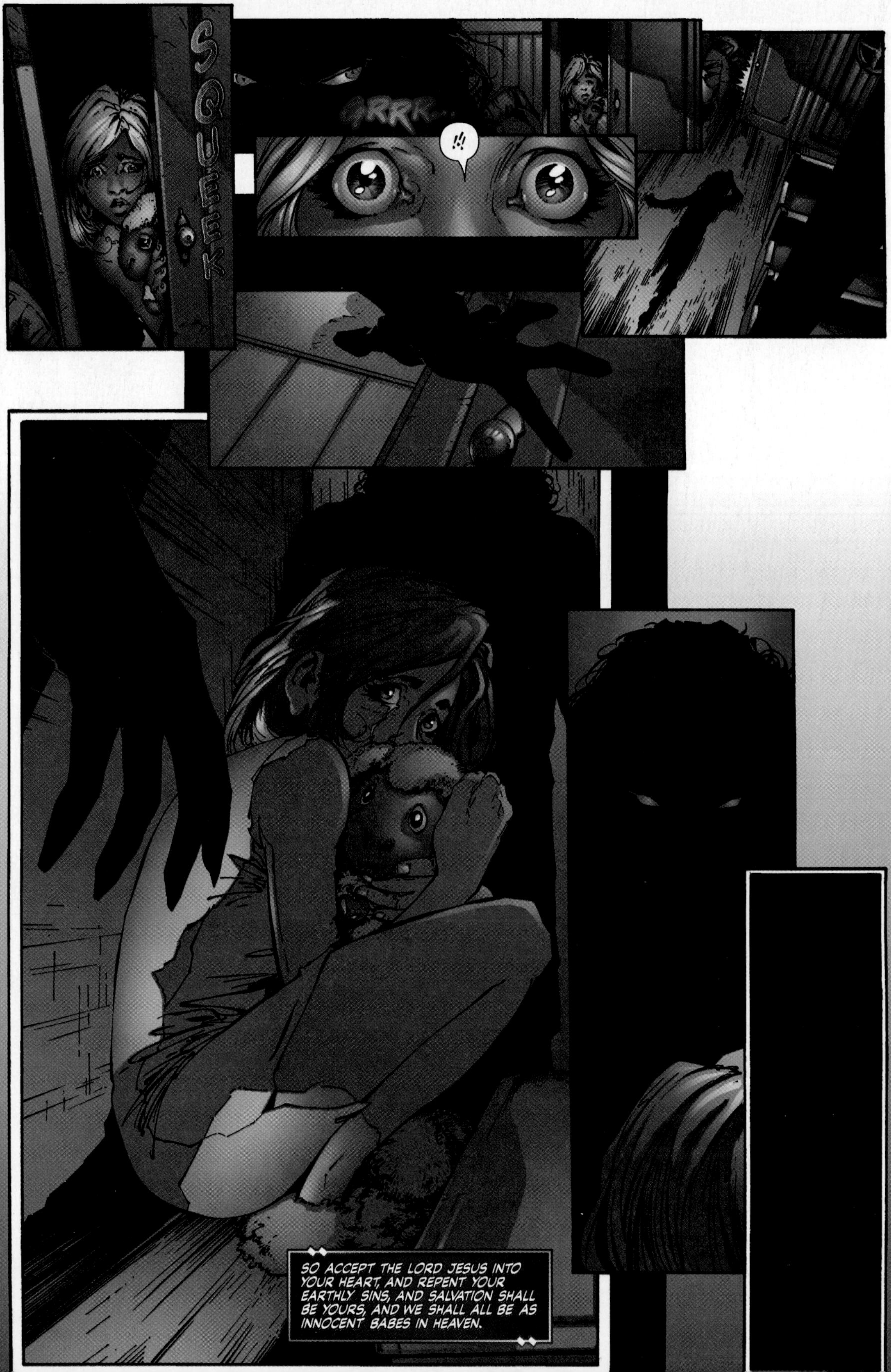
SQUEEK
GRRR...
!!!
SO ACCEPT THE LORD JESUS INTO YOUR HEART, AND REPENT YOUR EARTHLY SINS, AND SALVATION SHALL BE YOURS, AND WE SHALL ALL BE AS INNOCENT BABES IN HEAVEN.

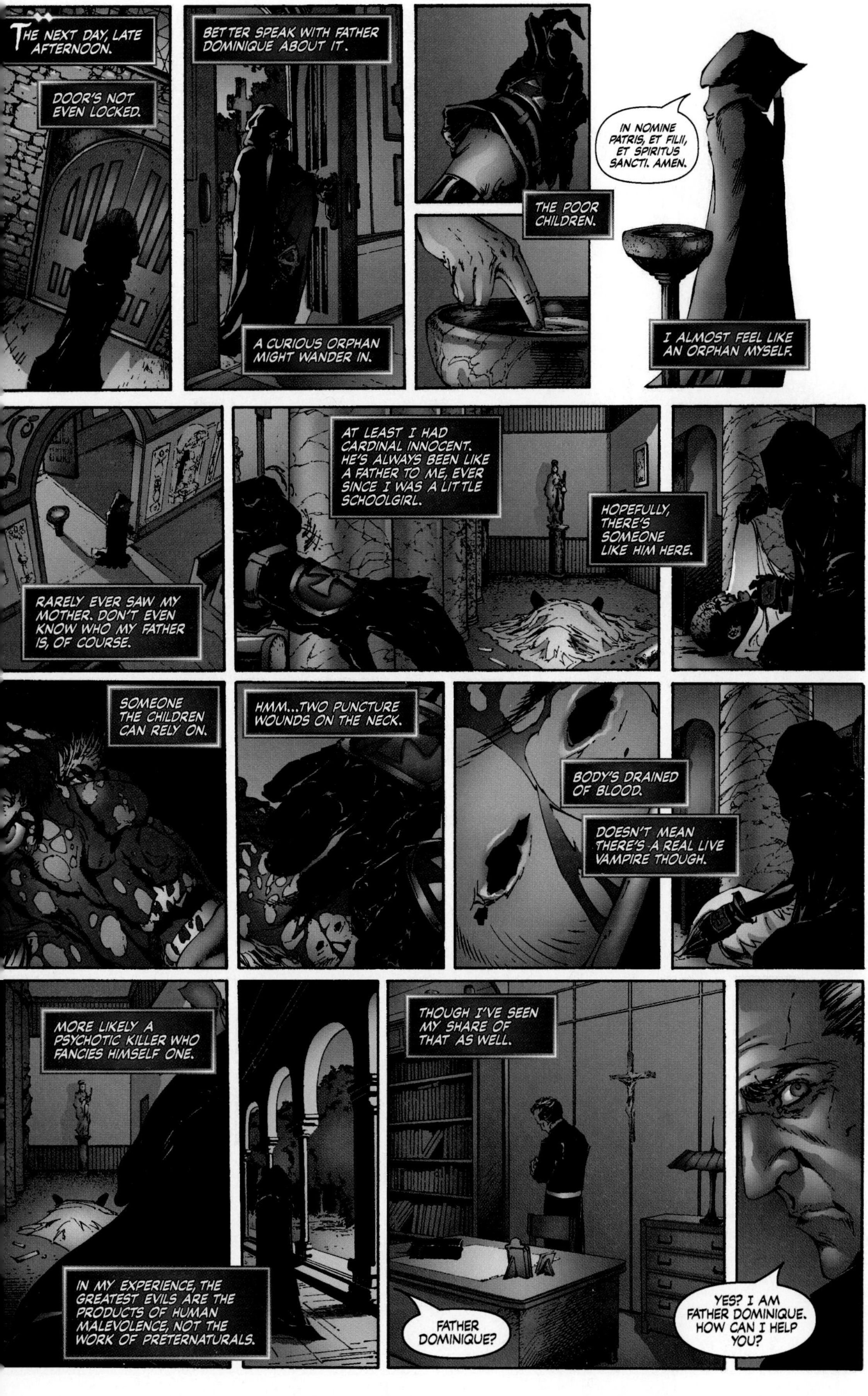
THE NEXT DAY, LATE AFTERNOON.
DOOR'S NOT EVEN LOCKED.
BETTER SPEAK WITH FATHER DOMINIQUE ABOUT IT.
A CURIOUS ORPHAN MIGHT WANDER IN.
THE POOR CHILDREN.
IN NOMINE PATRIS, ET FILII, ET SPIRITUS SANCTI. AMEN.
I ALMOST FEEL LIKE AN ORPHAN MYSELF.
RARELY EVER SAW MY MOTHER. DON'T EVEN KNOW WHO MY FATHER IS, OF COURSE.
AT LEAST I HAD CARDINAL INNOCENT. HE'S ALWAYS BEEN LIKE A FATHER TO ME, EVER SINCE I WAS A LITTLE SCHOOLGIRL.
HOPEFULLY, THERE'S SOMEONE LIKE HIM HERE.
SOMEONE THE CHILDREN CAN RELY ON.
HMM...TWO PUNCTURE WOUNDS ON THE NECK.
BODY'S DRAINED OF BLOOD.
DOESN'T MEAN THERE'S A REAL LIVE VAMPIRE THOUGH.
MORE LIKELY A PSYCHOTIC KILLER WHO FANCIES HIMSELF ONE.
IN MY EXPERIENCE, THE GREATEST EVILS ARE THE PRODUCTS OF HUMAN MALEVOLENCE, NOT THE WORK OF PRETERNATURALS.
THOUGH I'VE SEEN MY SHARE OF THAT AS WELL.
FATHER DOMINIQUE?
YES? I AM FATHER DOMINIQUE. HOW CAN I HELP YOU?

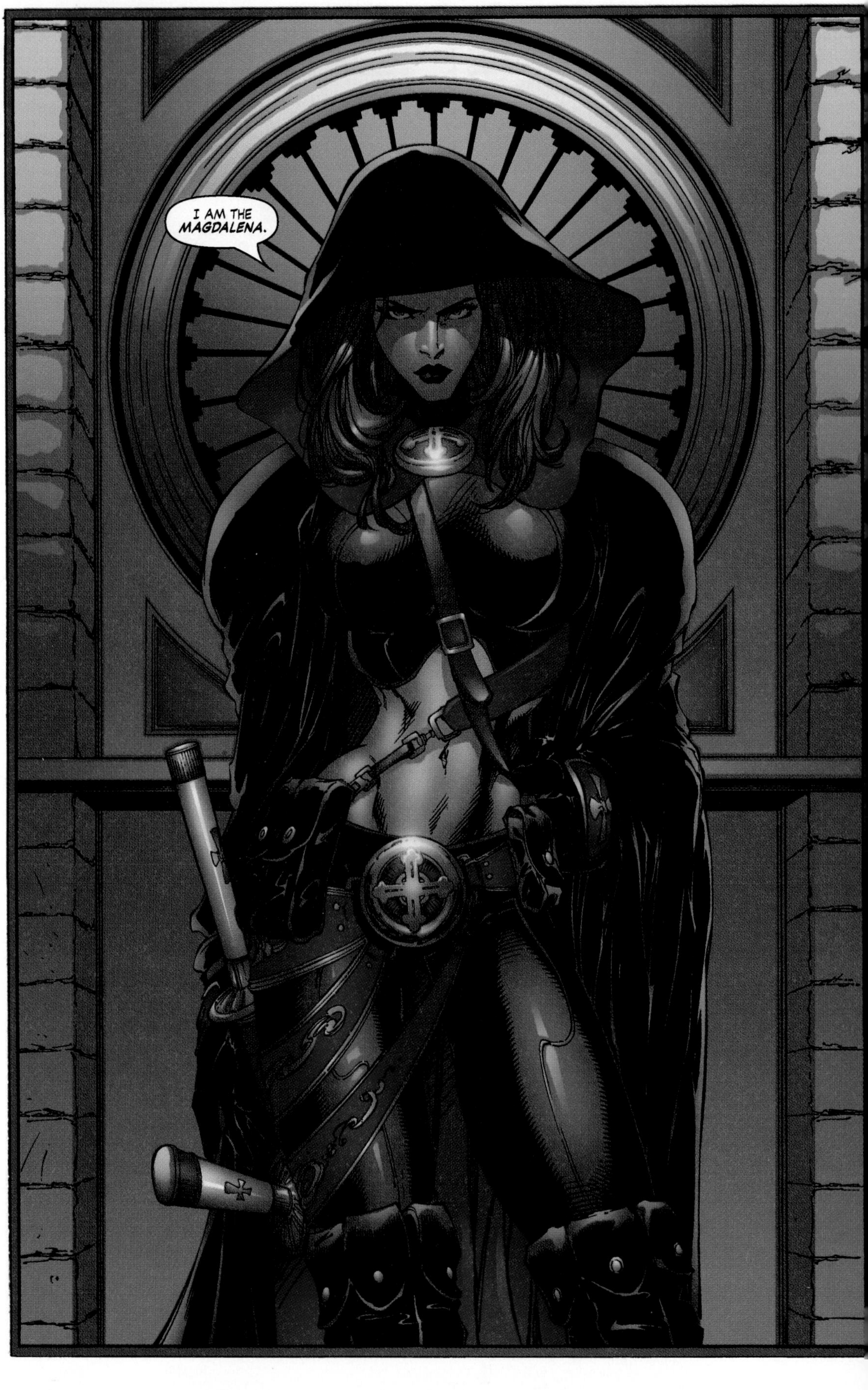
I AM THE MAGDALENA.

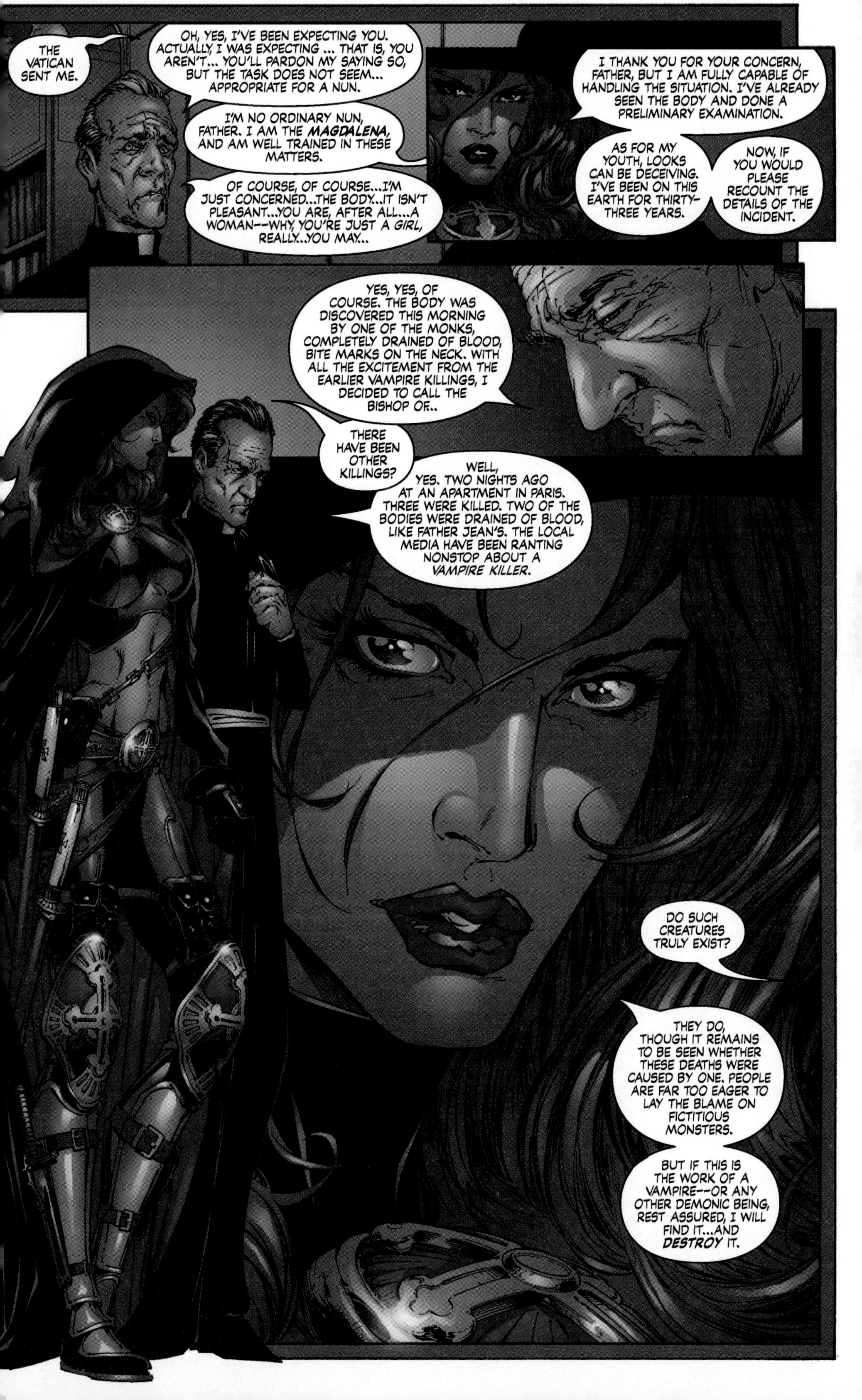

THE VATICAN SENT ME.
OH, YES, I'VE BEEN EXPECTING YOU. ACTUALLY, I WAS EXPECTING ... THAT IS, YOU AREN'T... YOU'LL PARDON MY SAYING SO, BUT THE TASK DOES NOT SEEM... APPROPRIATE FOR A NUN.
I'M NO ORDINARY NUN, FATHER. I AM THE *MAGDALENA,* AND AM WELL TRAINED IN THESE MATTERS.
OF COURSE, OF COURSE...I'M JUST CONCERNED...THE BODY...IT ISN'T PLEASANT...YOU ARE, AFTER ALL...A WOMAN--WHY, YOU'RE JUST A *GIRL,* REALLY...YOU MAY...
I THANK YOU FOR YOUR CONCERN, FATHER, BUT I AM FULLY CAPABLE OF HANDLING THE SITUATION. I'VE ALREADY SEEN THE BODY AND DONE A PRELIMINARY EXAMINATION.
AS FOR MY YOUTH, LOOKS CAN BE DECEIVING. I'VE BEEN ON THIS EARTH FOR THIRTY-THREE YEARS.
NOW, IF YOU WOULD PLEASE RECOUNT THE DETAILS OF THE INCIDENT.
YES, YES, OF COURSE. THE BODY WAS DISCOVERED THIS MORNING BY ONE OF THE MONKS, COMPLETELY DRAINED OF BLOOD, BITE MARKS ON THE NECK. WITH ALL THE EXCITEMENT FROM THE EARLIER VAMPIRE KILLINGS, I DECIDED TO CALL THE BISHOP OF..
THERE HAVE BEEN OTHER KILLINGS?
WELL, YES. TWO NIGHTS AGO AT AN APARTMENT IN PARIS. THREE WERE KILLED. TWO OF THE BODIES WERE DRAINED OF BLOOD, LIKE FATHER JEAN'S. THE LOCAL MEDIA HAVE BEEN RANTING NONSTOP ABOUT A *VAMPIRE KILLER.*
DO SUCH CREATURES TRULY EXIST?
THEY DO, THOUGH IT REMAINS TO BE SEEN WHETHER THESE DEATHS WERE CAUSED BY ONE. PEOPLE ARE FAR TOO EAGER TO LAY THE BLAME ON FICTITIOUS MONSTERS.
BUT IF THIS IS THE WORK OF A VAMPIRE--OR ANY OTHER DEMONIC BEING, REST ASSURED, I WILL FIND IT...AND ***DESTROY*** IT.

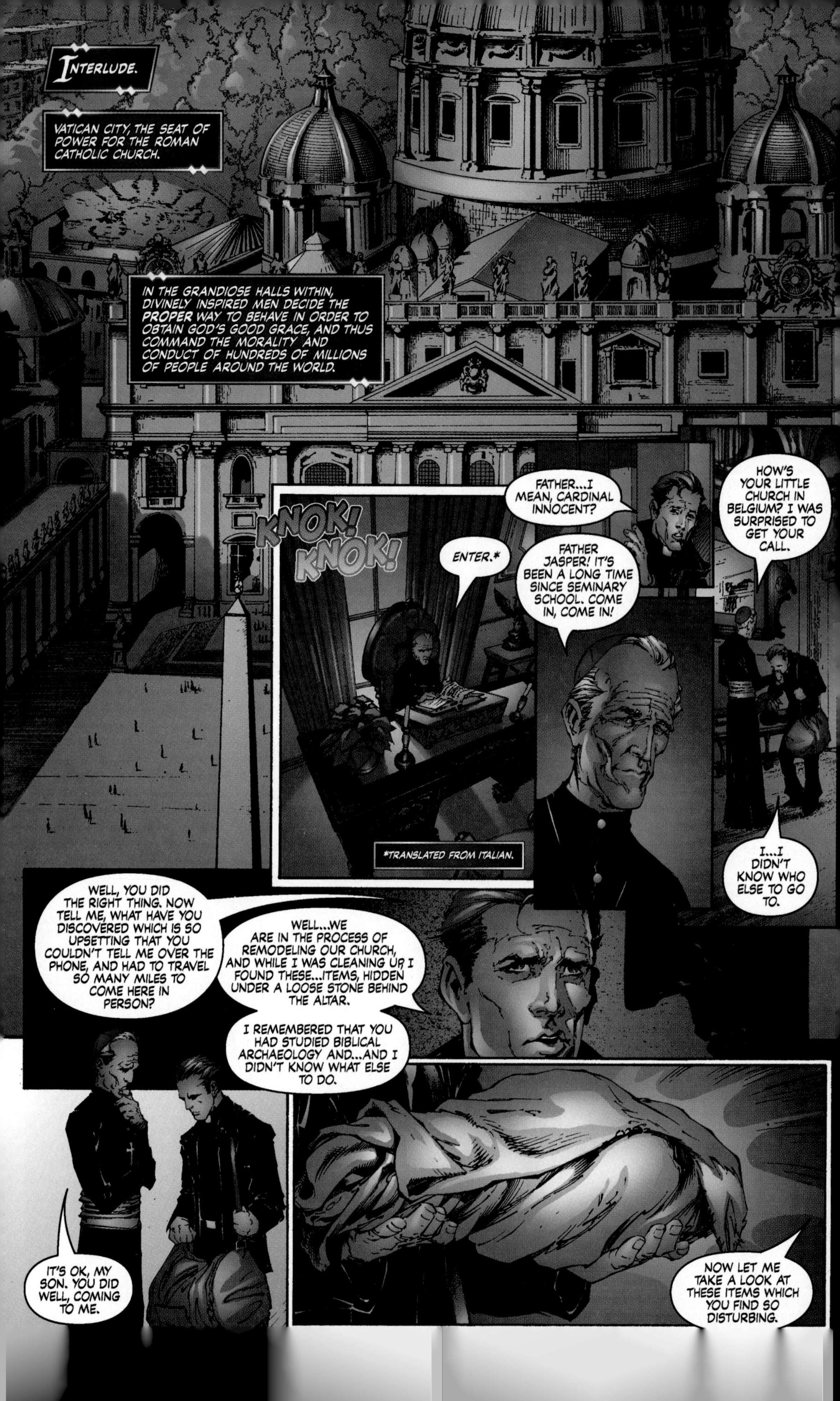
INTERLUDE.
VATICAN CITY, THE SEAT OF POWER FOR THE ROMAN CATHOLIC CHURCH.
IN THE GRANDIOSE HALLS WITHIN, DIVINELY INSPIRED MEN DECIDE THE PROPER WAY TO BEHAVE IN ORDER TO OBTAIN GOD'S GOOD GRACE, AND THUS COMMAND THE MORALITY AND CONDUCT OF HUNDREDS OF MILLIONS OF PEOPLE AROUND THE WORLD.
KNOK! KNOK!
ENTER.*
*TRANSLATED FROM ITALIAN.
FATHER...I MEAN, CARDINAL INNOCENT?
FATHER JASPER! IT'S BEEN A LONG TIME SINCE SEMINARY SCHOOL. COME IN, COME IN!
HOW'S YOUR LITTLE CHURCH IN BELGIUM? I WAS SURPRISED TO GET YOUR CALL.
I...I DIDN'T KNOW WHO ELSE TO GO TO.
WELL, YOU DID THE RIGHT THING. NOW TELL ME, WHAT HAVE YOU DISCOVERED WHICH IS SO UPSETTING THAT YOU COULDN'T TELL ME OVER THE PHONE, AND HAD TO TRAVEL SO MANY MILES TO COME HERE IN PERSON?
WELL...WE ARE IN THE PROCESS OF REMODELING OUR CHURCH, AND WHILE I WAS CLEANING UP, I FOUND THESE...ITEMS, HIDDEN UNDER A LOOSE STONE BEHIND THE ALTAR.
I REMEMBERED THAT YOU HAD STUDIED BIBLICAL ARCHAEOLOGY AND...AND I DIDN'T KNOW WHAT ELSE TO DO.
IT'S OK, MY SON. YOU DID WELL, COMING TO ME.
NOW LET ME TAKE A LOOK AT THESE ITEMS WHICH YOU FIND SO DISTURBING.

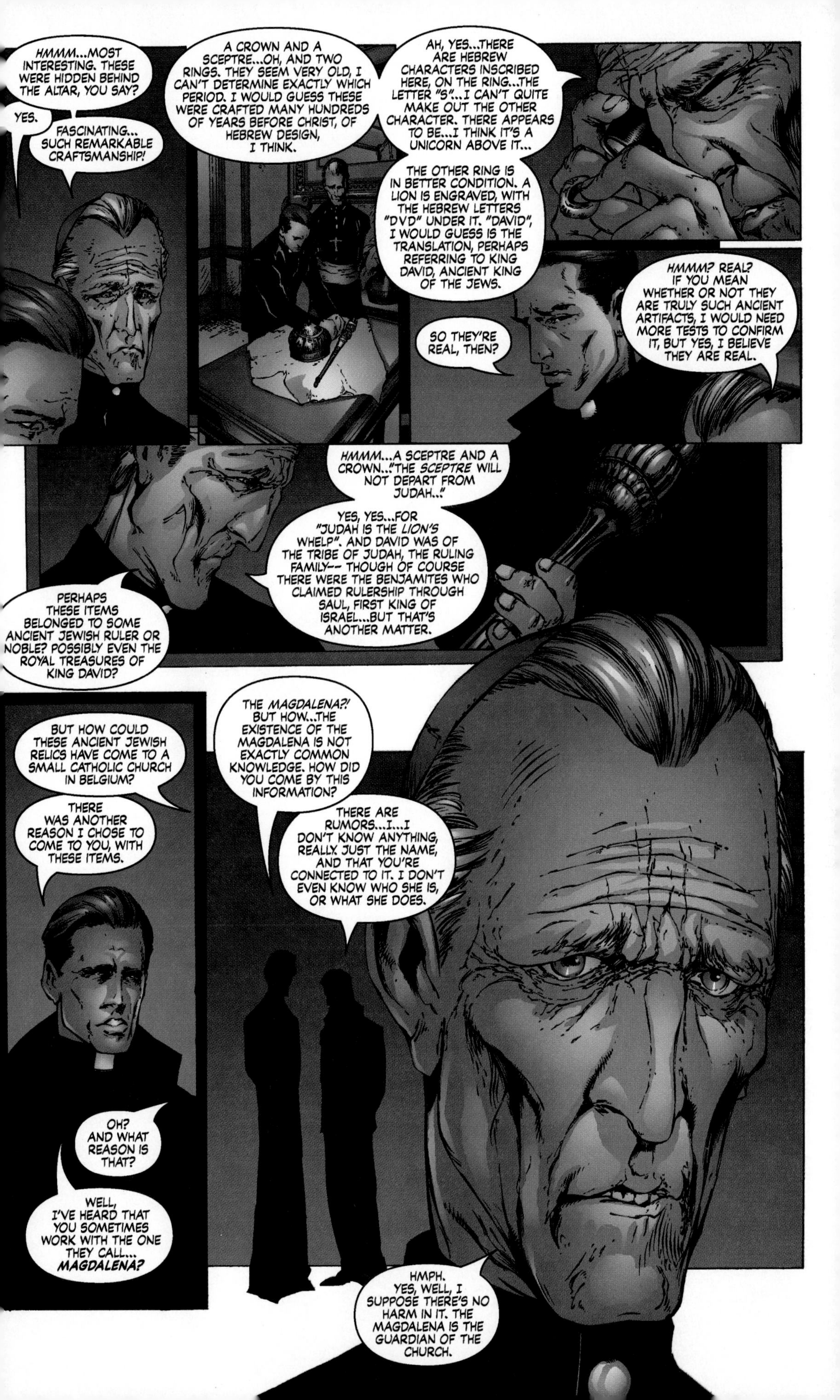
HMMM...MOST INTERESTING. THESE WERE HIDDEN BEHIND THE ALTAR, YOU SAY?
YES.
FASCINATING... SUCH REMARKABLE CRAFTSMANSHIP!
A CROWN AND A SCEPTRE...OH, AND TWO RINGS. THEY SEEM VERY OLD, I CAN'T DETERMINE EXACTLY WHICH PERIOD. I WOULD GUESS THESE WERE CRAFTED MANY HUNDREDS OF YEARS BEFORE CHRIST, OF HEBREW DESIGN, I THINK.
AH, YES...THERE ARE HEBREW CHARACTERS INSCRIBED HERE, ON THE RING...THE LETTER "S"...I CAN'T QUITE MAKE OUT THE OTHER CHARACTER. THERE APPEARS TO BE...I THINK IT'S A UNICORN ABOVE IT...
THE OTHER RING IS IN BETTER CONDITION. A LION IS ENGRAVED, WITH THE HEBREW LETTERS "DVD" UNDER IT. "DAVID", I WOULD GUESS IS THE TRANSLATION, PERHAPS REFERRING TO KING DAVID, ANCIENT KING OF THE JEWS.
SO THEY'RE REAL, THEN?
HMMM? REAL? IF YOU MEAN WHETHER OR NOT THEY ARE TRULY SUCH ANCIENT ARTIFACTS, I WOULD NEED MORE TESTS TO CONFIRM IT, BUT YES, I BELIEVE THEY ARE REAL.
HMMM...A SCEPTRE AND A CROWN..."THE SCEPTRE WILL NOT DEPART FROM JUDAH..."
YES, YES...FOR "JUDAH IS THE LION'S WHELP". AND DAVID WAS OF THE TRIBE OF JUDAH, THE RULING FAMILY-- THOUGH OF COURSE THERE WERE THE BENJAMITES WHO CLAIMED RULERSHIP THROUGH SAUL, FIRST KING OF ISRAEL...BUT THAT'S ANOTHER MATTER.
PERHAPS THESE ITEMS BELONGED TO SOME ANCIENT JEWISH RULER OR NOBLE? POSSIBLY EVEN THE ROYAL TREASURES OF KING DAVID?
BUT HOW COULD THESE ANCIENT JEWISH RELICS HAVE COME TO A SMALL CATHOLIC CHURCH IN BELGIUM?
THERE WAS ANOTHER REASON I CHOSE TO COME TO YOU, WITH THESE ITEMS.
OH? AND WHAT REASON IS THAT?
WELL, I'VE HEARD THAT YOU SOMETIMES WORK WITH THE ONE THEY CALL... MAGDALENA?
THE MAGDALENA?! BUT HOW...THE EXISTENCE OF THE MAGDALENA IS NOT EXACTLY COMMON KNOWLEDGE. HOW DID YOU COME BY THIS INFORMATION?
THERE ARE RUMORS...I...I DON'T KNOW ANYTHING, REALLY. JUST THE NAME, AND THAT YOU'RE CONNECTED TO IT. I DON'T EVEN KNOW WHO SHE IS, OR WHAT SHE DOES.
HMPH. YES, WELL, I SUPPOSE THERE'S NO HARM IN IT. THE MAGDALENA IS THE GUARDIAN OF THE CHURCH.

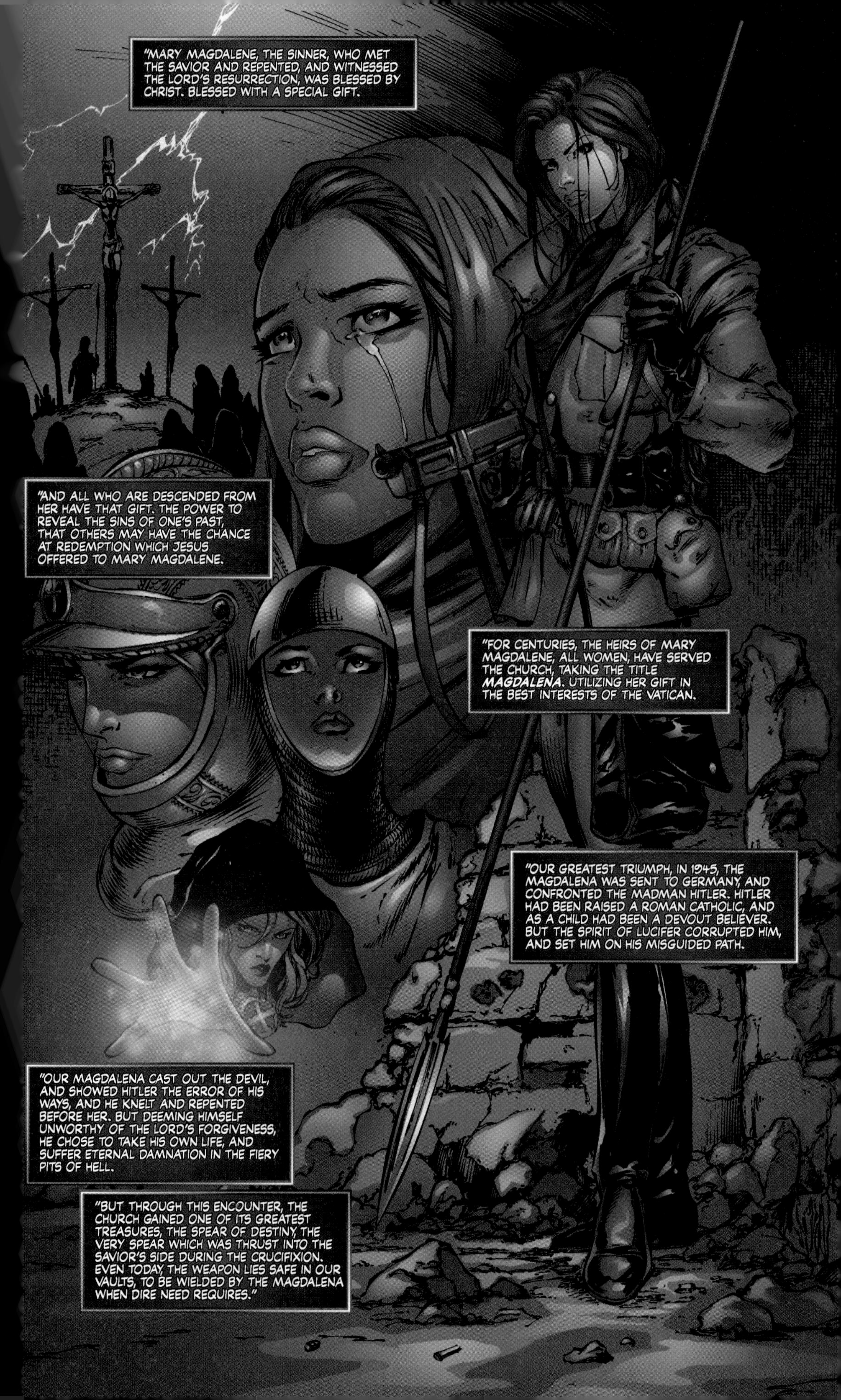
"MARY MAGDALENE, THE SINNER, WHO MET THE SAVIOR AND REPENTED, AND WITNESSED THE LORD'S RESURRECTION, WAS BLESSED BY CHRIST. BLESSED WITH A SPECIAL GIFT.
"AND ALL WHO ARE DESCENDED FROM HER HAVE THAT GIFT. THE POWER TO REVEAL THE SINS OF ONE'S PAST, THAT OTHERS MAY HAVE THE CHANCE AT REDEMPTION WHICH JESUS OFFERED TO MARY MAGDALENE.
"FOR CENTURIES, THE HEIRS OF MARY MAGDALENE, ALL WOMEN, HAVE SERVED THE CHURCH, TAKING THE TITLE *MAGDALENA*. UTILIZING HER GIFT IN THE BEST INTERESTS OF THE VATICAN.
"OUR GREATEST TRIUMPH, IN 1945, THE MAGDALENA WAS SENT TO GERMANY, AND CONFRONTED THE MADMAN HITLER. HITLER HAD BEEN RAISED A ROMAN CATHOLIC, AND AS A CHILD HAD BEEN A DEVOUT BELIEVER. BUT THE SPIRIT OF LUCIFER CORRUPTED HIM, AND SET HIM ON HIS MISGUIDED PATH.
"OUR MAGDALENA CAST OUT THE DEVIL, AND SHOWED HITLER THE ERROR OF HIS WAYS, AND HE KNELT AND REPENTED BEFORE HER. BUT DEEMING HIMSELF UNWORTHY OF THE LORD'S FORGIVENESS, HE CHOSE TO TAKE HIS OWN LIFE, AND SUFFER ETERNAL DAMNATION IN THE FIERY PITS OF HELL.
"BUT THROUGH THIS ENCOUNTER, THE CHURCH GAINED ONE OF ITS GREATEST TREASURES, THE SPEAR OF DESTINY, THE VERY SPEAR WHICH WAS THRUST INTO THE SAVIOR'S SIDE DURING THE CRUCIFIXION. EVEN TODAY, THE WEAPON LIES SAFE IN OUR VAULTS, TO BE WIELDED BY THE MAGDALENA WHEN DIRE NEED REQUIRES."

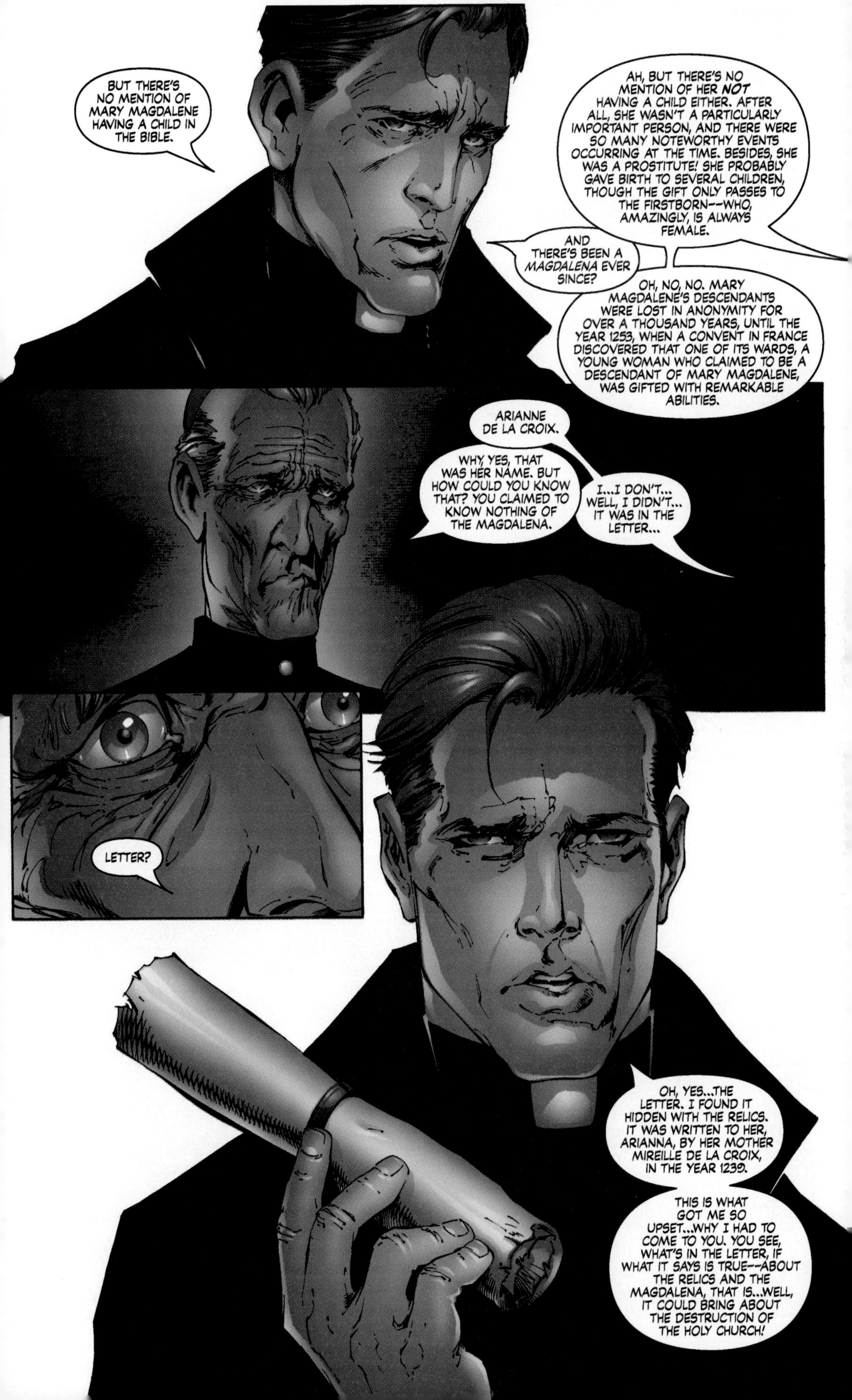
BUT THERE'S NO MENTION OF MARY MAGDALENE HAVING A CHILD IN THE BIBLE.
AH, BUT THERE'S NO MENTION OF HER *NOT* HAVING A CHILD EITHER. AFTER ALL, SHE WASN'T A PARTICULARLY IMPORTANT PERSON, AND THERE WERE SO MANY NOTEWORTHY EVENTS OCCURRING AT THE TIME. BESIDES, SHE WAS A PROSTITUTE! SHE PROBABLY GAVE BIRTH TO SEVERAL CHILDREN, THOUGH THE GIFT ONLY PASSES TO THE FIRSTBORN--WHO, AMAZINGLY, IS ALWAYS FEMALE.
AND THERE'S BEEN A *MAGDALENA* EVER SINCE?
OH, NO, NO. MARY MAGDALENE'S DESCENDANTS WERE LOST IN ANONYMITY FOR OVER A THOUSAND YEARS, UNTIL THE YEAR 1253, WHEN A CONVENT IN FRANCE DISCOVERED THAT ONE OF ITS WARDS, A YOUNG WOMAN WHO CLAIMED TO BE A DESCENDANT OF MARY MAGDALENE, WAS GIFTED WITH REMARKABLE ABILITIES.
ARIANNE DE LA CROIX.
WHY, YES, THAT WAS HER NAME. BUT HOW COULD YOU KNOW THAT? YOU CLAIMED TO KNOW NOTHING OF THE MAGDALENA.
I...I DON'T... WELL, I DIDN'T... IT WAS IN THE LETTER...
LETTER?
OH, YES...THE LETTER. I FOUND IT HIDDEN WITH THE RELICS. IT WAS WRITTEN TO HER, ARIANNA, BY HER MOTHER MIREILLE DE LA CROIX, IN THE YEAR 1239.
THIS IS WHAT GOT ME SO UPSET...WHY I HAD TO COME TO YOU. YOU SEE, WHAT'S IN THE LETTER, IF WHAT IT SAYS IS TRUE--ABOUT THE RELICS AND THE MAGDALENA, THAT IS...WELL, IT COULD BRING ABOUT THE DESTRUCTION OF THE HOLY CHURCH!

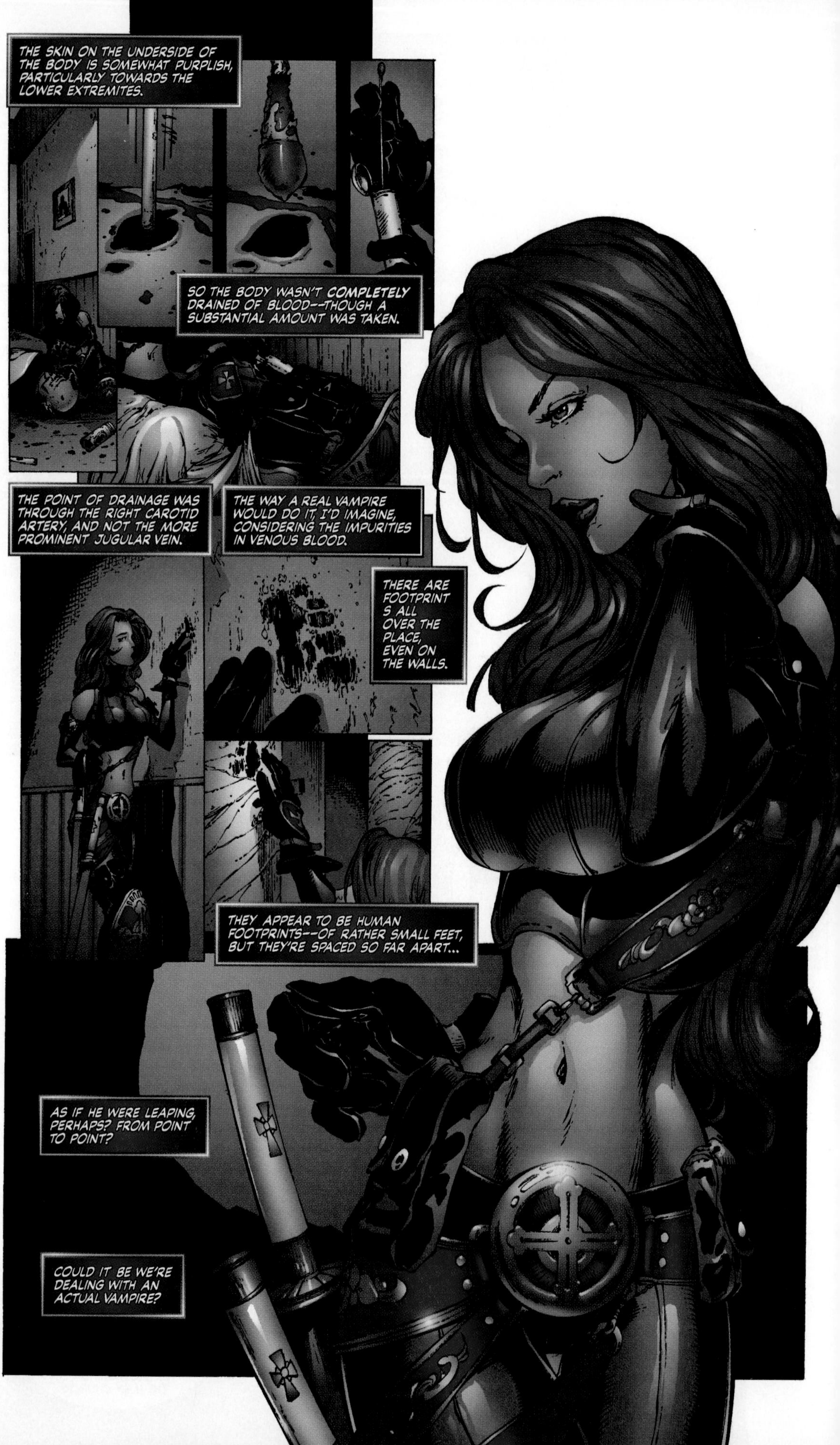
THE SKIN ON THE UNDERSIDE OF THE BODY IS SOMEWHAT PURPLISH, PARTICULARLY TOWARDS THE LOWER EXTREMITES.
SO THE BODY WASN'T COMPLETELY DRAINED OF BLOOD--THOUGH A SUBSTANTIAL AMOUNT WAS TAKEN.
THE POINT OF DRAINAGE WAS THROUGH THE RIGHT CAROTID ARTERY, AND NOT THE MORE PROMINENT JUGULAR VEIN.
THE WAY A REAL VAMPIRE WOULD DO IT, I'D IMAGINE, CONSIDERING THE IMPURITIES IN VENOUS BLOOD.
THERE ARE FOOTPRINT S ALL OVER THE PLACE, EVEN ON THE WALLS.
THEY APPEAR TO BE HUMAN FOOTPRINTS--OF RATHER SMALL FEET, BUT THEY'RE SPACED SO FAR APART...
AS IF HE WERE LEAPING, PERHAPS? FROM POINT TO POINT?
COULD IT BE WE'RE DEALING WITH AN ACTUAL VAMPIRE?

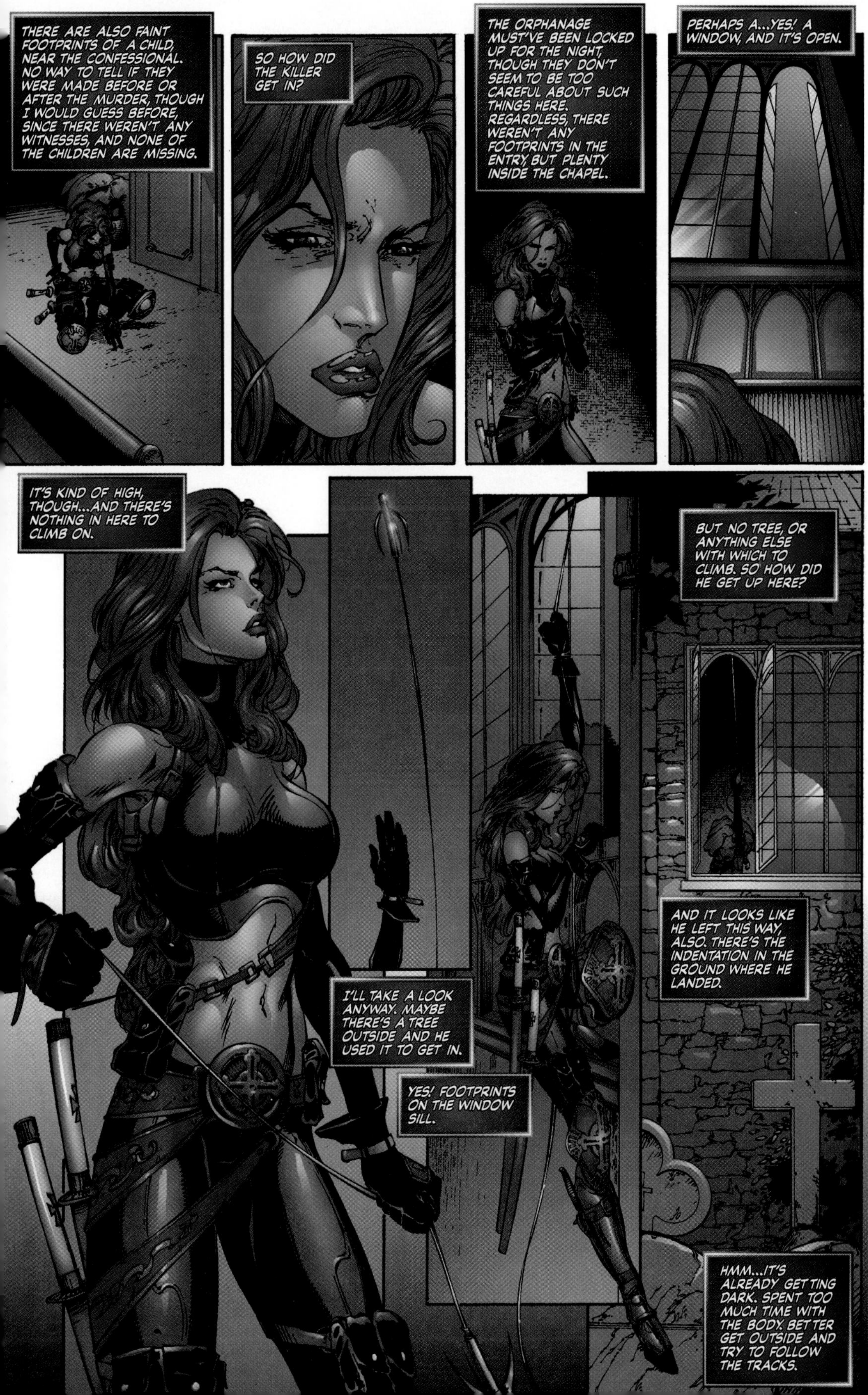
THERE ARE ALSO FAINT FOOTPRINTS OF A CHILD, NEAR THE CONFESSIONAL. NO WAY TO TELL IF THEY WERE MADE BEFORE OR AFTER THE MURDER, THOUGH I WOULD GUESS BEFORE, SINCE THERE WEREN'T ANY WITNESSES, AND NONE OF THE CHILDREN ARE MISSING.
SO HOW DID THE KILLER GET IN?
THE ORPHANAGE MUST'VE BEEN LOCKED UP FOR THE NIGHT, THOUGH THEY DON'T SEEM TO BE TOO CAREFUL ABOUT SUCH THINGS HERE. REGARDLESS, THERE WEREN'T ANY FOOTPRINTS IN THE ENTRY, BUT PLENTY INSIDE THE CHAPEL.
PERHAPS A...YES! A WINDOW, AND IT'S OPEN.
IT'S KIND OF HIGH, THOUGH...AND THERE'S NOTHING IN HERE TO CLIMB ON.
I'LL TAKE A LOOK ANYWAY. MAYBE THERE'S A TREE OUTSIDE AND HE USED IT TO GET IN.
YES! FOOTPRINTS ON THE WINDOW SILL.
BUT NO TREE, OR ANYTHING ELSE WITH WHICH TO CLIMB. SO HOW DID HE GET UP HERE?
AND IT LOOKS LIKE HE LEFT THIS WAY, ALSO. THERE'S THE INDENTATION IN THE GROUND WHERE HE LANDED.
HMM...IT'S ALREADY GETTING DARK. SPENT TOO MUCH TIME WITH THE BODY. BETTER GET OUTSIDE AND TRY TO FOLLOW THE TRACKS.

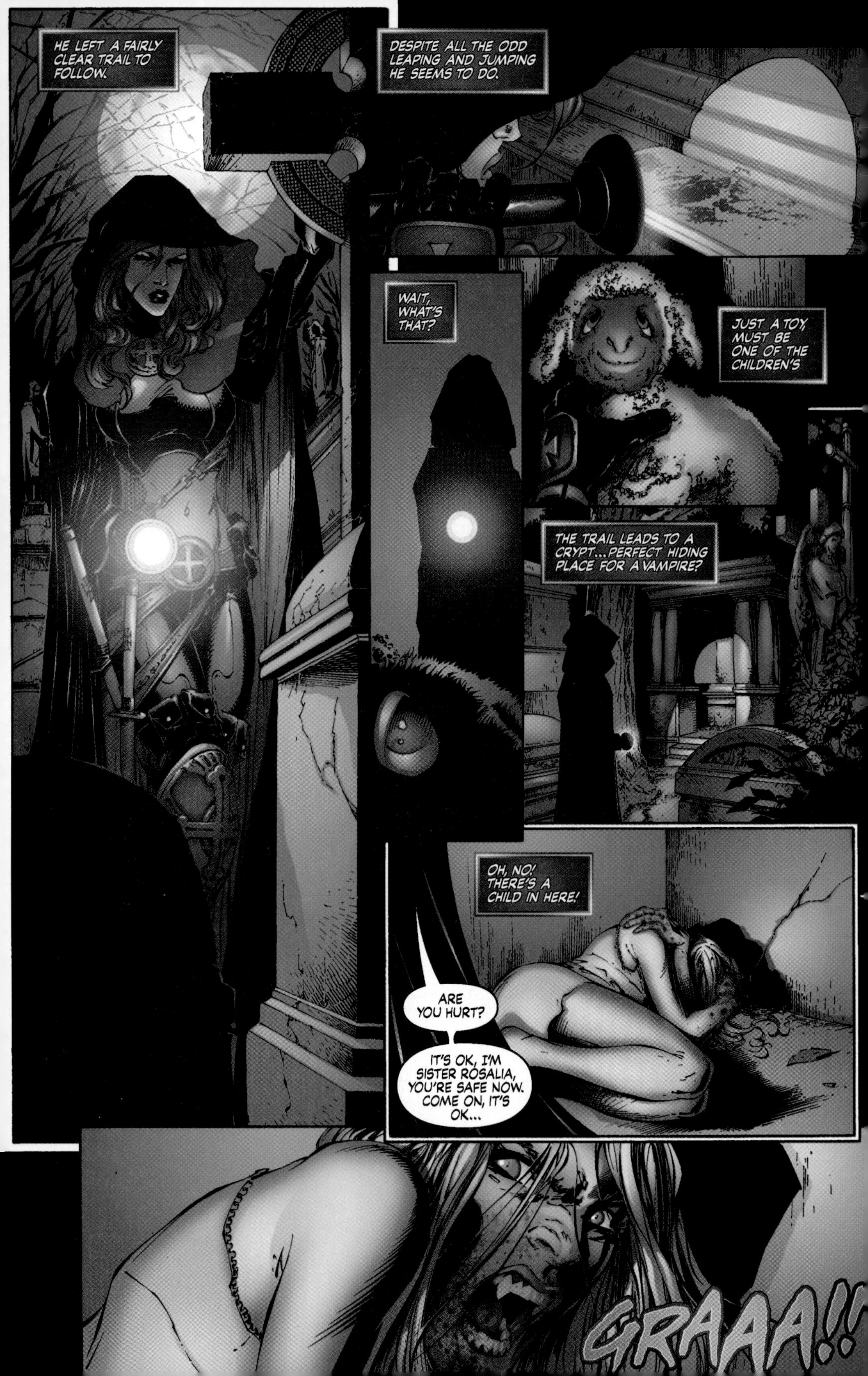
HE LEFT A FAIRLY CLEAR TRAIL TO FOLLOW.
DESPITE ALL THE ODD LEAPING AND JUMPING HE SEEMS TO DO.
WAIT, WHAT'S THAT?
JUST A TOY, MUST BE ONE OF THE CHILDREN'S
THE TRAIL LEADS TO A CRYPT...PERFECT HIDING PLACE FOR A VAMPIRE?
OH, NO! THERE'S A CHILD IN HERE!
ARE YOU HURT?
IT'S OK, I'M SISTER ROSALIA, YOU'RE SAFE NOW. COME ON, IT'S OK...
GRAAA!!

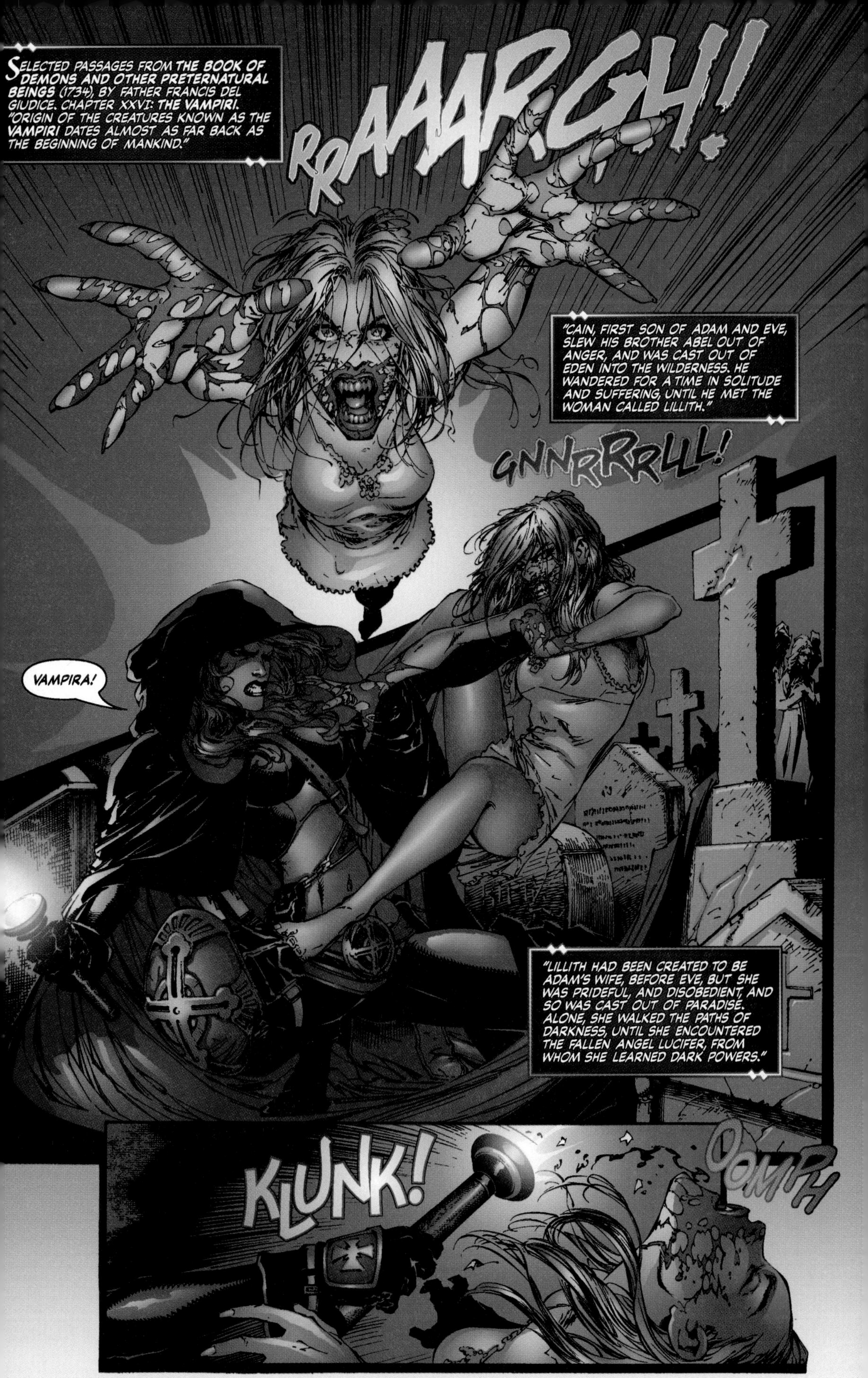
SELECTED PASSAGES FROM THE BOOK OF DEMONS AND OTHER PRETERNATURAL BEINGS (1734), BY FATHER FRANCIS DEL GIUDICE. CHAPTER XXVI: THE VAMPIRI. "ORIGIN OF THE CREATURES KNOWN AS THE VAMPIRI DATES ALMOST AS FAR BACK AS THE BEGINNING OF MANKIND."
RRAAAARGH!
"CAIN, FIRST SON OF ADAM AND EVE, SLEW HIS BROTHER ABEL OUT OF ANGER, AND WAS CAST OUT OF EDEN INTO THE WILDERNESS. HE WANDERED FOR A TIME IN SOLITUDE AND SUFFERING, UNTIL HE MET THE WOMAN CALLED LILLITH."
GNNRRRLL!
VAMPIRA!
"LILLITH HAD BEEN CREATED TO BE ADAM'S WIFE, BEFORE EVE, BUT SHE WAS PRIDEFUL, AND DISOBEDIENT, AND SO WAS CAST OUT OF PARADISE. ALONE, SHE WALKED THE PATHS OF DARKNESS, UNTIL SHE ENCOUNTERED THE FALLEN ANGEL LUCIFER, FROM WHOM SHE LEARNED DARK POWERS."
KLUNK!
OOMPH

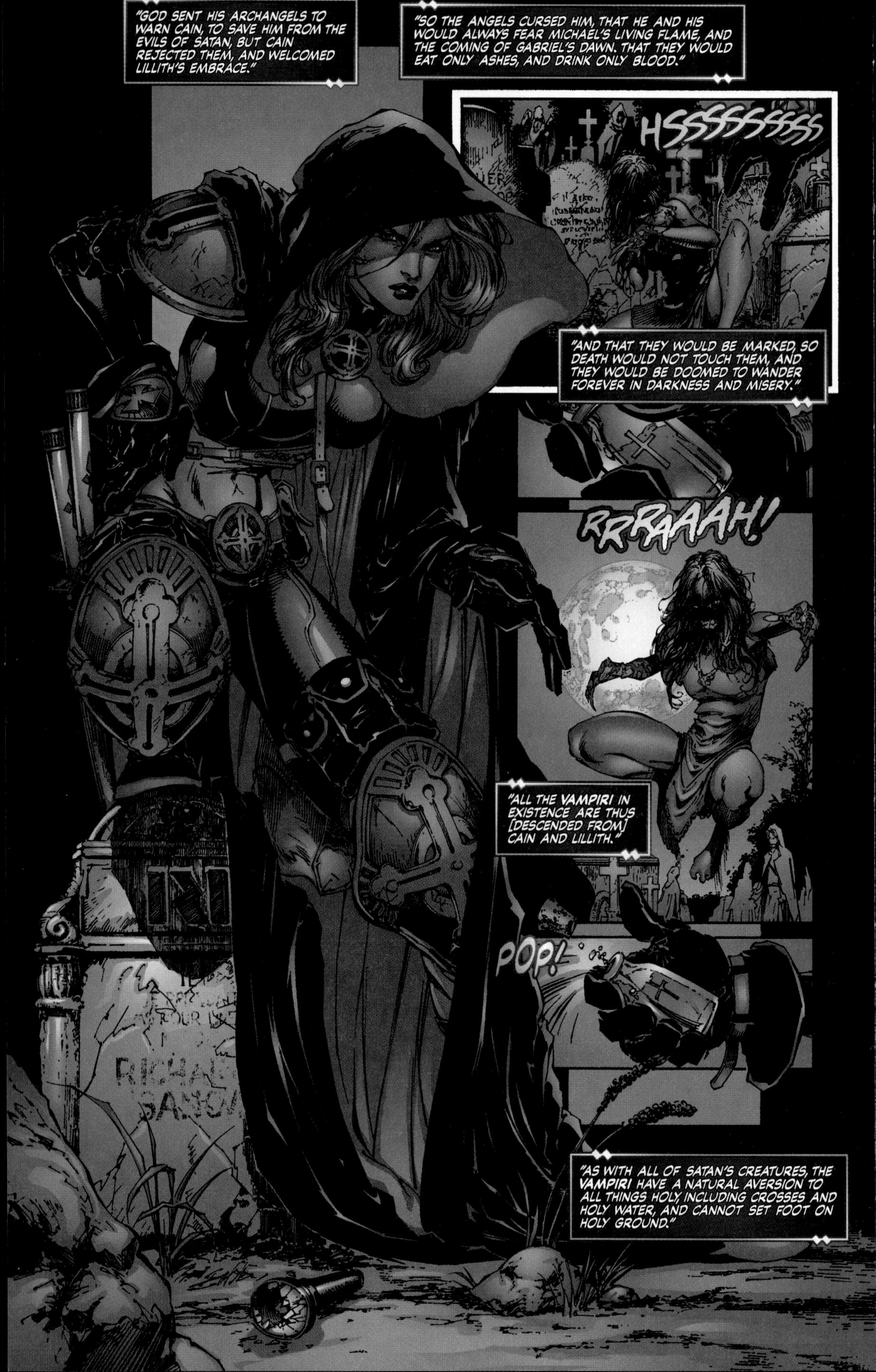
"GOD SENT HIS ARCHANGELS TO WARN CAIN, TO SAVE HIM FROM THE EVILS OF SATAN, BUT CAIN REJECTED THEM, AND WELCOMED LILLITH'S EMBRACE."
"SO THE ANGELS CURSED HIM, THAT HE AND HIS WOULD ALWAYS FEAR MICHAEL'S LIVING FLAME, AND THE COMING OF GABRIEL'S DAWN. THAT THEY WOULD EAT ONLY ASHES, AND DRINK ONLY BLOOD."
HSSSSSSSSS
"AND THAT THEY WOULD BE MARKED, SO DEATH WOULD NOT TOUCH THEM, AND THEY WOULD BE DOOMED TO WANDER FOREVER IN DARKNESS AND MISERY."
RRRAAAH!
"ALL THE VAMPIRI IN EXISTENCE ARE THUS [DESCENDED FROM] CAIN AND LILLITH."
POP!
"AS WITH ALL OF SATAN'S CREATURES, THE VAMPIRI HAVE A NATURAL AVERSION TO ALL THINGS HOLY, INCLUDING CROSSES AND HOLY WATER, AND CANNOT SET FOOT ON HOLY GROUND."

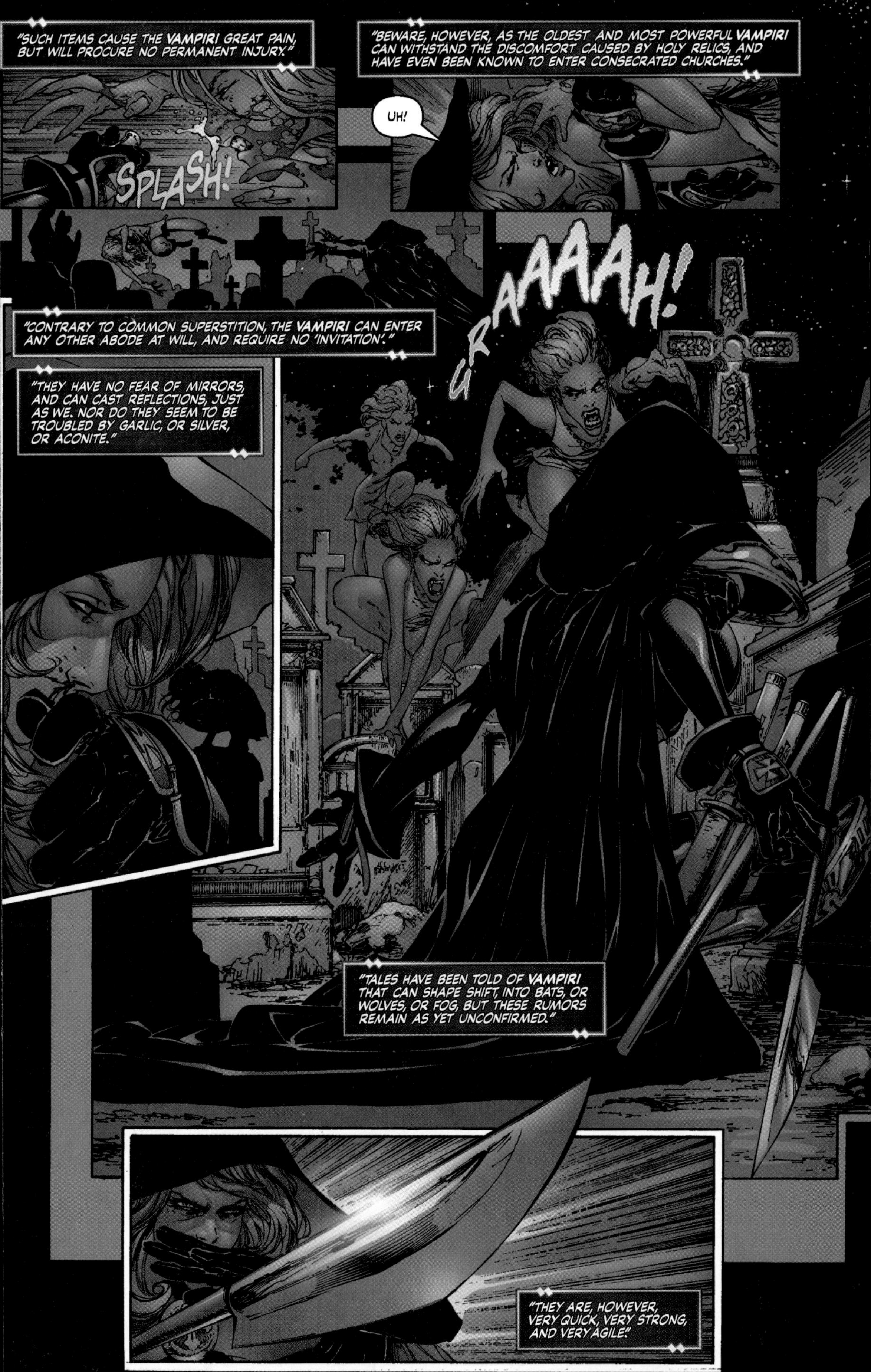
"SUCH ITEMS CAUSE THE VAMPIRI GREAT PAIN, BUT WILL PROCURE NO PERMANENT INJURY."
SPLASH!
"BEWARE, HOWEVER, AS THE OLDEST AND MOST POWERFUL VAMPIRI CAN WITHSTAND THE DISCOMFORT CAUSED BY HOLY RELICS, AND HAVE EVEN BEEN KNOWN TO ENTER CONSECRATED CHURCHES."
UH!
"CONTRARY TO COMMON SUPERSTITION, THE VAMPIRI CAN ENTER ANY OTHER ABODE AT WILL, AND REQUIRE NO 'INVITATION'."
GRAAAAAH!
"THEY HAVE NO FEAR OF MIRRORS, AND CAN CAST REFLECTIONS, JUST AS WE. NOR DO THEY SEEM TO BE TROUBLED BY GARLIC, OR SILVER, OR ACONITE."
"TALES HAVE BEEN TOLD OF VAMPIRI THAT CAN SHAPE SHIFT, INTO BATS, OR WOLVES, OR FOG, BUT THESE RUMORS REMAIN AS YET UNCONFIRMED."
"THEY ARE, HOWEVER, VERY QUICK, VERY STRONG, AND VERY AGILE."

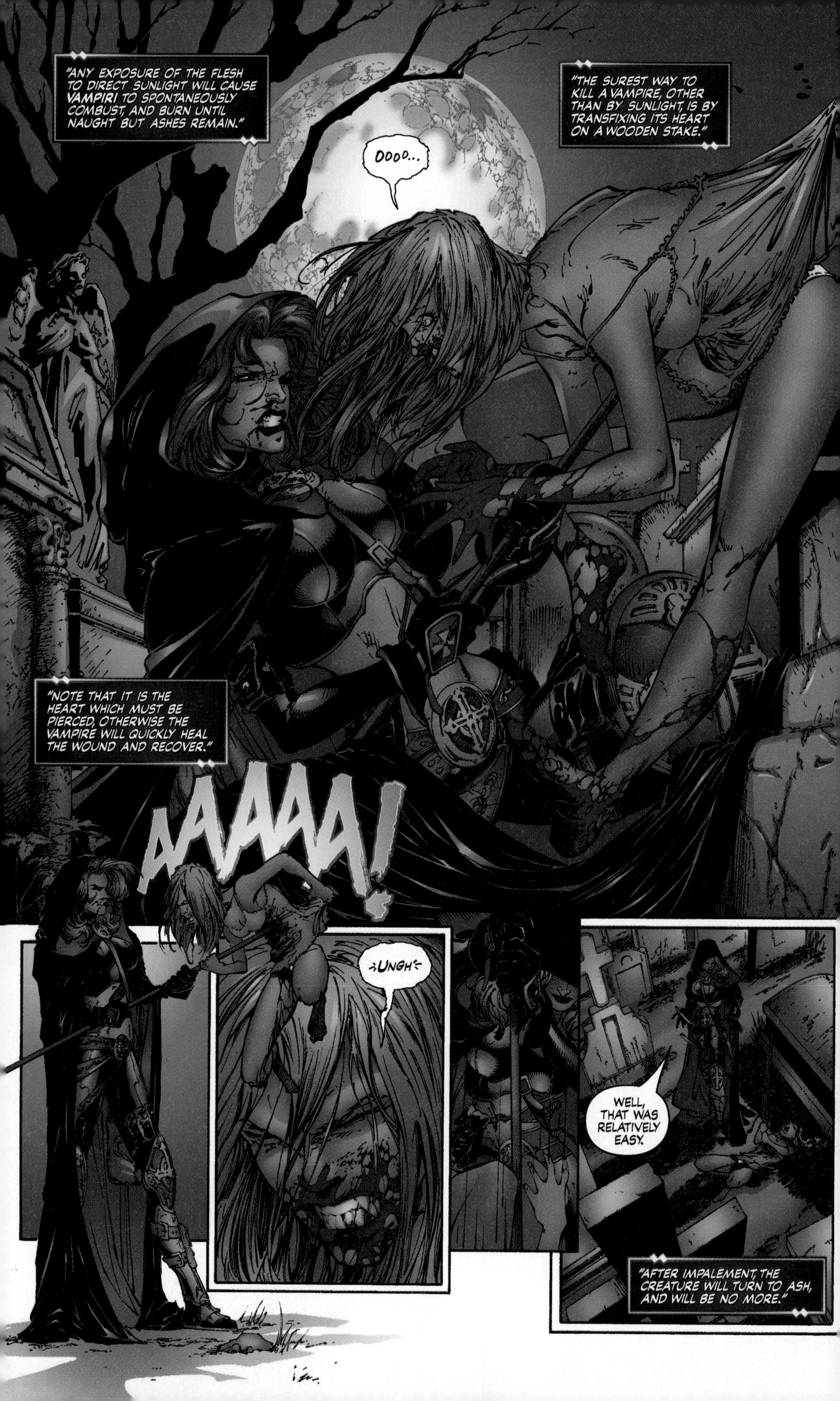
"ANY EXPOSURE OF THE FLESH TO DIRECT SUNLIGHT WILL CAUSE VAMPIRI TO SPONTANEOUSLY COMBUST, AND BURN UNTIL NAUGHT BUT ASHES REMAIN."
"THE SUREST WAY TO KILL A VAMPIRE, OTHER THAN BY SUNLIGHT, IS BY TRANSFIXING ITS HEART ON A WOODEN STAKE."
OOOO...
"NOTE THAT IT IS THE HEART WHICH MUST BE PIERCED, OTHERWISE THE VAMPIRE WILL QUICKLY HEAL THE WOUND AND RECOVER."
AAAAA!
UNGH
WELL, THAT WAS RELATIVELY EASY.
"AFTER IMPALEMENT, THE CREATURE WILL TURN TO ASH, AND WILL BE NO MORE."

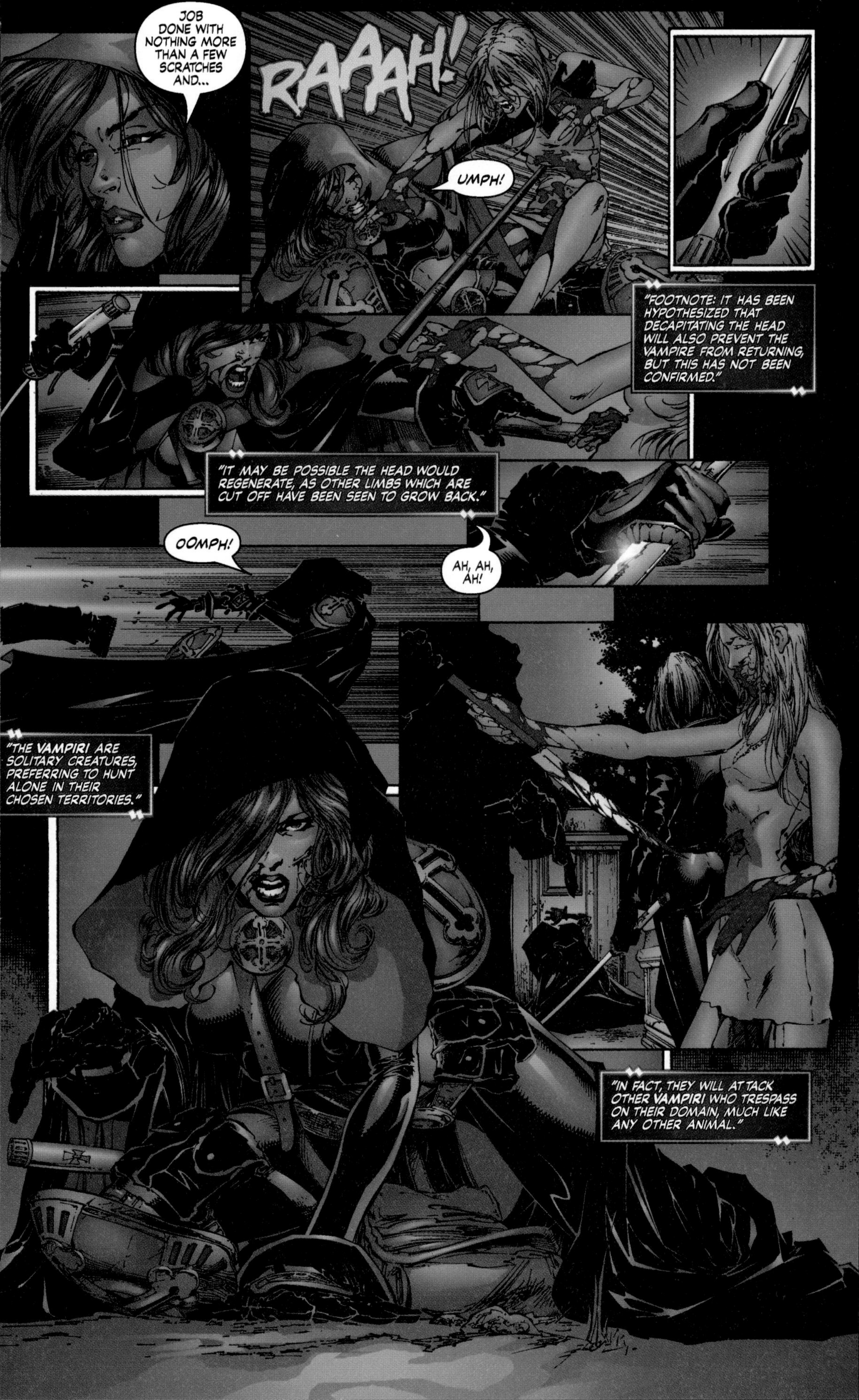
JOB DONE WITH NOTHING MORE THAN A FEW SCRATCHES AND...
RAAAH!
UMPH!
"FOOTNOTE: IT HAS BEEN HYPOTHESIZED THAT DECAPITATING THE HEAD WILL ALSO PREVENT THE VAMPIRE FROM RETURNING, BUT THIS HAS NOT BEEN CONFIRMED."
"IT MAY BE POSSIBLE THE HEAD WOULD REGENERATE, AS OTHER LIMBS WHICH ARE CUT OFF HAVE BEEN SEEN TO GROW BACK."
OOMPH!
AH, AH, AH!
"THE VAMPIRI ARE SOLITARY CREATURES, PREFERRING TO HUNT ALONE IN THEIR CHOSEN TERRITORIES."
"IN FACT, THEY WILL ATTACK OTHER VAMPIRI WHO TRESPASS ON THEIR DOMAIN, MUCH LIKE ANY OTHER ANIMAL."

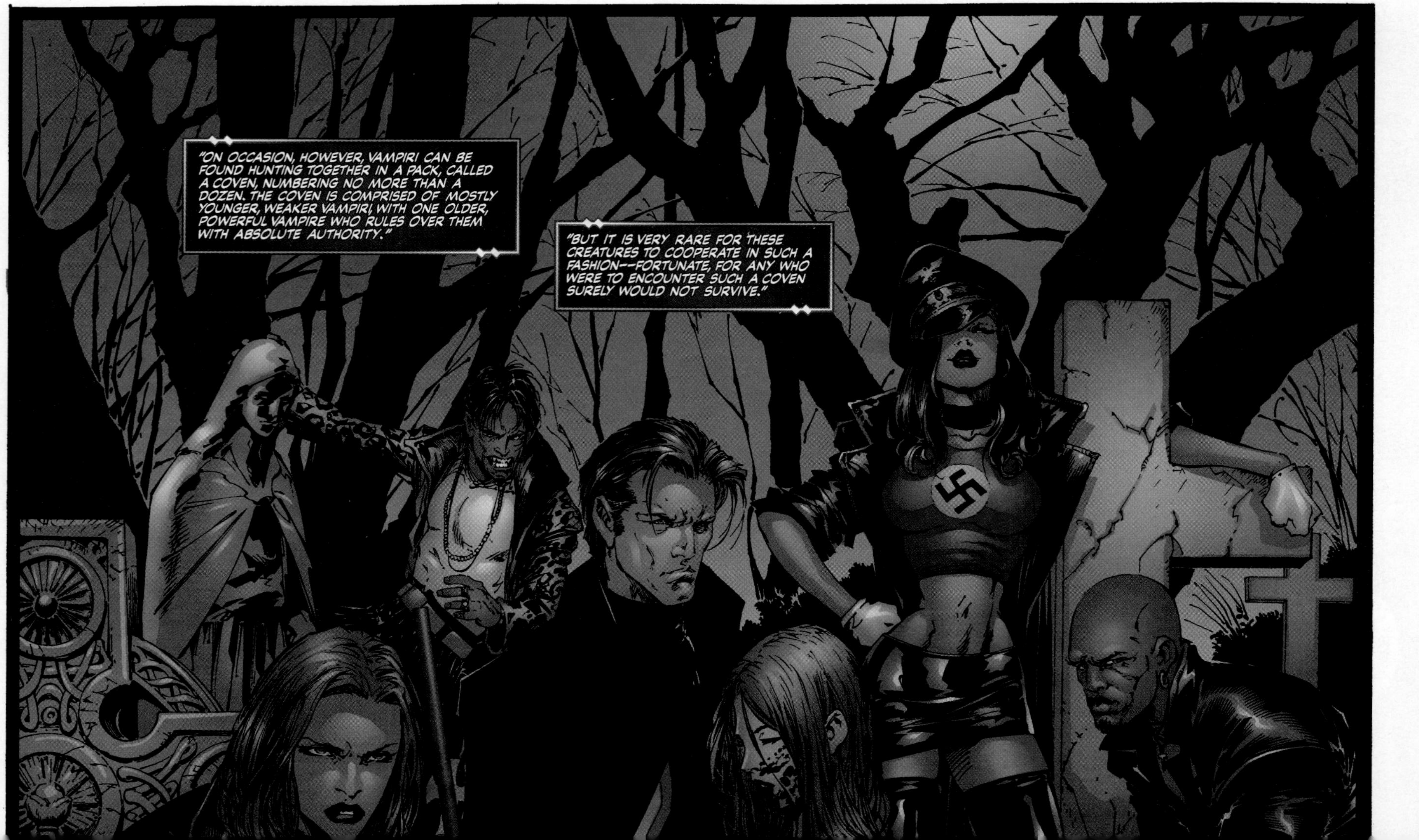
"ON OCCASION, HOWEVER, VAMPIRI CAN BE FOUND HUNTING TOGETHER IN A PACK, CALLED A COVEN, NUMBERING NO MORE THAN A DOZEN. THE COVEN IS COMPRISED OF MOSTLY YOUNGER, WEAKER VAMPIRI, WITH ONE OLDER, POWERFUL VAMPIRE WHO RULES OVER THEM WITH ABSOLUTE AUTHORITY."
"BUT IT IS VERY RARE FOR THESE CREATURES TO COOPERATE IN SUCH A FASHION--FORTUNATE, FOR ANY WHO WERE TO ENCOUNTER SUCH A COVEN SURELY WOULD NOT SURVIVE."

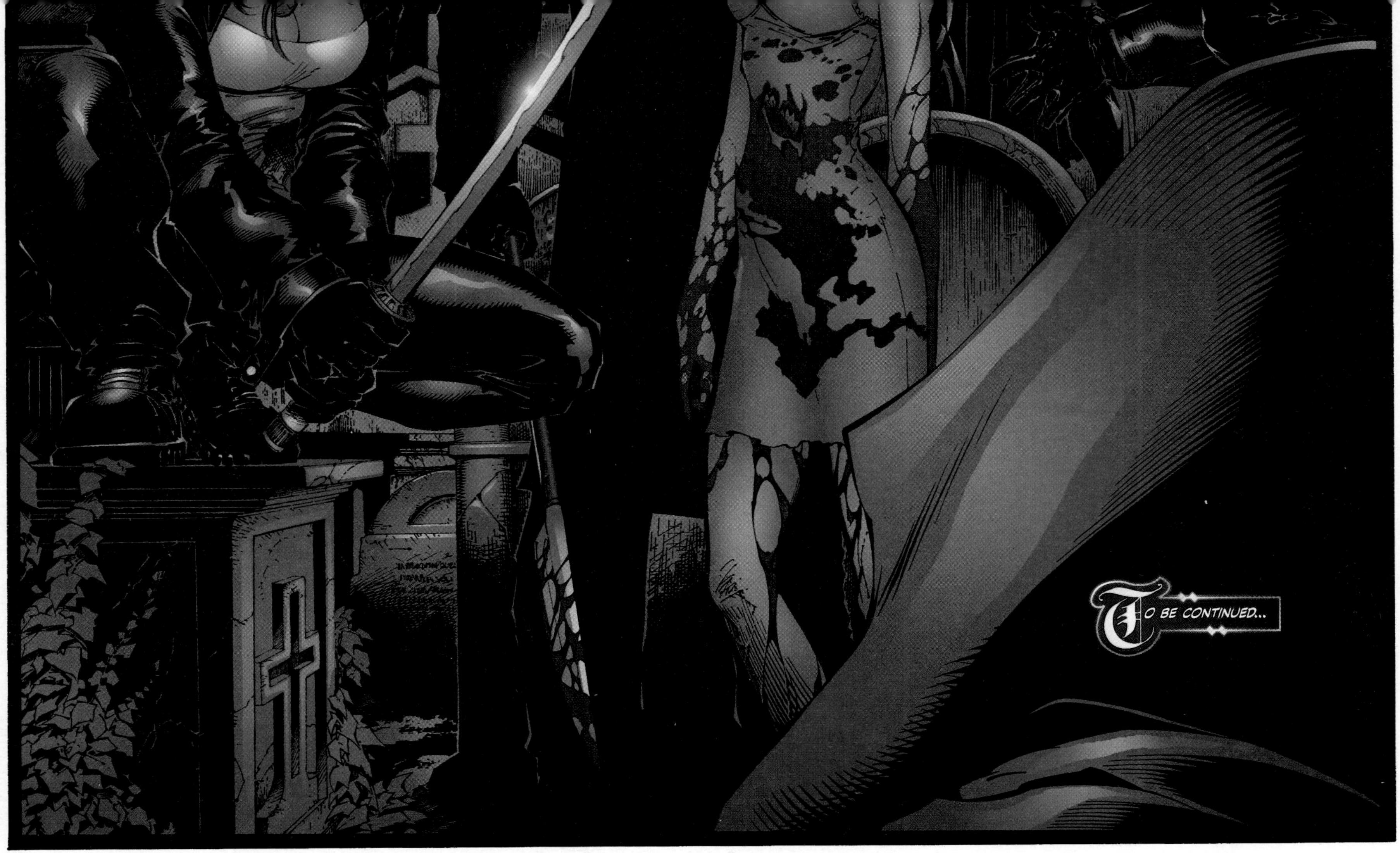
TO BE CONTINUED...

Blood Divine

CHAPTER TWO

Written by **Marcia Chen** · Penciled by **Joe Benitez**
[Pencil Assists by Mun Kao]

Inks by **Joe Weems V**
[with Billy Tan & Kevin Conrad]
[Ink Assists by Marco Galli & Eric Basaldua]

Colors by **Jonathan D. Smith**

Letters by **Dreamer Design's**
Robin Spehar & Dennis Heisler

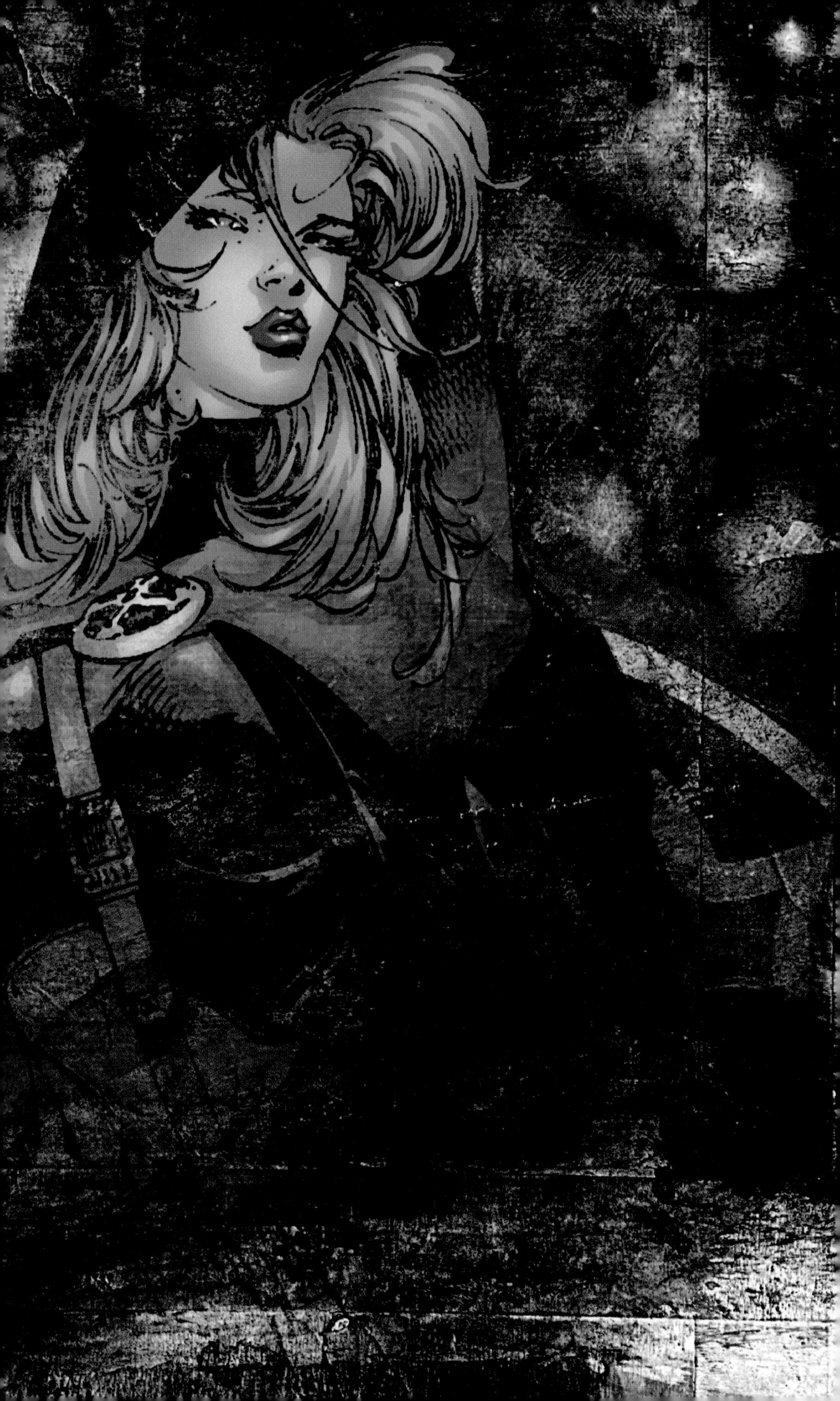

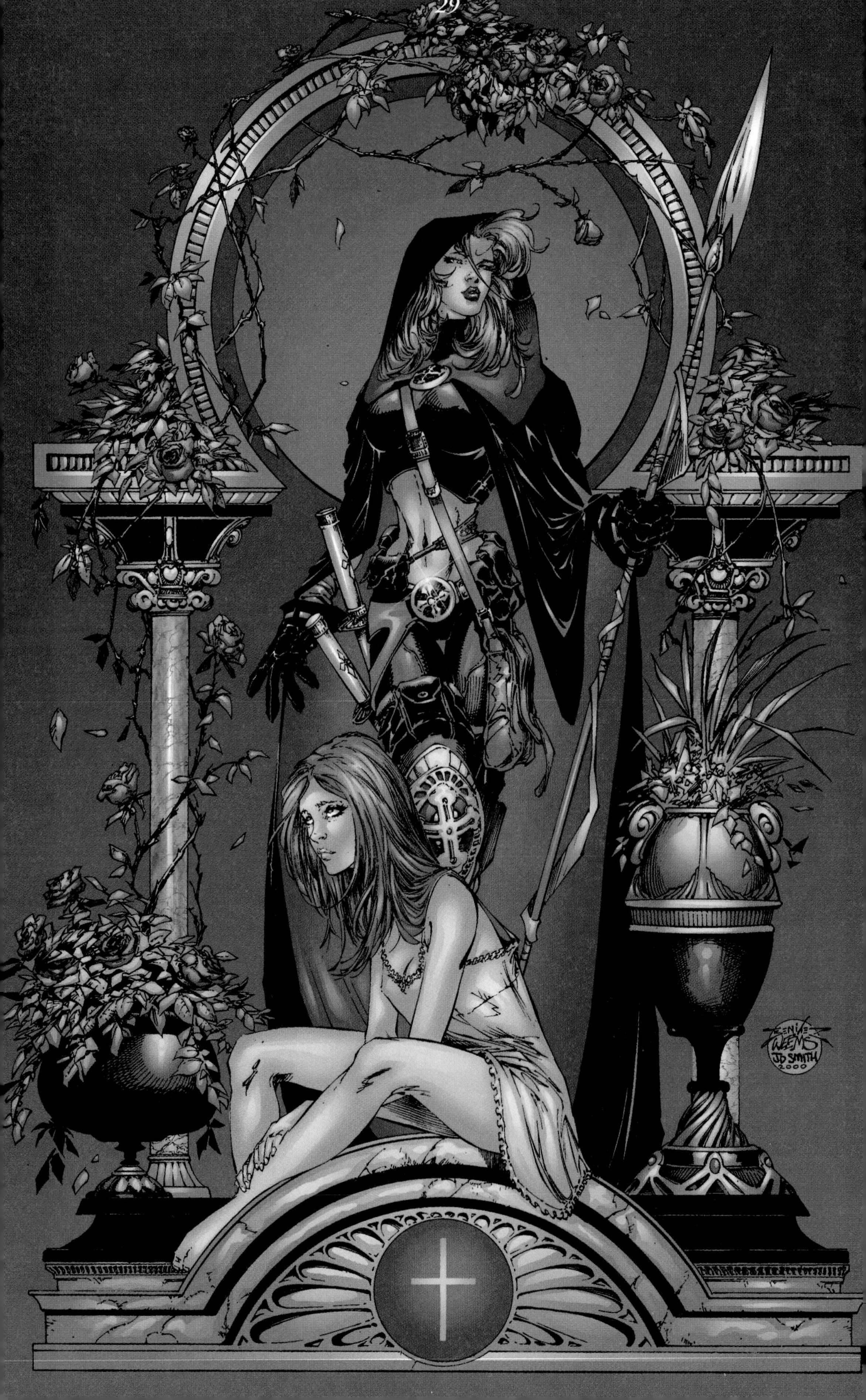
JD SMITH
2000

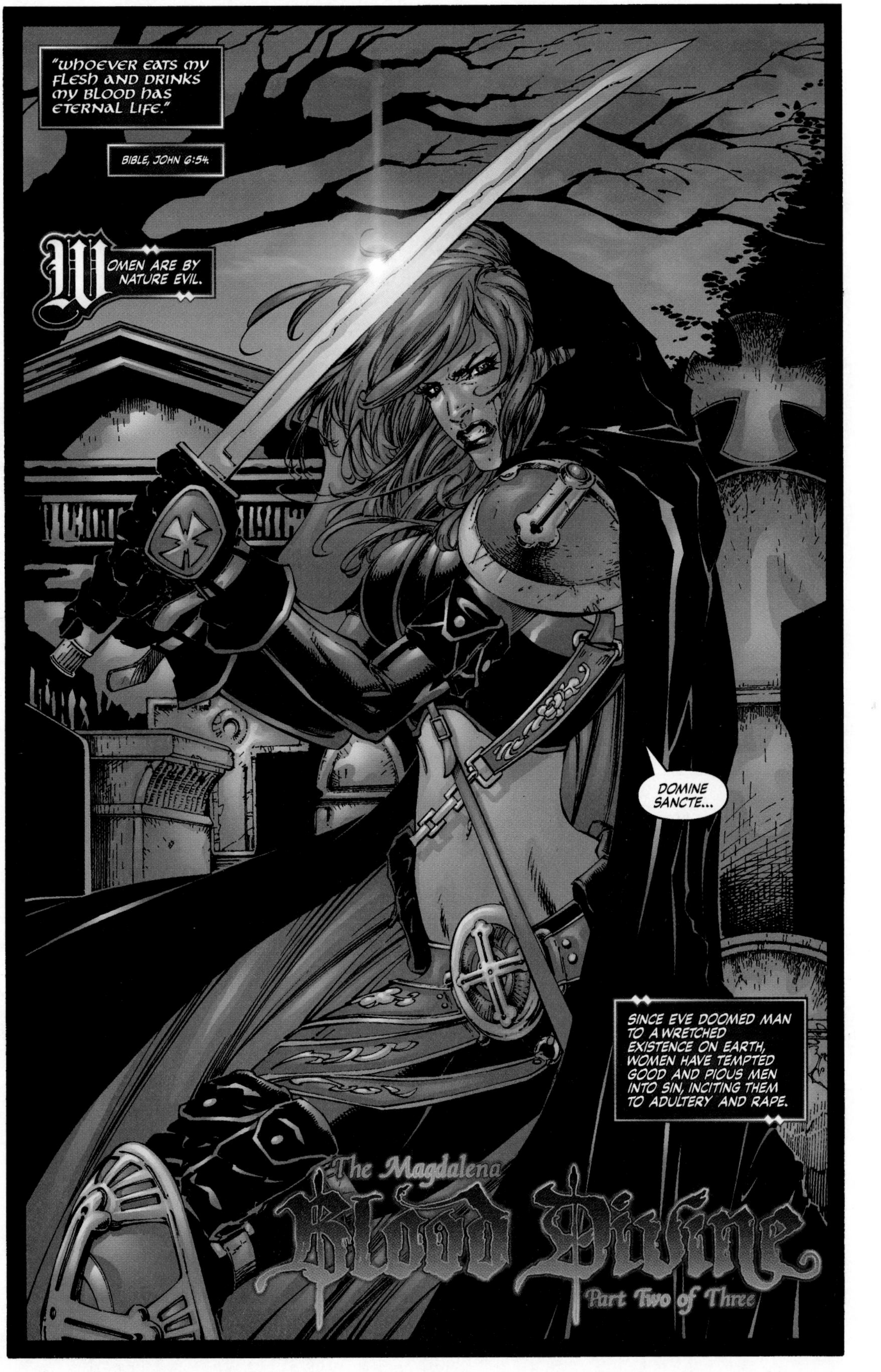

"WHOEVER EATS MY FLESH AND DRINKS MY BLOOD HAS ETERNAL LIFE."
BIBLE, JOHN 6:54.
WOMEN ARE BY NATURE EVIL.
DOMINE SANCTE...
SINCE EVE DOOMED MAN TO A WRETCHED EXISTENCE ON EARTH, WOMEN HAVE TEMPTED GOOD AND PIOUS MEN INTO SIN, INCITING THEM TO ADULTERY AND RAPE.
The Magdalena
Blood Divine
Part Two of Three

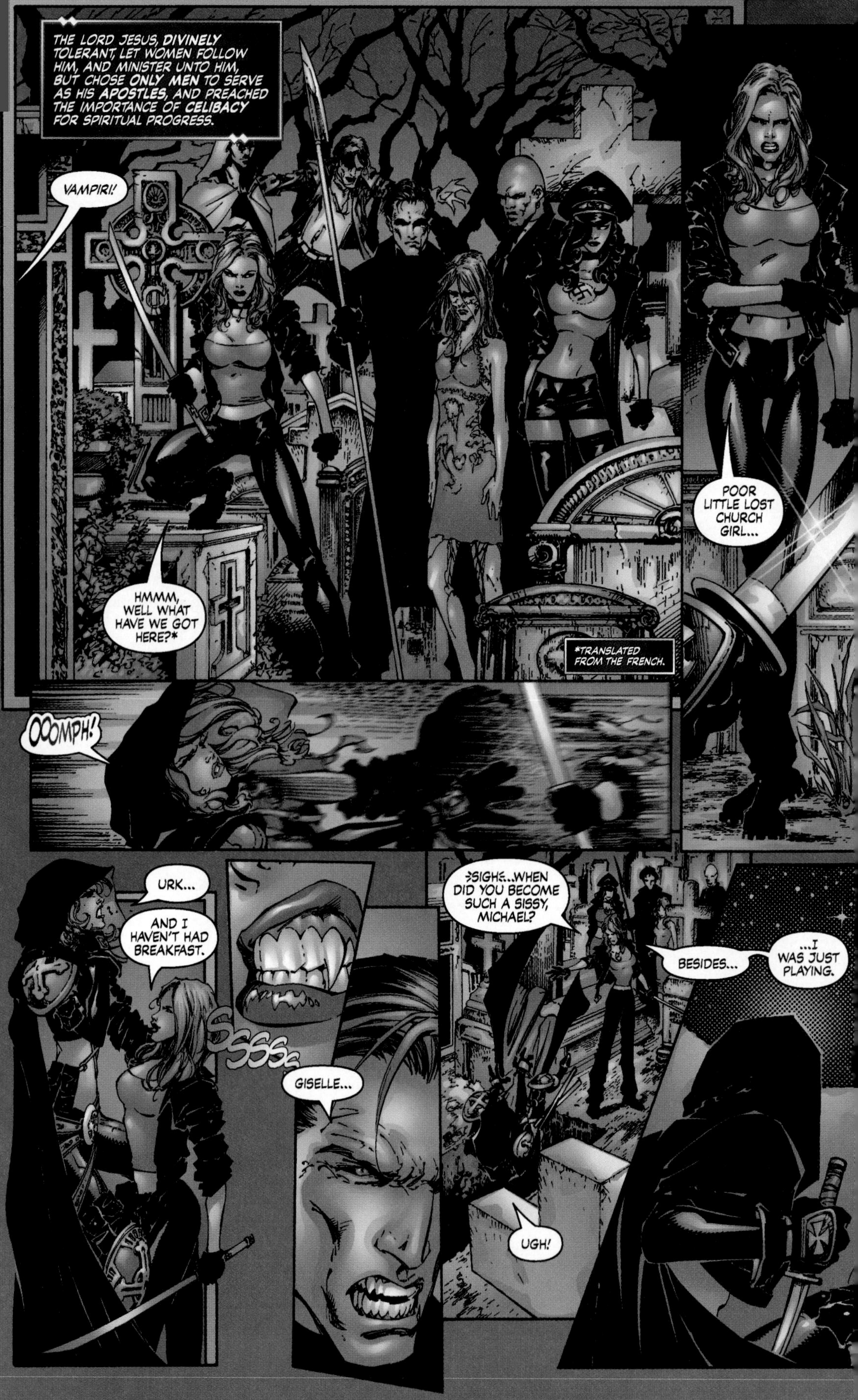
THE LORD JESUS, DIVINELY TOLERANT, LET WOMEN FOLLOW HIM, AND MINISTER UNTO HIM, BUT CHOSE ONLY MEN TO SERVE AS HIS APOSTLES, AND PREACHED THE IMPORTANCE OF CELIBACY FOR SPIRITUAL PROGRESS.
VAMPIRI!
HMMM, WELL WHAT HAVE WE GOT HERE?*
*TRANSLATED FROM THE FRENCH.
POOR LITTLE LOST CHURCH GIRL...
OOOMPH!
URK...
AND I HAVEN'T HAD BREAKFAST.
SSSSS
GISELLE...
>SIGH<...WHEN DID YOU BECOME SUCH A SISSY, MICHAEL?
UGH!
BESIDES...
...I WAS JUST PLAYING.

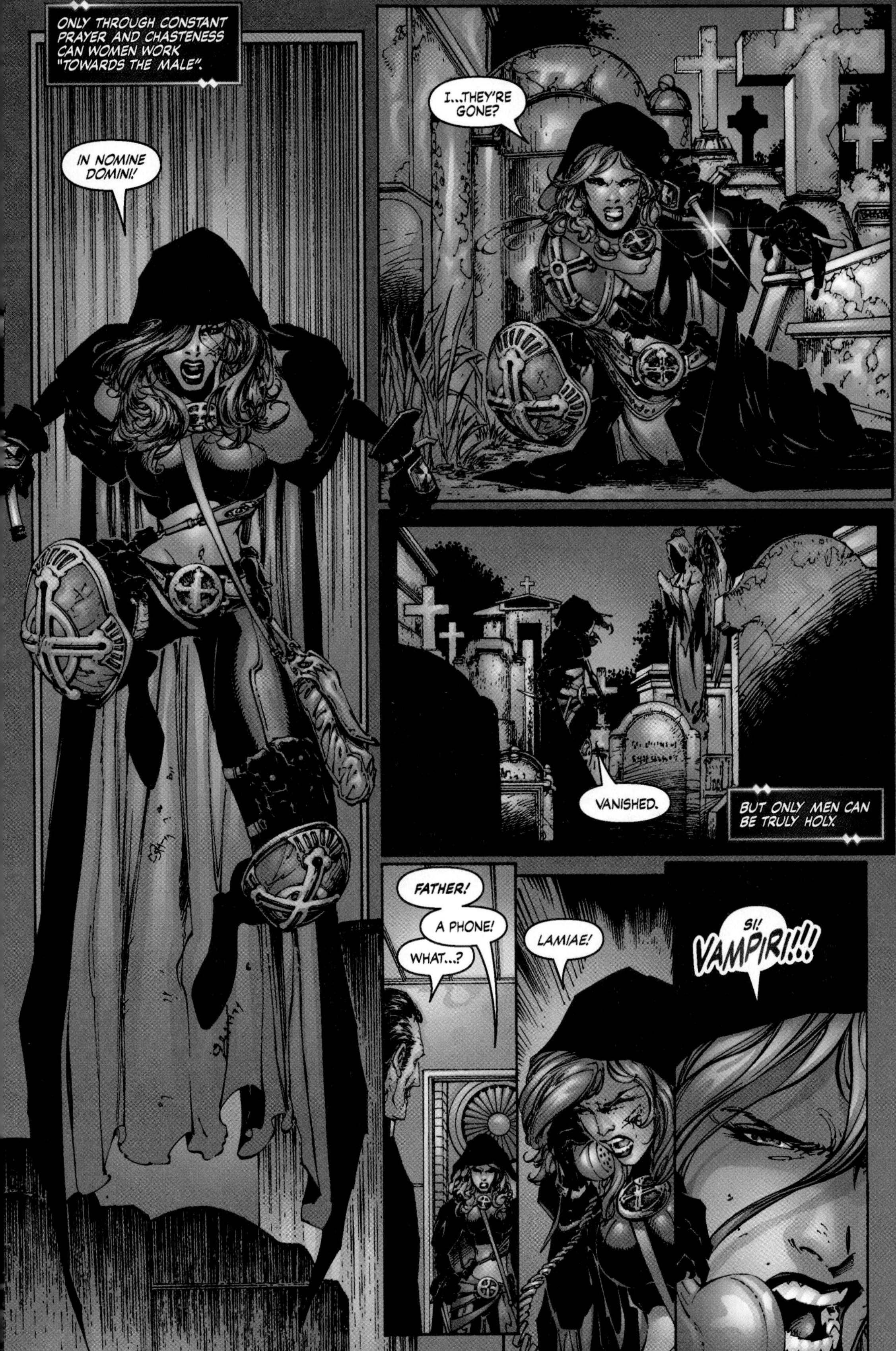

ONLY THROUGH CONSTANT PRAYER AND CHASTENESS CAN WOMEN WORK "TOWARDS THE MALE".
IN NOMINE DOMINI!
I...THEY'RE GONE?
VANISHED.
BUT ONLY MEN CAN BE TRULY HOLY.
FATHER!
A PHONE!
WHAT...?
LAMIAE!
SI!
VAMPIRI!!!

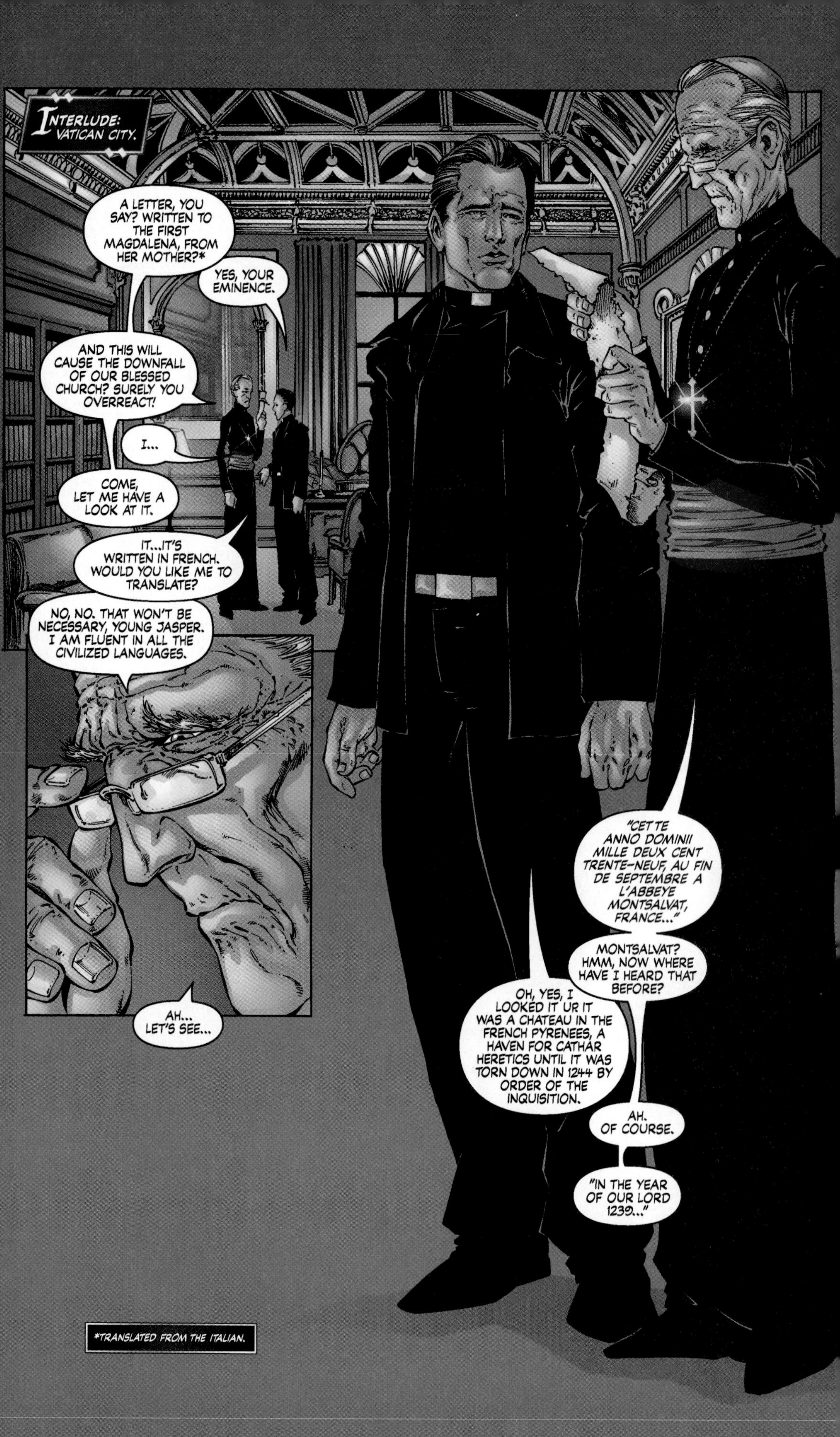
INTERLUDE: VATICAN CITY.
A LETTER, YOU SAY? WRITTEN TO THE FIRST MAGDALENA, FROM HER MOTHER?*
YES, YOUR EMINENCE.
AND THIS WILL CAUSE THE DOWNFALL OF OUR BLESSED CHURCH? SURELY YOU OVERREACT!
I...
COME, LET ME HAVE A LOOK AT IT.
IT...IT'S WRITTEN IN FRENCH. WOULD YOU LIKE ME TO TRANSLATE?
NO, NO. THAT WON'T BE NECESSARY, YOUNG JASPER. I AM FLUENT IN ALL THE CIVILIZED LANGUAGES.
AH... LET'S SEE...
"CETTE ANNO DOMINII MILLE DEUX CENT TRENTE-NEUF, AU FIN DE SEPTEMBRE A L'ABBEYE MONTSALVAT, FRANCE..."
MONTSALVAT? HMM, NOW WHERE HAVE I HEARD THAT BEFORE?
OH, YES, I LOOKED IT UP. IT WAS A CHATEAU IN THE FRENCH PYRENEES, A HAVEN FOR CATHAR HERETICS UNTIL IT WAS TORN DOWN IN 1244 BY ORDER OF THE INQUISITION.
AH. OF COURSE.
"IN THE YEAR OF OUR LORD 1239..."
*TRANSLATED FROM THE ITALIAN.

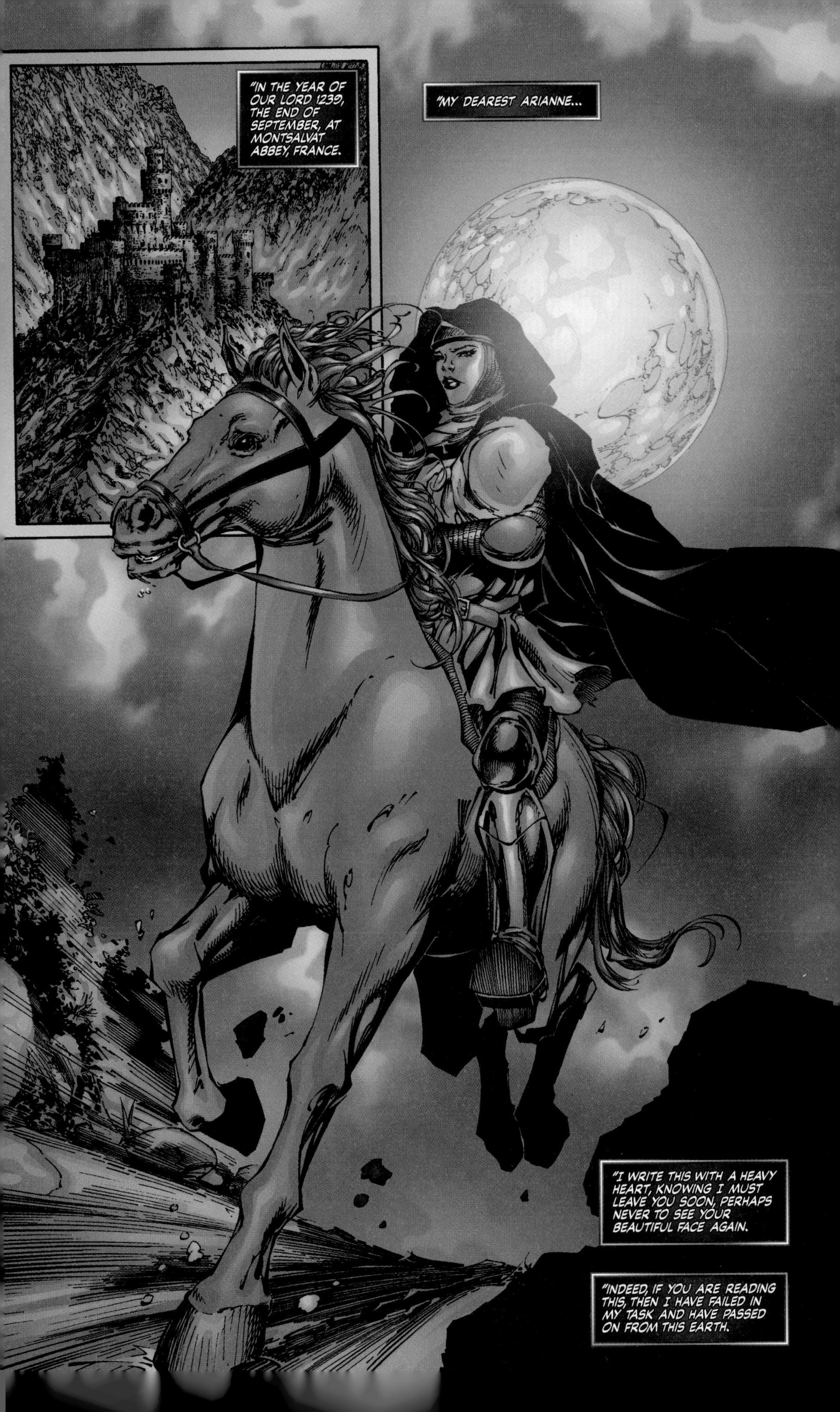
"IN THE YEAR OF OUR LORD 1239, THE END OF SEPTEMBER, AT MONTSALVAT ABBEY, FRANCE.
"MY DEAREST ARIANNE...
"I WRITE THIS WITH A HEAVY HEART, KNOWING I MUST LEAVE YOU SOON, PERHAPS NEVER TO SEE YOUR BEAUTIFUL FACE AGAIN.
"INDEED, IF YOU ARE READING THIS, THEN I HAVE FAILED IN MY TASK AND HAVE PASSED ON FROM THIS EARTH.

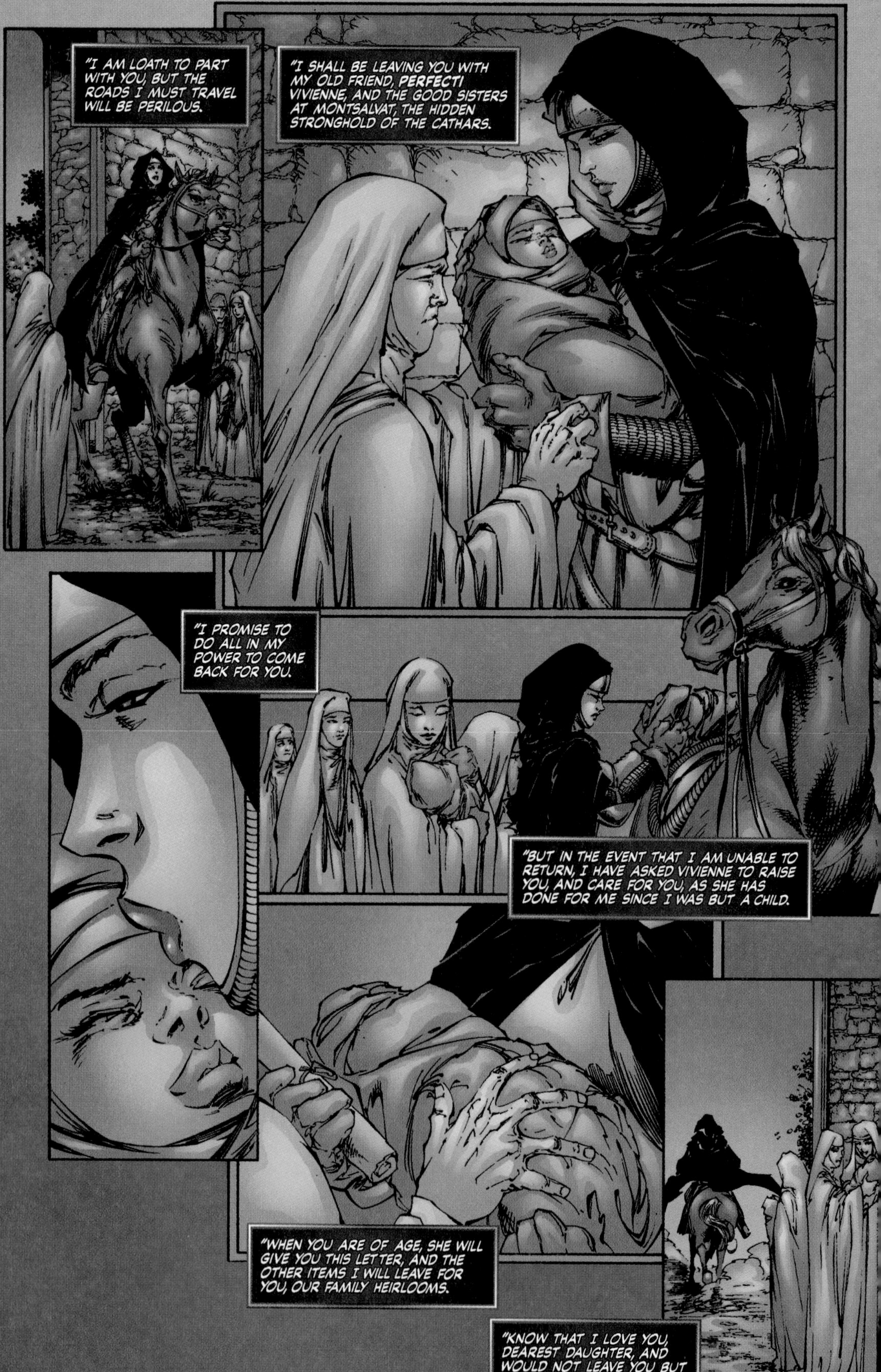
"I AM LOATH TO PART WITH YOU, BUT THE ROADS I MUST TRAVEL WILL BE PERILOUS.
"I SHALL BE LEAVING YOU WITH MY OLD FRIEND, PERFECTI VIVIENNE, AND THE GOOD SISTERS AT MONTSALVAT, THE HIDDEN STRONGHOLD OF THE CATHARS.
"I PROMISE TO DO ALL IN MY POWER TO COME BACK FOR YOU.
"BUT IN THE EVENT THAT I AM UNABLE TO RETURN, I HAVE ASKED VIVIENNE TO RAISE YOU, AND CARE FOR YOU, AS SHE HAS DONE FOR ME SINCE I WAS BUT A CHILD.
"WHEN YOU ARE OF AGE, SHE WILL GIVE YOU THIS LETTER, AND THE OTHER ITEMS I WILL LEAVE FOR YOU, OUR FAMILY HEIRLOOMS.
"KNOW THAT I LOVE YOU, DEAREST DAUGHTER, AND WOULD NOT LEAVE YOU BUT FOR THE GRAVEST NEED.

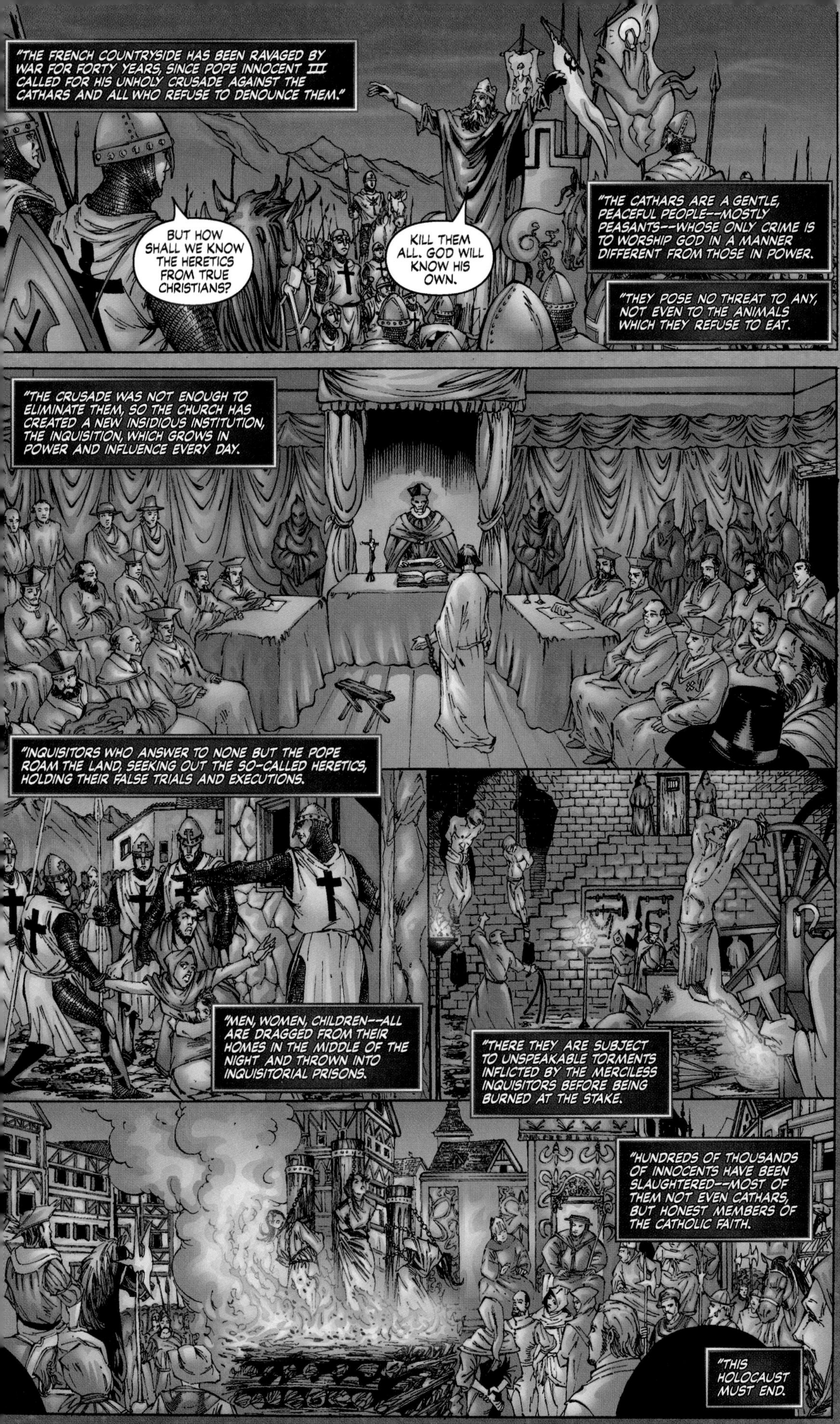
"THE FRENCH COUNTRYSIDE HAS BEEN RAVAGED BY WAR FOR FORTY YEARS, SINCE POPE INNOCENT III CALLED FOR HIS UNHOLY CRUSADE AGAINST THE CATHARS AND ALL WHO REFUSE TO DENOUNCE THEM."
BUT HOW SHALL WE KNOW THE HERETICS FROM TRUE CHRISTIANS?
KILL THEM ALL. GOD WILL KNOW HIS OWN.
"THE CATHARS ARE A GENTLE, PEACEFUL PEOPLE--MOSTLY PEASANTS--WHOSE ONLY CRIME IS TO WORSHIP GOD IN A MANNER DIFFERENT FROM THOSE IN POWER.
"THEY POSE NO THREAT TO ANY, NOT EVEN TO THE ANIMALS WHICH THEY REFUSE TO EAT.
"THE CRUSADE WAS NOT ENOUGH TO ELIMINATE THEM, SO THE CHURCH HAS CREATED A NEW INSIDIOUS INSTITUTION, THE INQUISITION, WHICH GROWS IN POWER AND INFLUENCE EVERY DAY.
"INQUISITORS WHO ANSWER TO NONE BUT THE POPE ROAM THE LAND, SEEKING OUT THE SO-CALLED HERETICS, HOLDING THEIR FALSE TRIALS AND EXECUTIONS.
"MEN, WOMEN, CHILDREN--ALL ARE DRAGGED FROM THEIR HOMES IN THE MIDDLE OF THE NIGHT AND THROWN INTO INQUISITORIAL PRISONS.
"THERE THEY ARE SUBJECT TO UNSPEAKABLE TORMENTS INFLICTED BY THE MERCILESS INQUISITORS BEFORE BEING BURNED AT THE STAKE.
"HUNDREDS OF THOUSANDS OF INNOCENTS HAVE BEEN SLAUGHTERED--MOST OF THEM NOT EVEN CATHARS, BUT HONEST MEMBERS OF THE CATHOLIC FAITH.
"THIS HOLOCAUST MUST END.

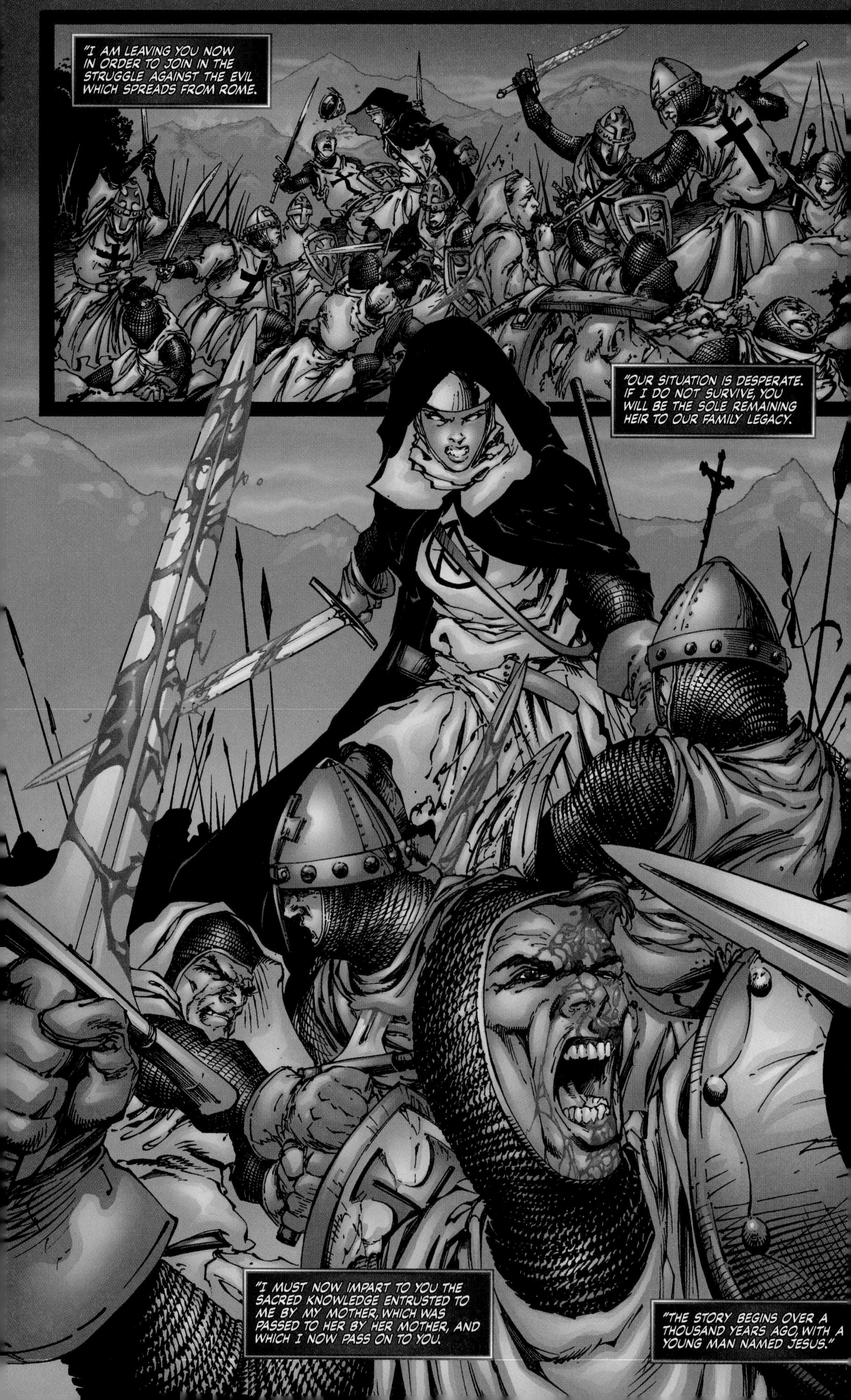
"I AM LEAVING YOU NOW IN ORDER TO JOIN IN THE STRUGGLE AGAINST THE EVIL WHICH SPREADS FROM ROME.
"OUR SITUATION IS DESPERATE. IF I DO NOT SURVIVE, YOU WILL BE THE SOLE REMAINING HEIR TO OUR FAMILY LEGACY.
"I MUST NOW IMPART TO YOU THE SACRED KNOWLEDGE ENTRUSTED TO ME BY MY MOTHER, WHICH WAS PASSED TO HER BY HER MOTHER, AND WHICH I NOW PASS ON TO YOU.
"THE STORY BEGINS OVER A THOUSAND YEARS AGO, WITH A YOUNG MAN NAMED JESUS."

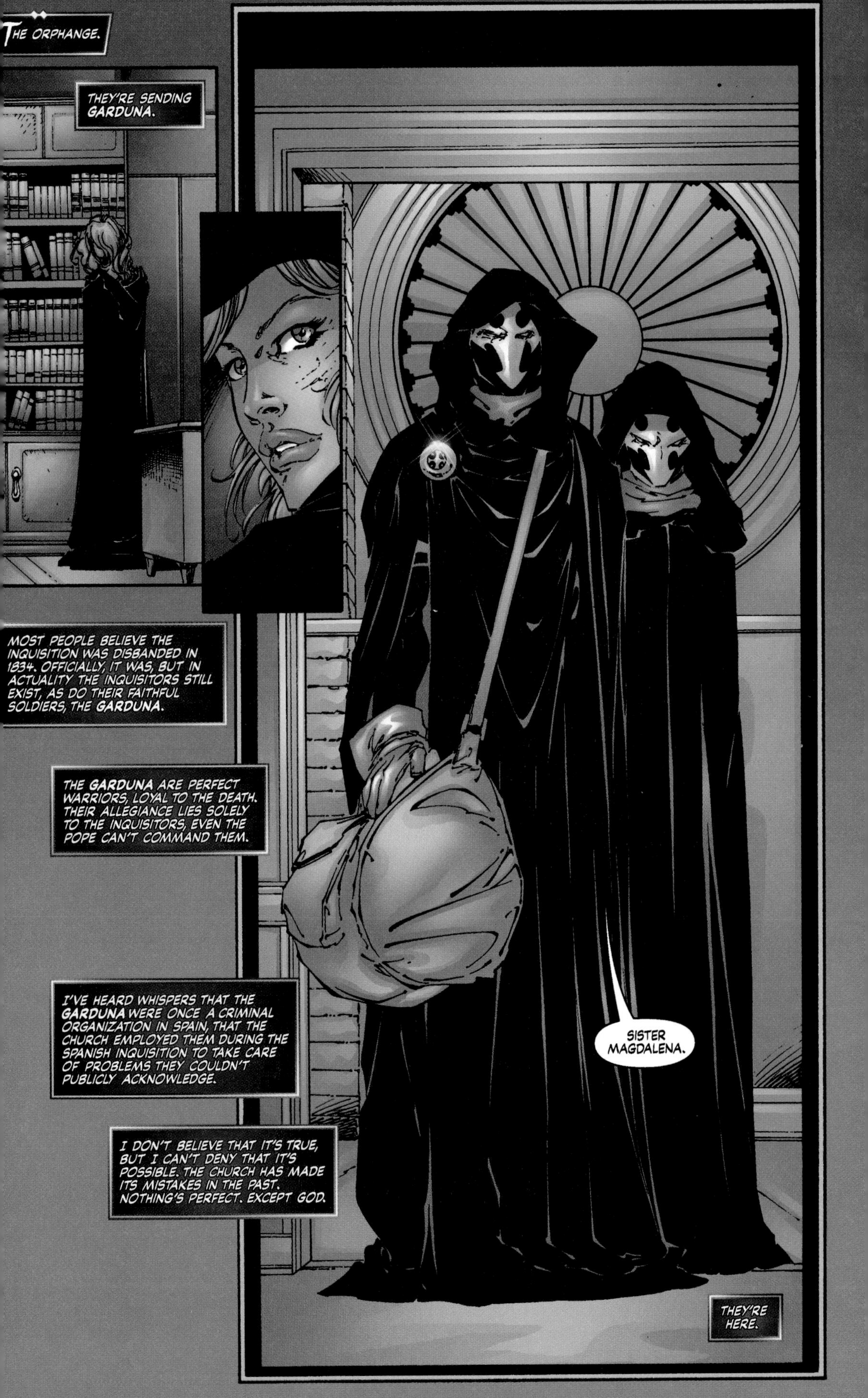
THE ORPHANGE.
THEY'RE SENDING GARDUNA.
MOST PEOPLE BELIEVE THE INQUISITION WAS DISBANDED IN 1834. OFFICIALLY, IT WAS, BUT IN ACTUALITY THE INQUISITORS STILL EXIST, AS DO THEIR FAITHFUL SOLDIERS, THE GARDUNA.
THE GARDUNA ARE PERFECT WARRIORS, LOYAL TO THE DEATH. THEIR ALLEGIANCE LIES SOLELY TO THE INQUISITORS, EVEN THE POPE CAN'T COMMAND THEM.
I'VE HEARD WHISPERS THAT THE GARDUNA WERE ONCE A CRIMINAL ORGANIZATION IN SPAIN, THAT THE CHURCH EMPLOYED THEM DURING THE SPANISH INQUISITION TO TAKE CARE OF PROBLEMS THEY COULDN'T PUBLICLY ACKNOWLEDGE.
I DON'T BELIEVE THAT IT'S TRUE, BUT I CAN'T DENY THAT IT'S POSSIBLE. THE CHURCH HAS MADE ITS MISTAKES IN THE PAST. NOTHING'S PERFECT. EXCEPT GOD.
SISTER MAGDALENA.
THEY'RE HERE.

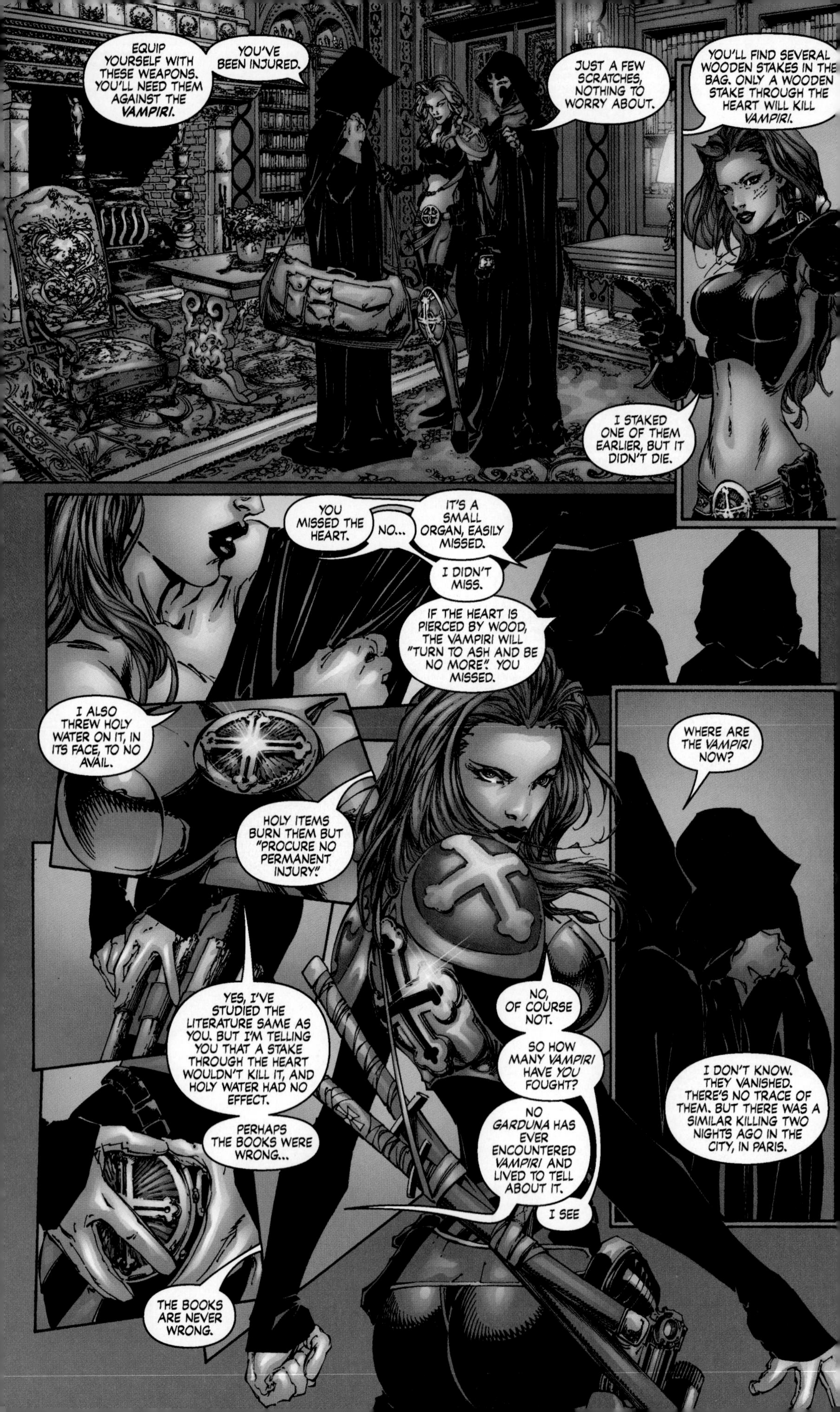
EQUIP YOURSELF WITH THESE WEAPONS. YOU'LL NEED THEM AGAINST THE VAMPIRI.
YOU'VE BEEN INJURED.
JUST A FEW SCRATCHES, NOTHING TO WORRY ABOUT.
YOU'LL FIND SEVERAL WOODEN STAKES IN THE BAG. ONLY A WOODEN STAKE THROUGH THE HEART WILL KILL VAMPIRI.
I STAKED ONE OF THEM EARLIER, BUT IT DIDN'T DIE.
YOU MISSED THE HEART.
NO...
IT'S A SMALL ORGAN, EASILY MISSED.
I DIDN'T MISS.
IF THE HEART IS PIERCED BY WOOD, THE VAMPIRI WILL "TURN TO ASH AND BE NO MORE". YOU MISSED.
I ALSO THREW HOLY WATER ON IT, IN ITS FACE, TO NO AVAIL.
HOLY ITEMS BURN THEM BUT "PROCURE NO PERMANENT INJURY."
YES, I'VE STUDIED THE LITERATURE SAME AS YOU. BUT I'M TELLING YOU THAT A STAKE THROUGH THE HEART WOULDN'T KILL IT, AND HOLY WATER HAD NO EFFECT.
PERHAPS THE BOOKS WERE WRONG...
THE BOOKS ARE NEVER WRONG.
NO, OF COURSE NOT.
SO HOW MANY VAMPIRI HAVE YOU FOUGHT?
NO GARDUNA HAS EVER ENCOUNTERED VAMPIRI AND LIVED TO TELL ABOUT IT.
I SEE
WHERE ARE THE VAMPIRI NOW?
I DON'T KNOW. THEY VANISHED. THERE'S NO TRACE OF THEM. BUT THERE WAS A SIMILAR KILLING TWO NIGHTS AGO IN THE CITY, IN PARIS.

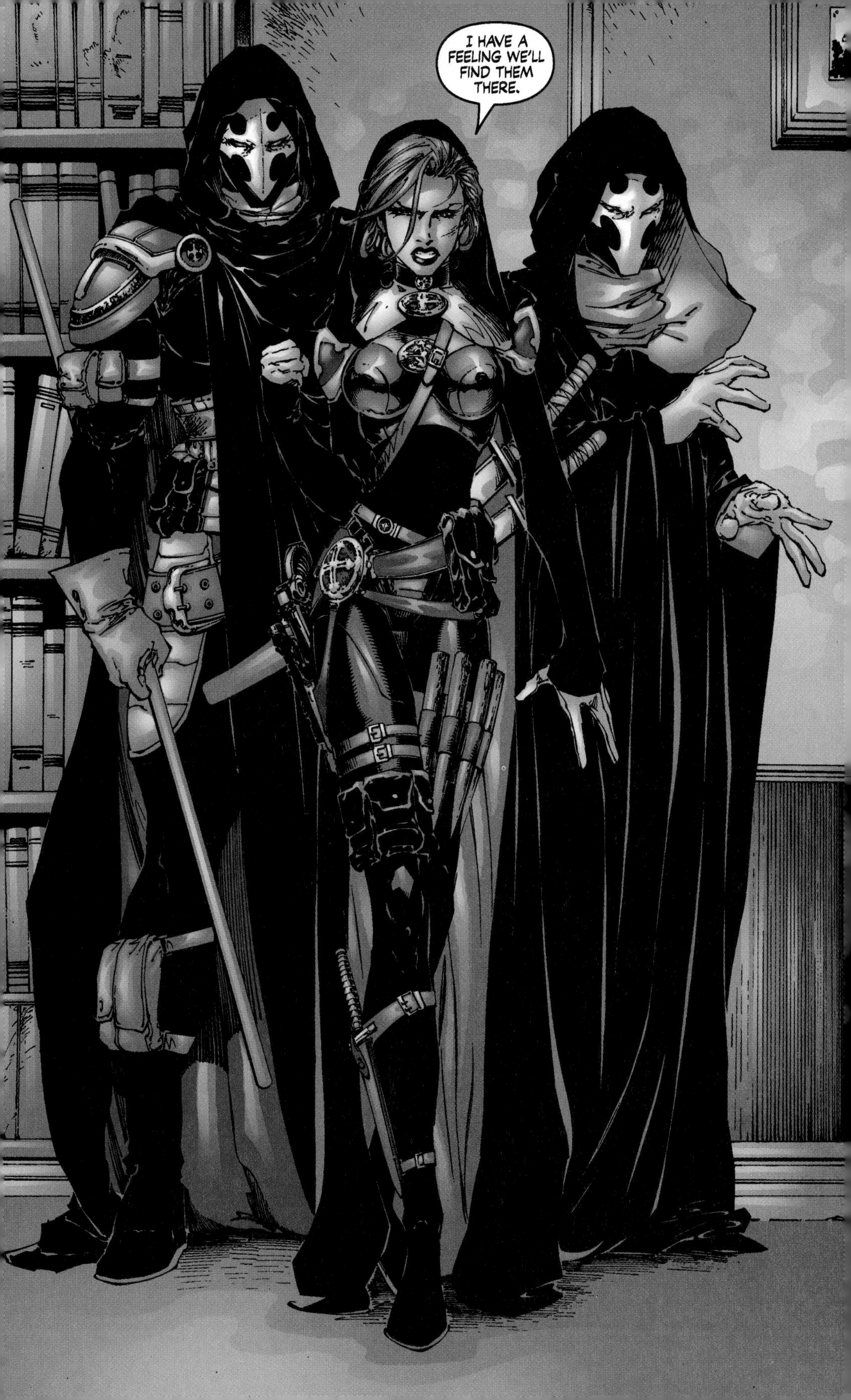
I HAVE A FEELING WE'LL FIND THEM THERE.

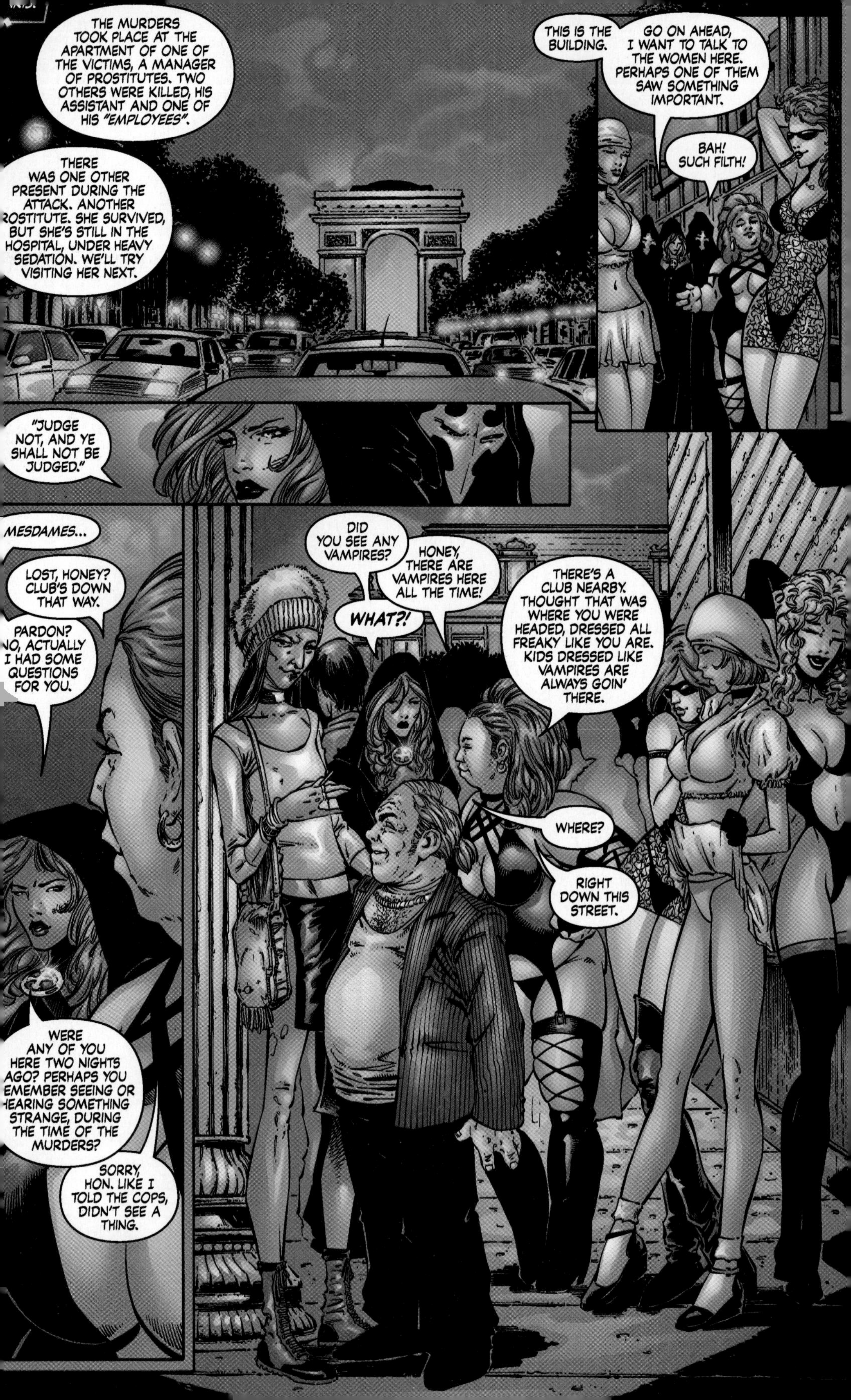

THE MURDERS TOOK PLACE AT THE APARTMENT OF ONE OF THE VICTIMS, A MANAGER OF PROSTITUTES. TWO OTHERS WERE KILLED, HIS ASSISTANT AND ONE OF HIS "EMPLOYEES".
THERE WAS ONE OTHER PRESENT DURING THE ATTACK. ANOTHER ROSTITUTE. SHE SURVIVED, BUT SHE'S STILL IN THE HOSPITAL, UNDER HEAVY SEDATION. WE'LL TRY VISITING HER NEXT.
THIS IS THE BUILDING.
GO ON AHEAD, I WANT TO TALK TO THE WOMEN HERE. PERHAPS ONE OF THEM SAW SOMETHING IMPORTANT.
BAH! SUCH FILTH!
"JUDGE NOT, AND YE SHALL NOT BE JUDGED."
MESDAMES...
LOST, HONEY? CLUB'S DOWN THAT WAY.
PARDON? IO, ACTUALLY I HAD SOME QUESTIONS FOR YOU.
DID YOU SEE ANY VAMPIRES?
HONEY, THERE ARE VAMPIRES HERE ALL THE TIME!
WHAT?!
THERE'S A CLUB NEARBY. THOUGHT THAT WAS WHERE YOU WERE HEADED, DRESSED ALL FREAKY LIKE YOU ARE. KIDS DRESSED LIKE VAMPIRES ARE ALWAYS GOIN' THERE.
WHERE?
RIGHT DOWN THIS STREET.
WERE ANY OF YOU HERE TWO NIGHTS AGO? PERHAPS YOU EMEMBER SEEING OR IEARING SOMETHING STRANGE, DURING THE TIME OF THE MURDERS?
SORRY, HON. LIKE I TOLD THE COPS, DIDN'T SEE A THING.

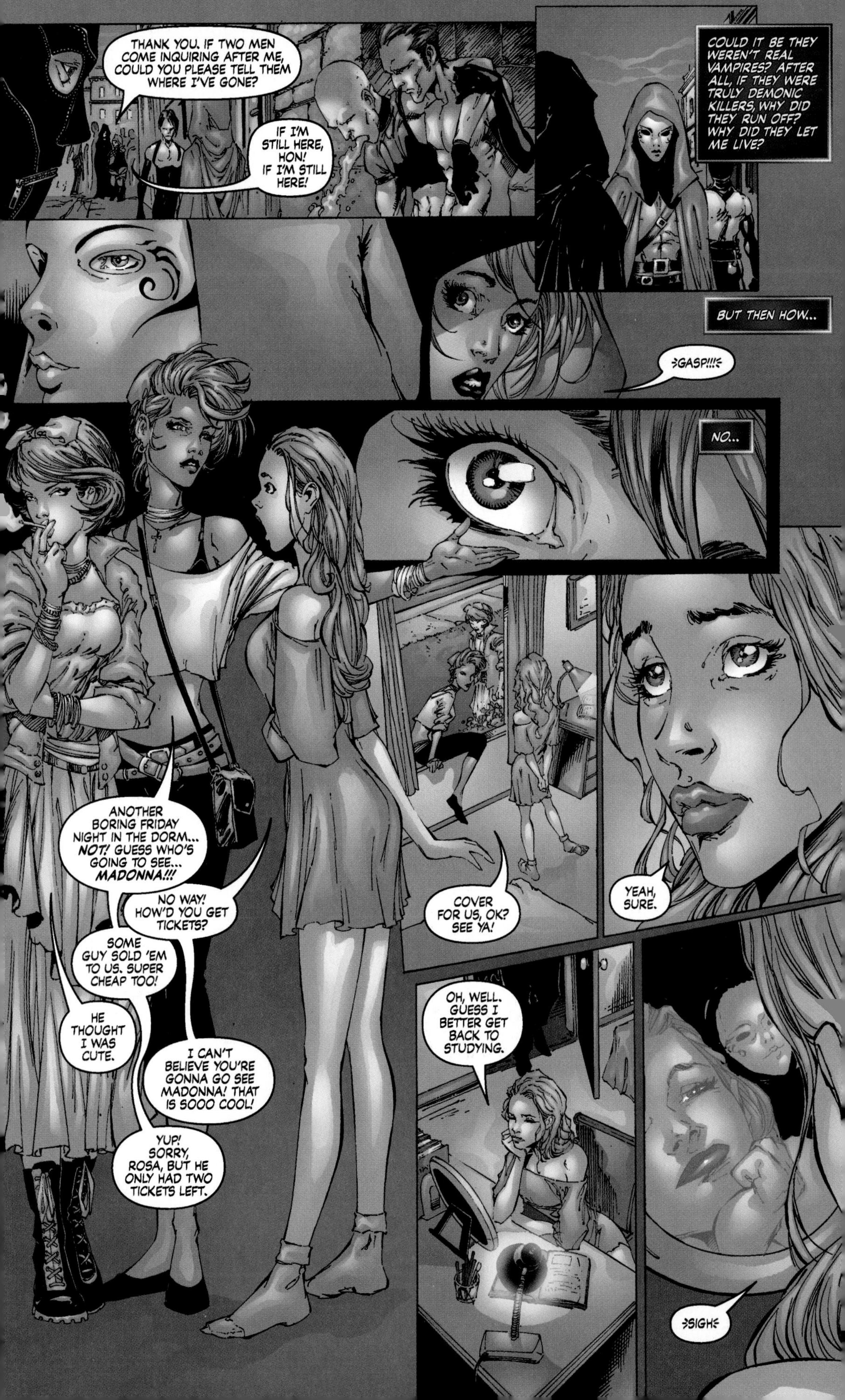
THANK YOU. IF TWO MEN COME INQUIRING AFTER ME, COULD YOU PLEASE TELL THEM WHERE I'VE GONE?
IF I'M STILL HERE, HON! IF I'M STILL HERE!
COULD IT BE THEY WEREN'T REAL VAMPIRES? AFTER ALL, IF THEY WERE TRULY DEMONIC KILLERS, WHY DID THEY RUN OFF? WHY DID THEY LET ME LIVE?
BUT THEN HOW...
GASP!!!
NO...
ANOTHER BORING FRIDAY NIGHT IN THE DORM... NOT! GUESS WHO'S GOING TO SEE... MADONNA!!!
NO WAY! HOW'D YOU GET TICKETS?
SOME GUY SOLD 'EM TO US. SUPER CHEAP TOO!
HE THOUGHT I WAS CUTE.
I CAN'T BELIEVE YOU'RE GONNA GO SEE MADONNA! THAT IS SOOO COOL!
YUP! SORRY, ROSA, BUT HE ONLY HAD TWO TICKETS LEFT.
COVER FOR US, OK? SEE YA!
YEAH, SURE.
OH, WELL. GUESS I BETTER GET BACK TO STUDYING.
SIGH

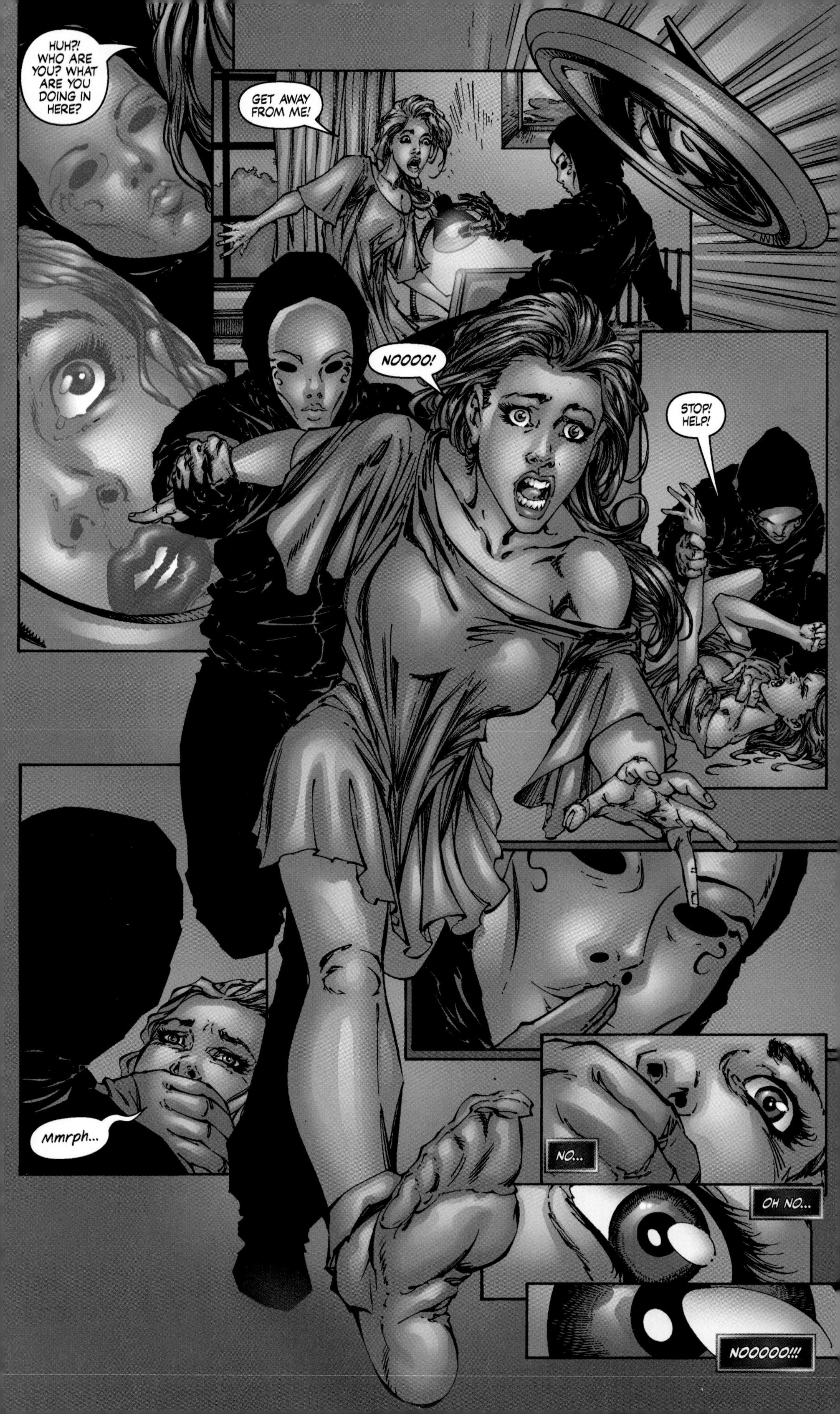

HUH?! WHO ARE YOU? WHAT ARE YOU DOING IN HERE?
GET AWAY FROM ME!
NOOOO!
STOP! HELP!
Mmrph...
NO...
OH NO...
NOOOOO!!!

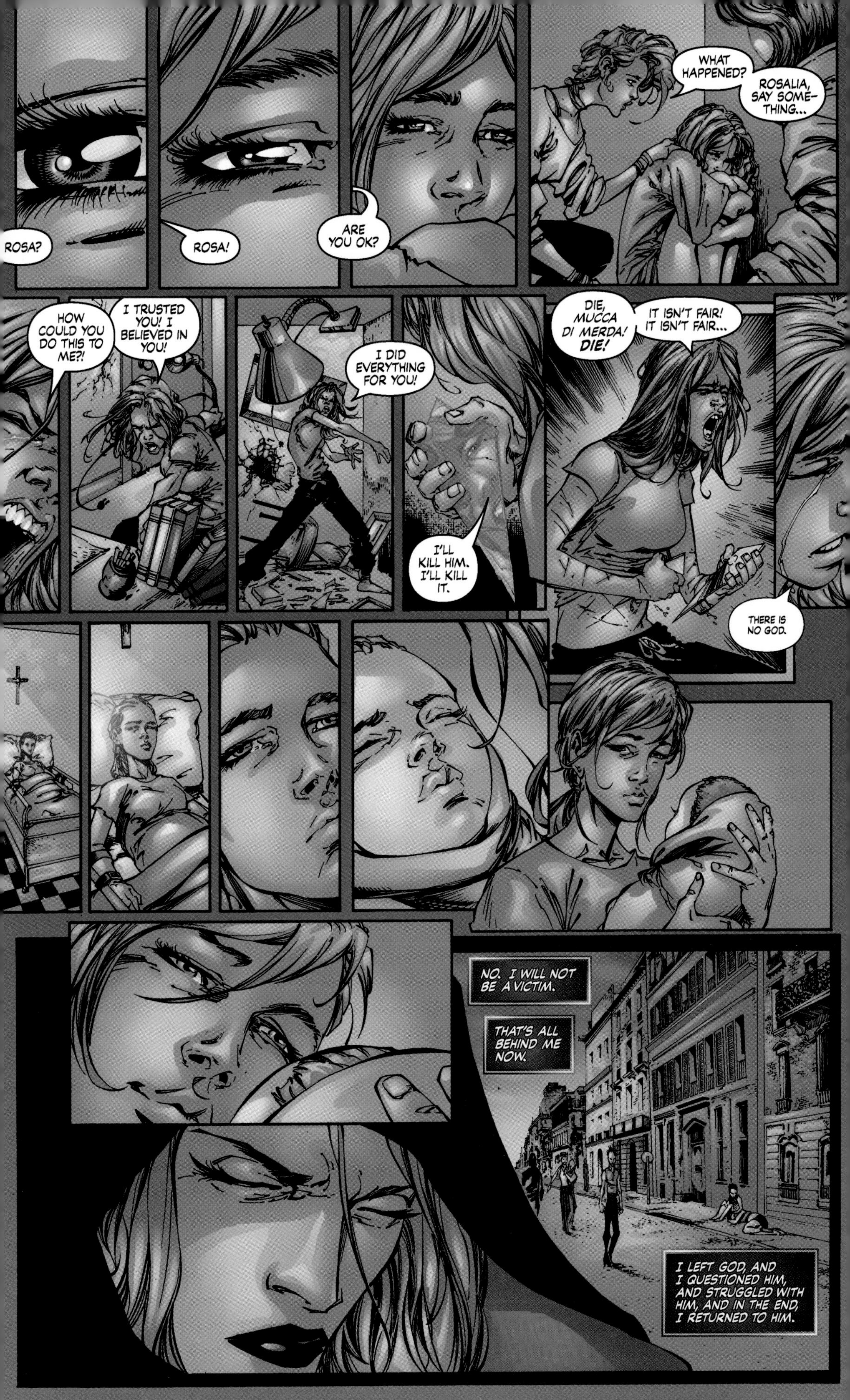

ROSA?
ROSA!
ARE YOU OK?
WHAT HAPPENED?
ROSALIA, SAY SOME-THING...
HOW COULD YOU DO THIS TO ME?!
I TRUSTED YOU! I BELIEVED IN YOU!
I DID EVERYTHING FOR YOU!
I'LL KILL HIM. I'LL KILL IT.
DIE, MUCCA DI MERDA! DIE!
IT ISN'T FAIR! IT ISN'T FAIR...
THERE IS NO GOD.
NO. I WILL NOT BE A VICTIM.
THAT'S ALL BEHIND ME NOW.
I LEFT GOD, AND I QUESTIONED HIM, AND STRUGGLED WITH HIM, AND IN THE END, I RETURNED TO HIM.

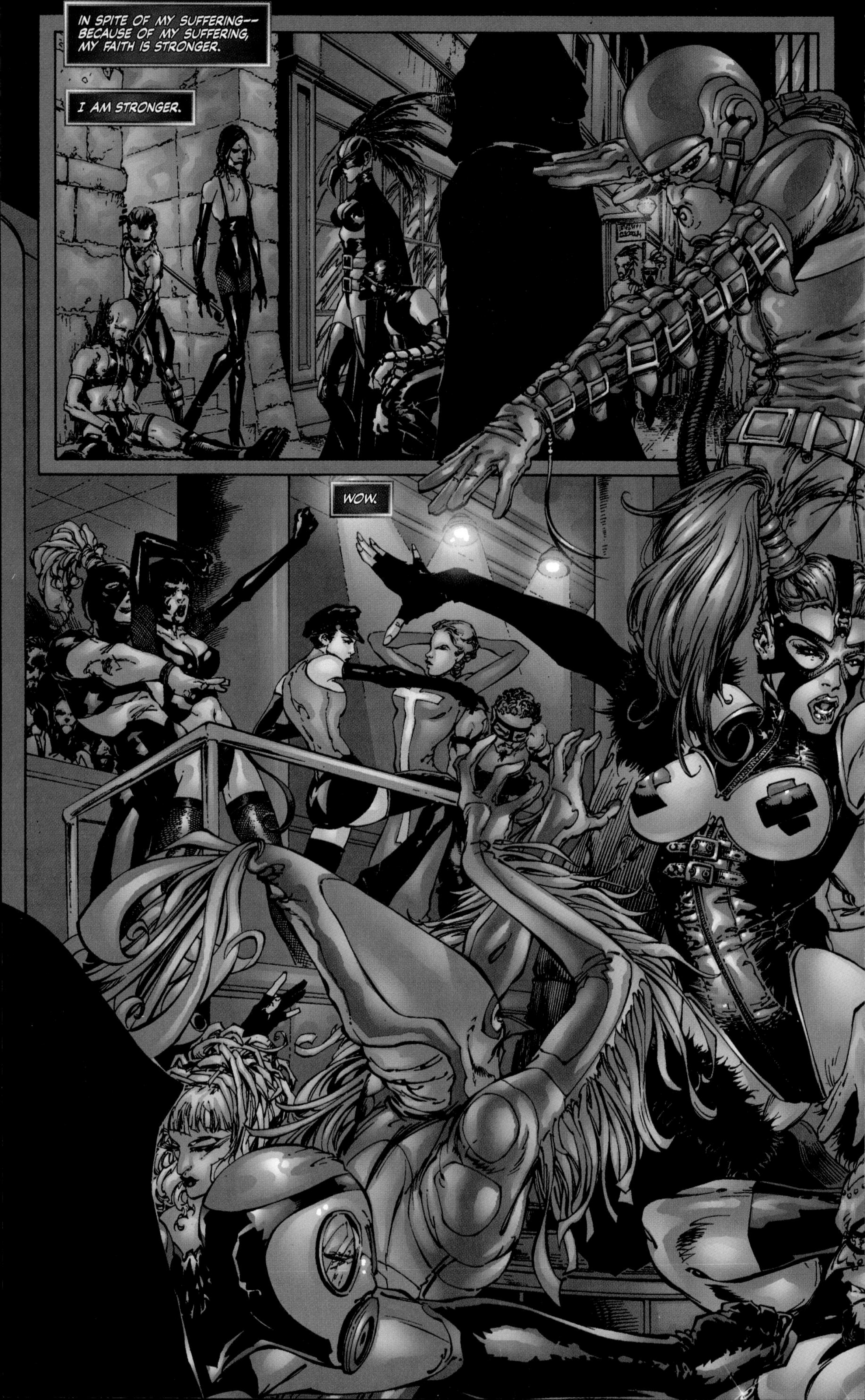
IN SPITE OF MY SUFFERING--
BECAUSE OF MY SUFFERING,
MY FAITH IS STRONGER.
I AM STRONGER.
WOW.

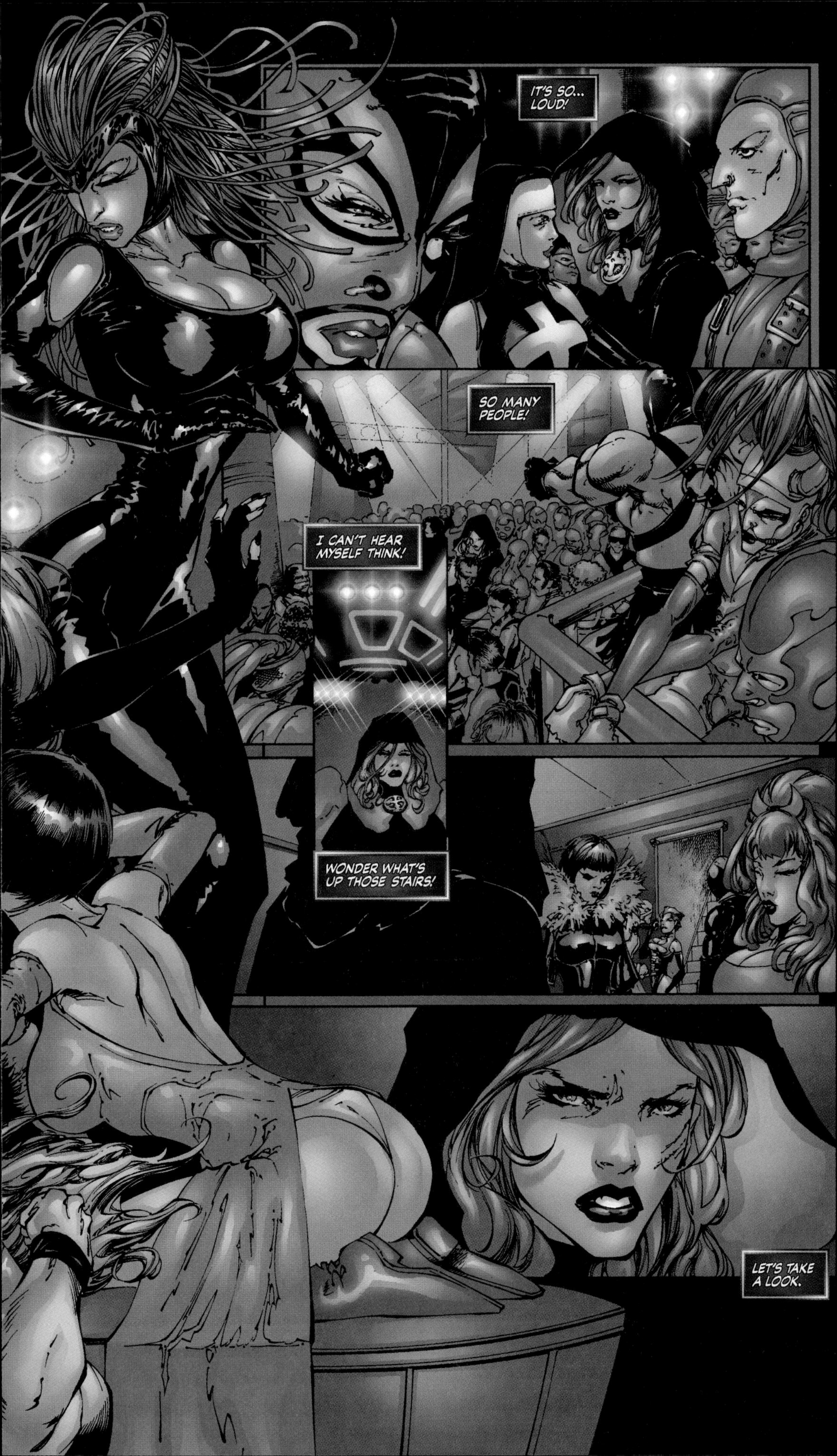

IT'S SO... LOUD!
SO MANY PEOPLE!
I CAN'T HEAR MYSELF THINK!
WONDER WHAT'S UP THOSE STAIRS!
LET'S TAKE A LOOK.

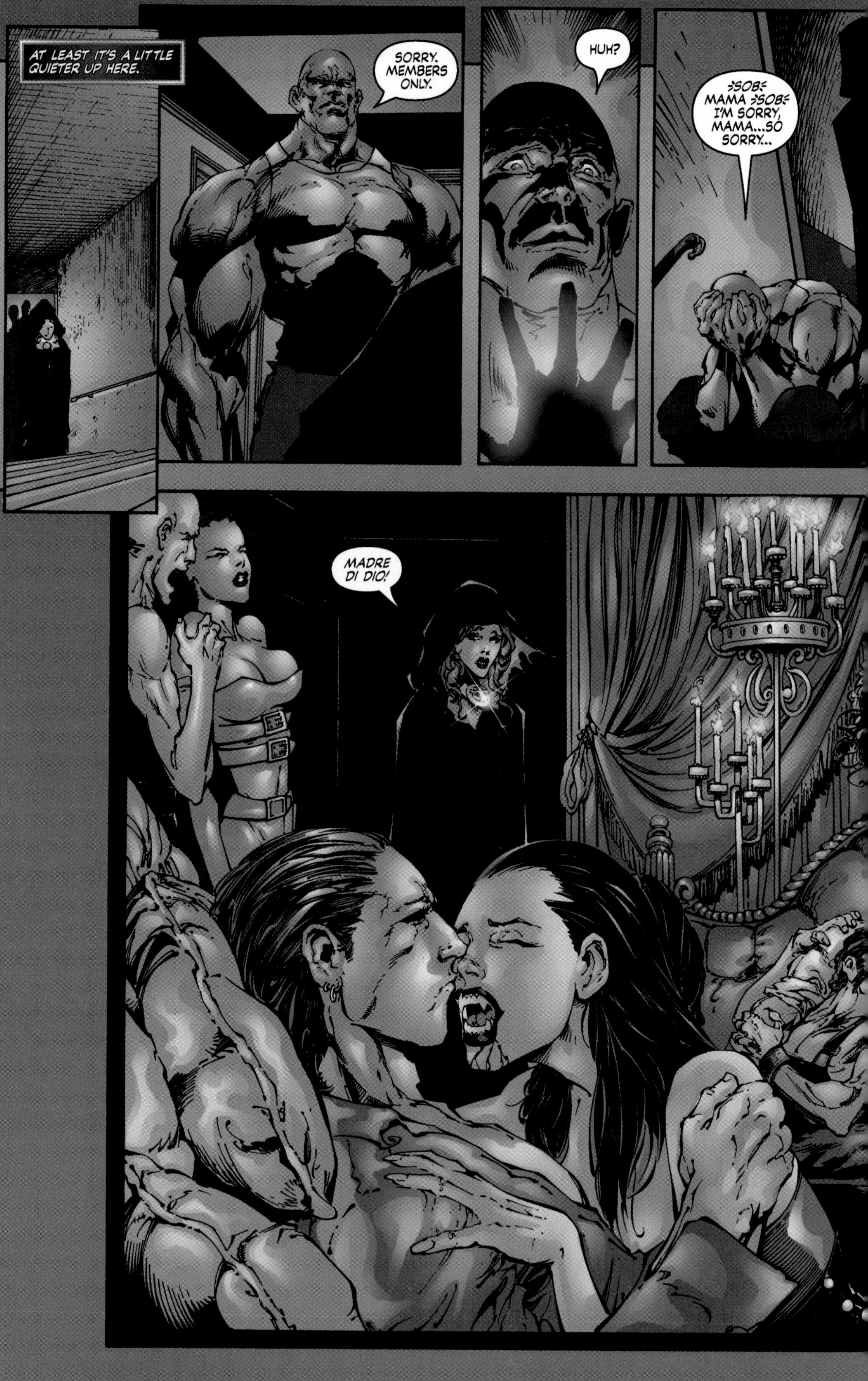
AT LEAST IT'S A LITTLE QUIETER UP HERE.
SORRY. MEMBERS ONLY.
HUH?
>SOB< MAMA >SOB< I'M SORRY, MAMA...SO SORRY...
MADRE DI DIO!

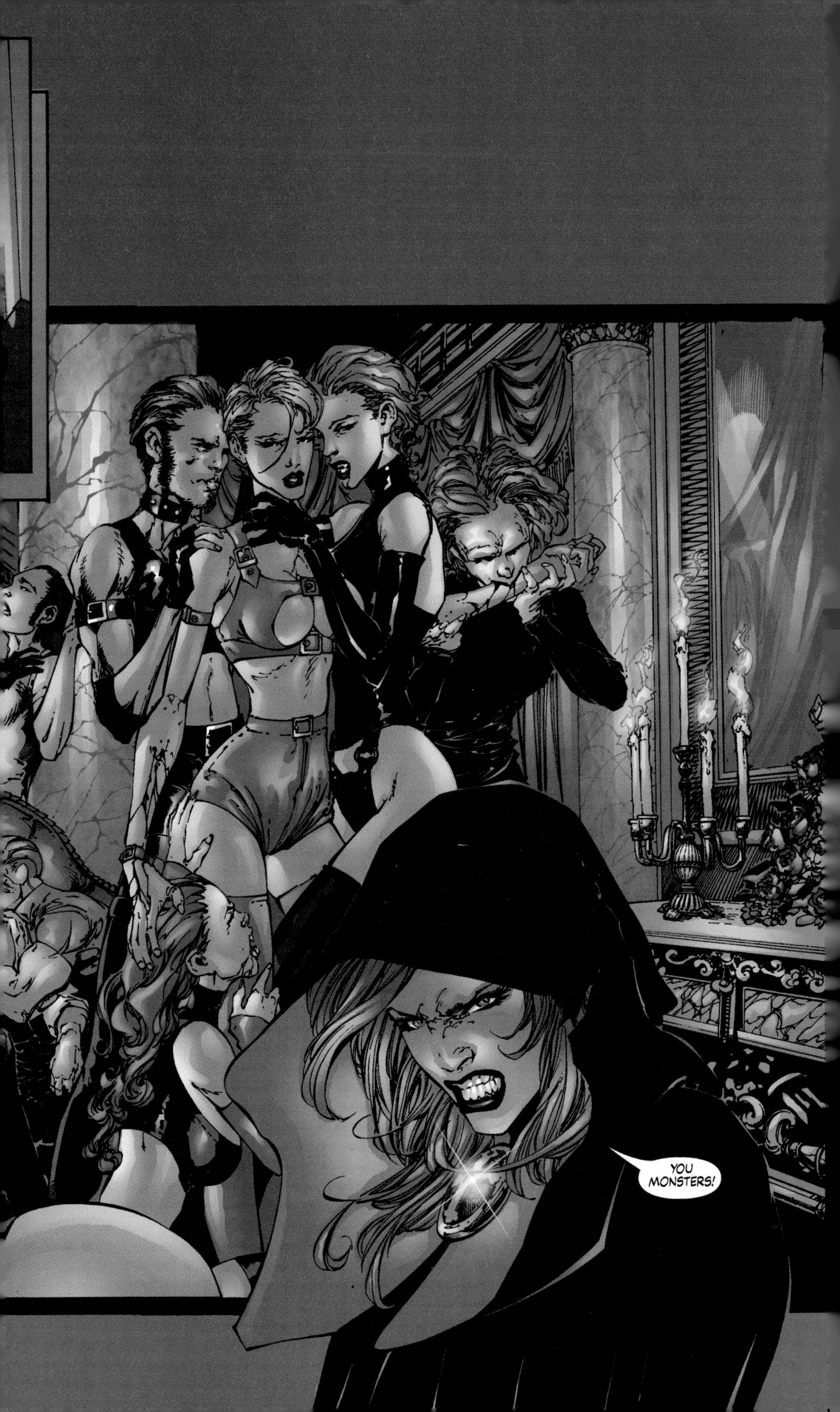
YOU MONSTERS!

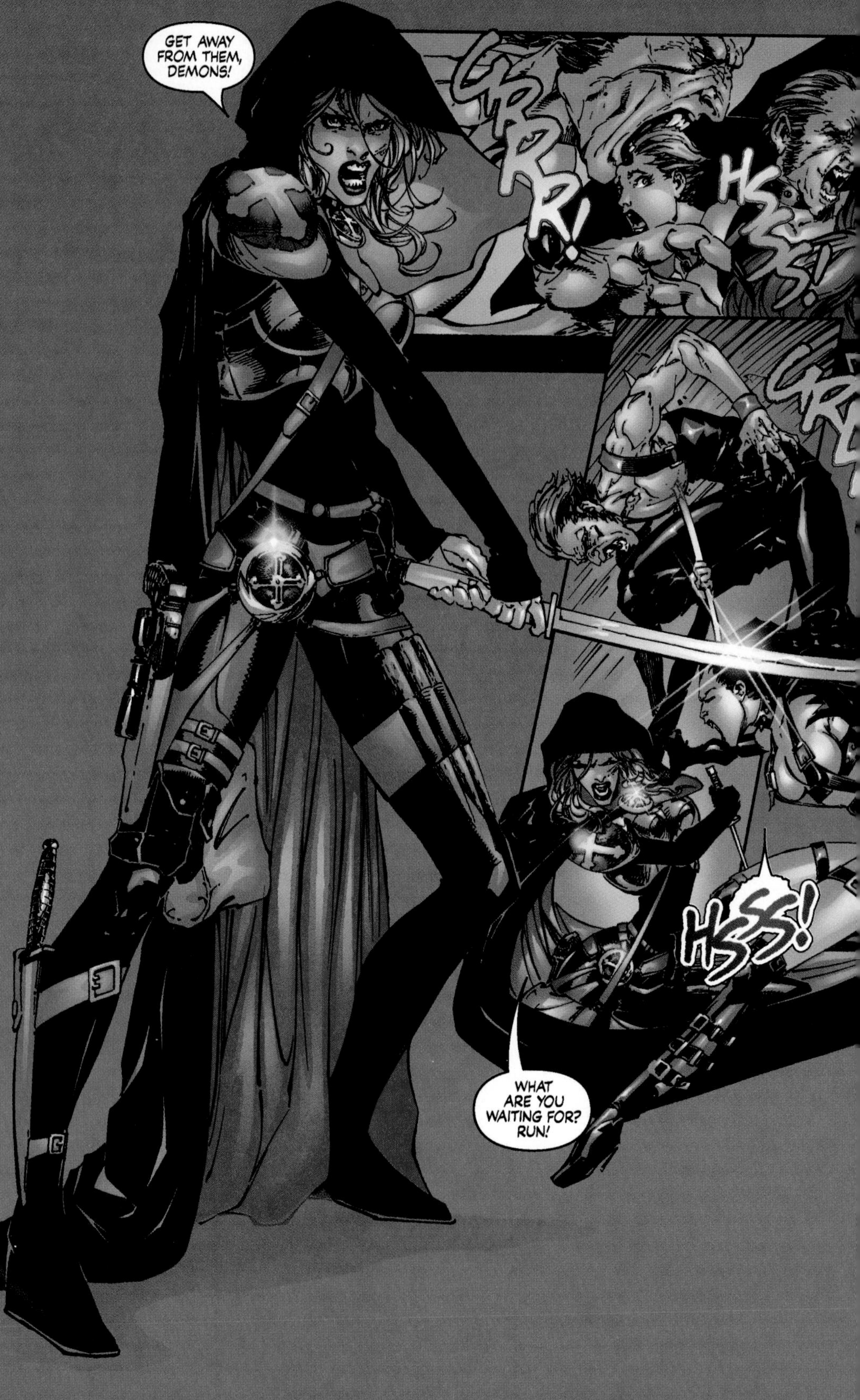
GET AWAY FROM THEM, DEMONS!
GRRR!
HSSS!
HSSS!
WHAT ARE YOU WAITING FOR? RUN!

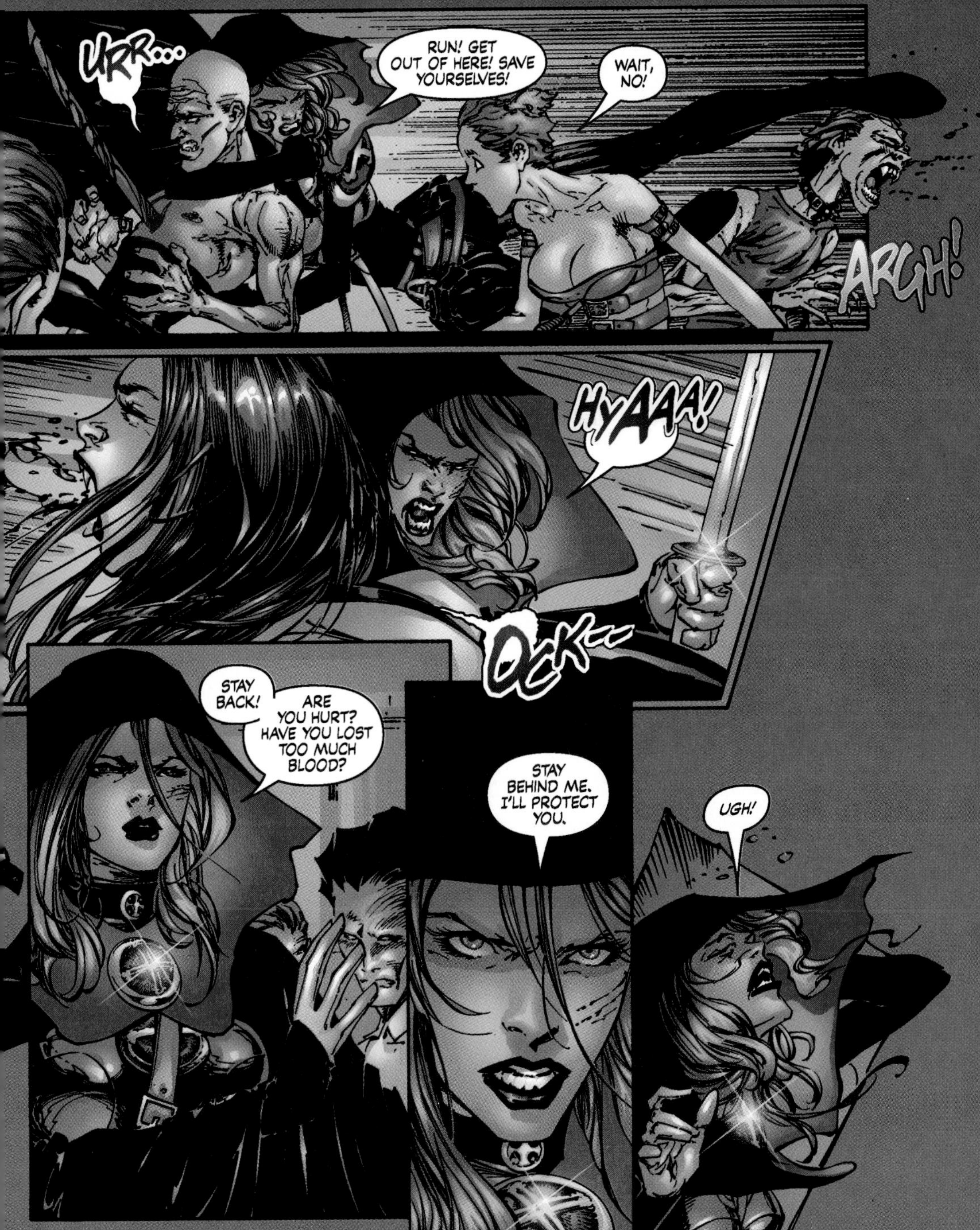
URR...
RUN! GET OUT OF HERE! SAVE YOURSELVES!
WAIT, NO!
ARGH!
HYAAA!
OCK--
STAY BACK!
ARE YOU HURT? HAVE YOU LOST TOO MUCH BLOOD?
STAY BEHIND ME. I'LL PROTECT YOU.
UGH!

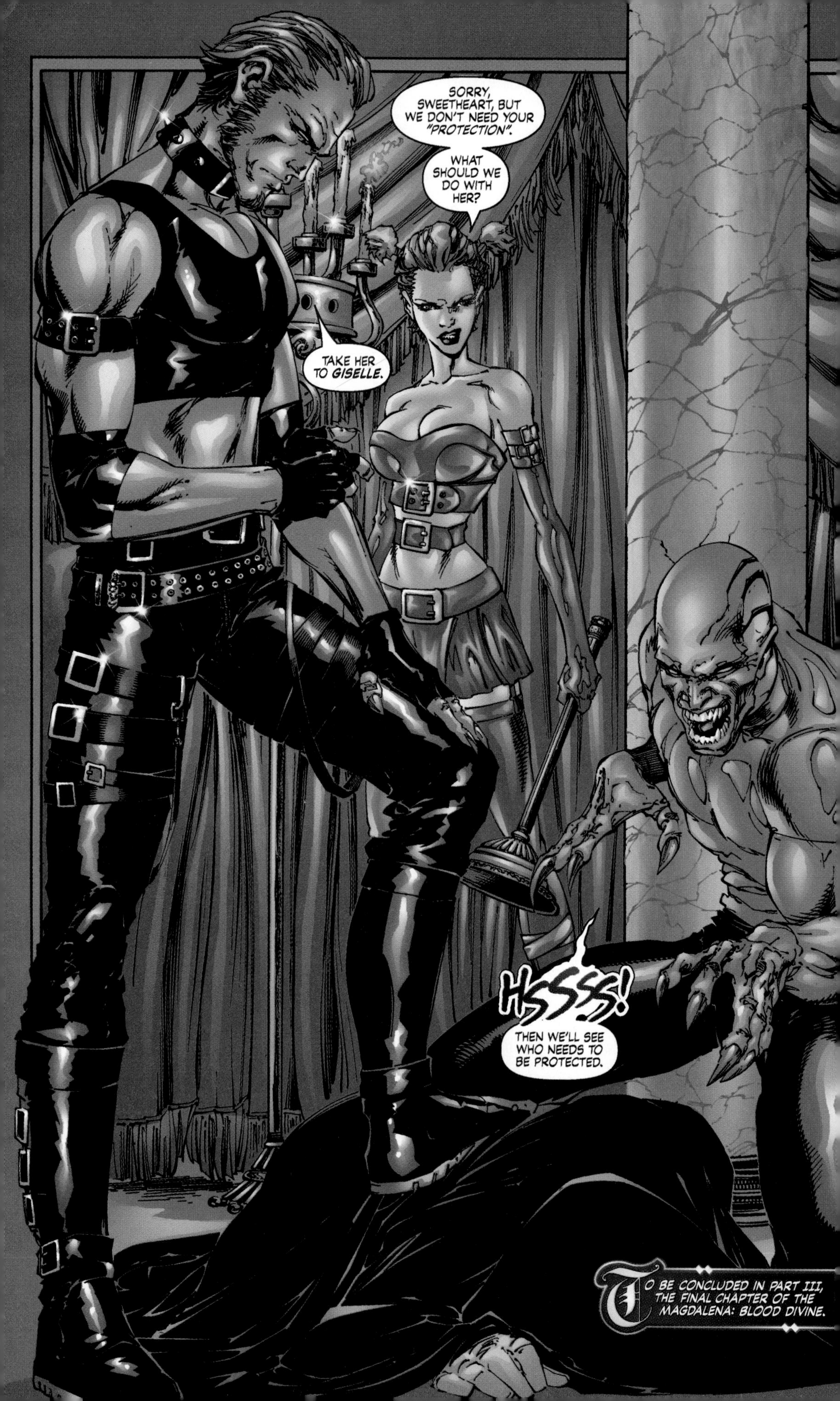

SORRY, SWEETHEART, BUT WE DON'T NEED YOUR "PROTECTION".
WHAT SHOULD WE DO WITH HER?
TAKE HER TO GISELLE.
HSSSS!
THEN WE'LL SEE WHO NEEDS TO BE PROTECTED.
TO BE CONCLUDED IN PART III, THE FINAL CHAPTER OF THE MAGDALENA: BLOOD DIVINE.

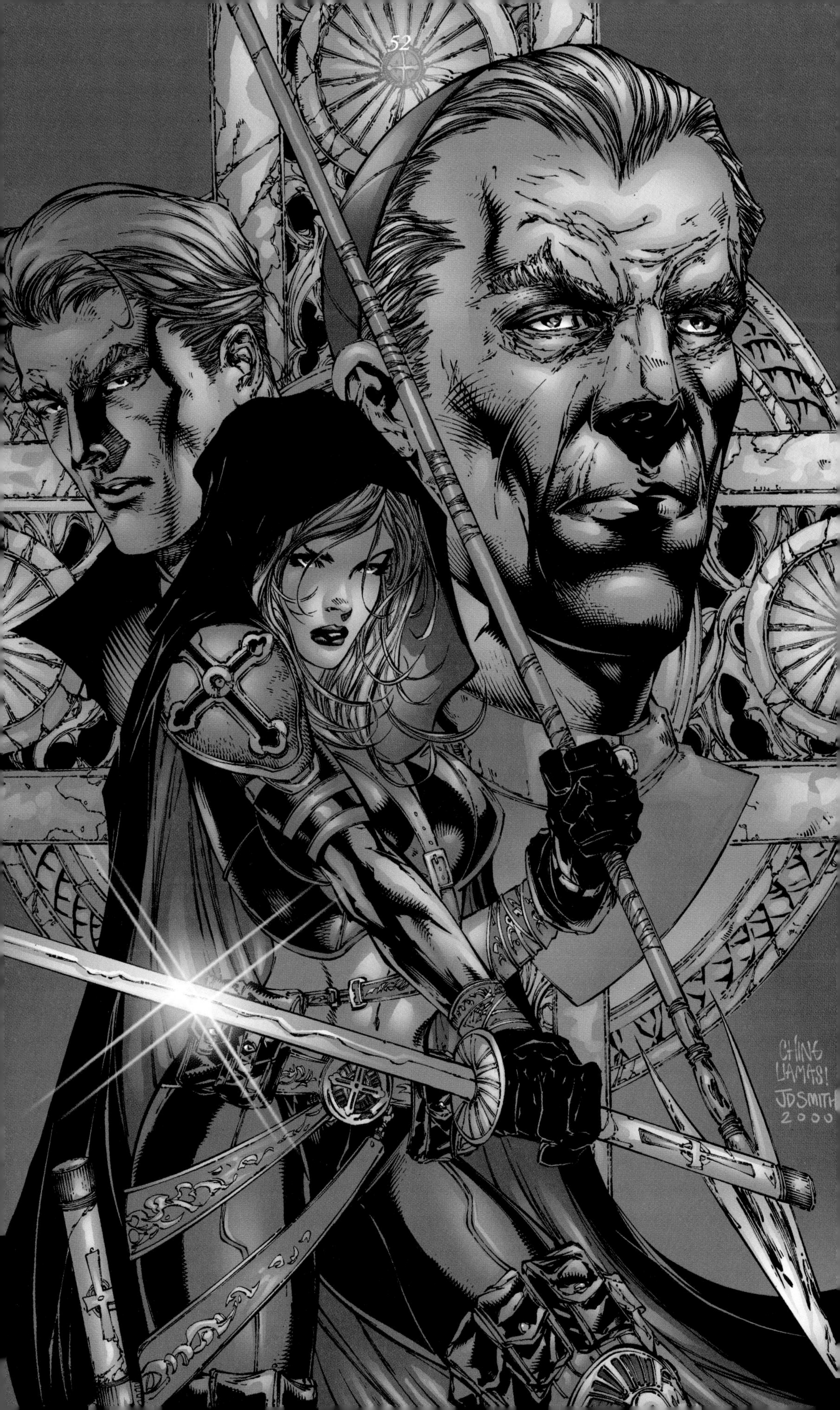
CHING
LLAMAS!
JD SMITH
2000

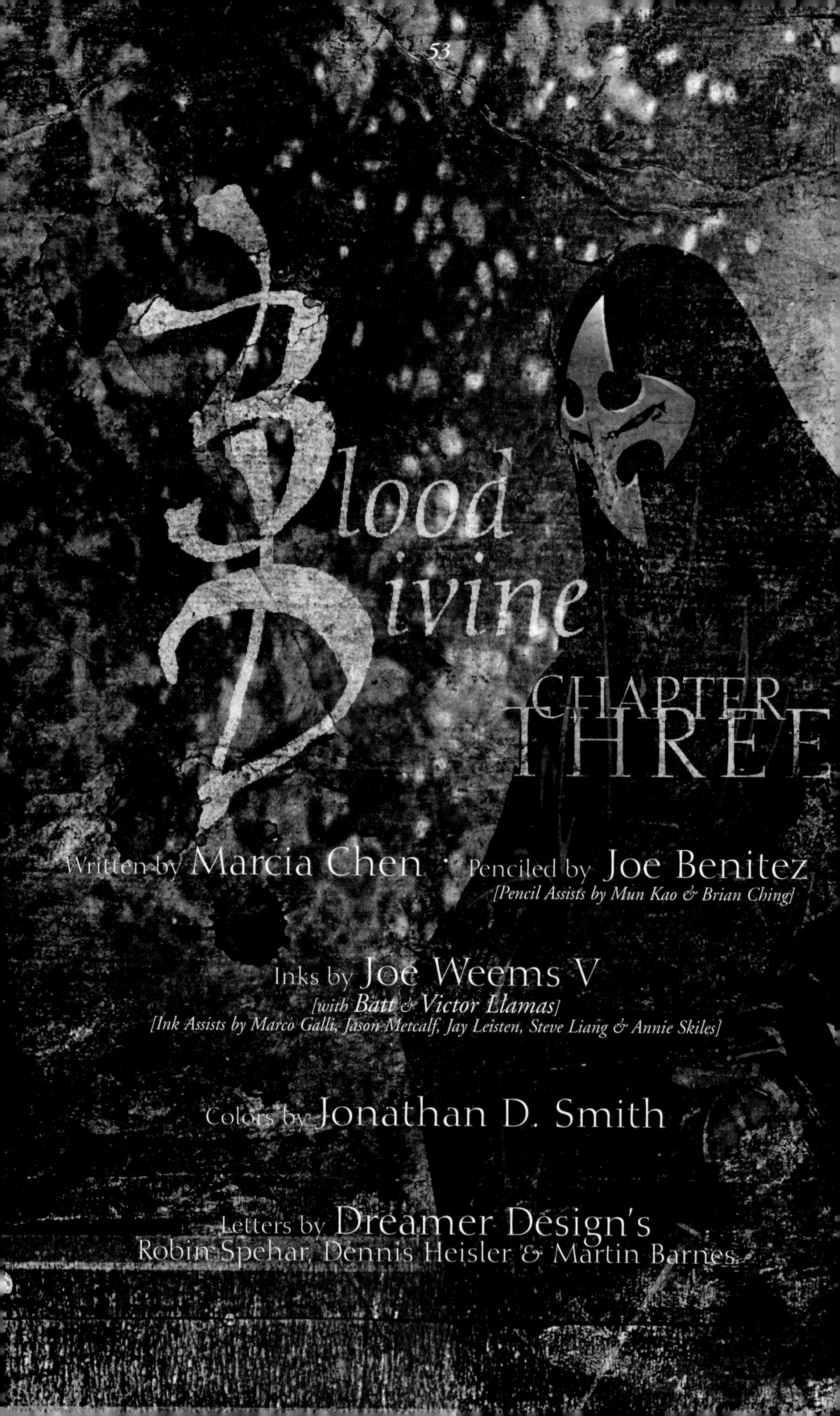
Blood Divine
CHAPTER THREE
Written by Marcia Chen · Penciled by Joe Benitez
[Pencil Assists by Mun Kao & Brian Ching]
Inks by Joe Weems V
[with Batt & Victor Llamas]
[Ink Assists by Marco Galli, Jason Metcalf, Jay Leisten, Steve Liang & Annie Skiles]
Colors by Jonathan D. Smith
Letters by Dreamer Design's
Robin Spehar, Dennis Heisler & Martin Barnes

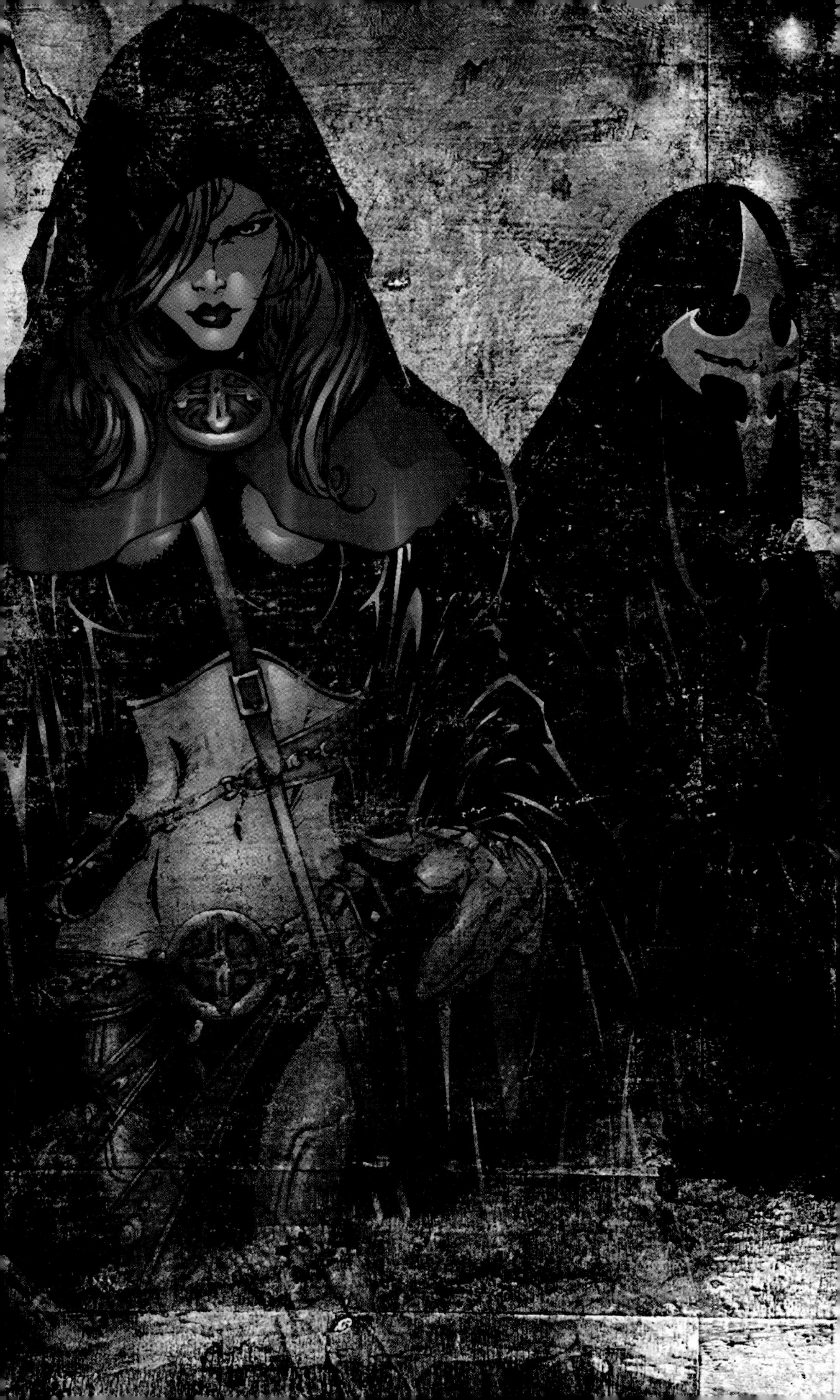

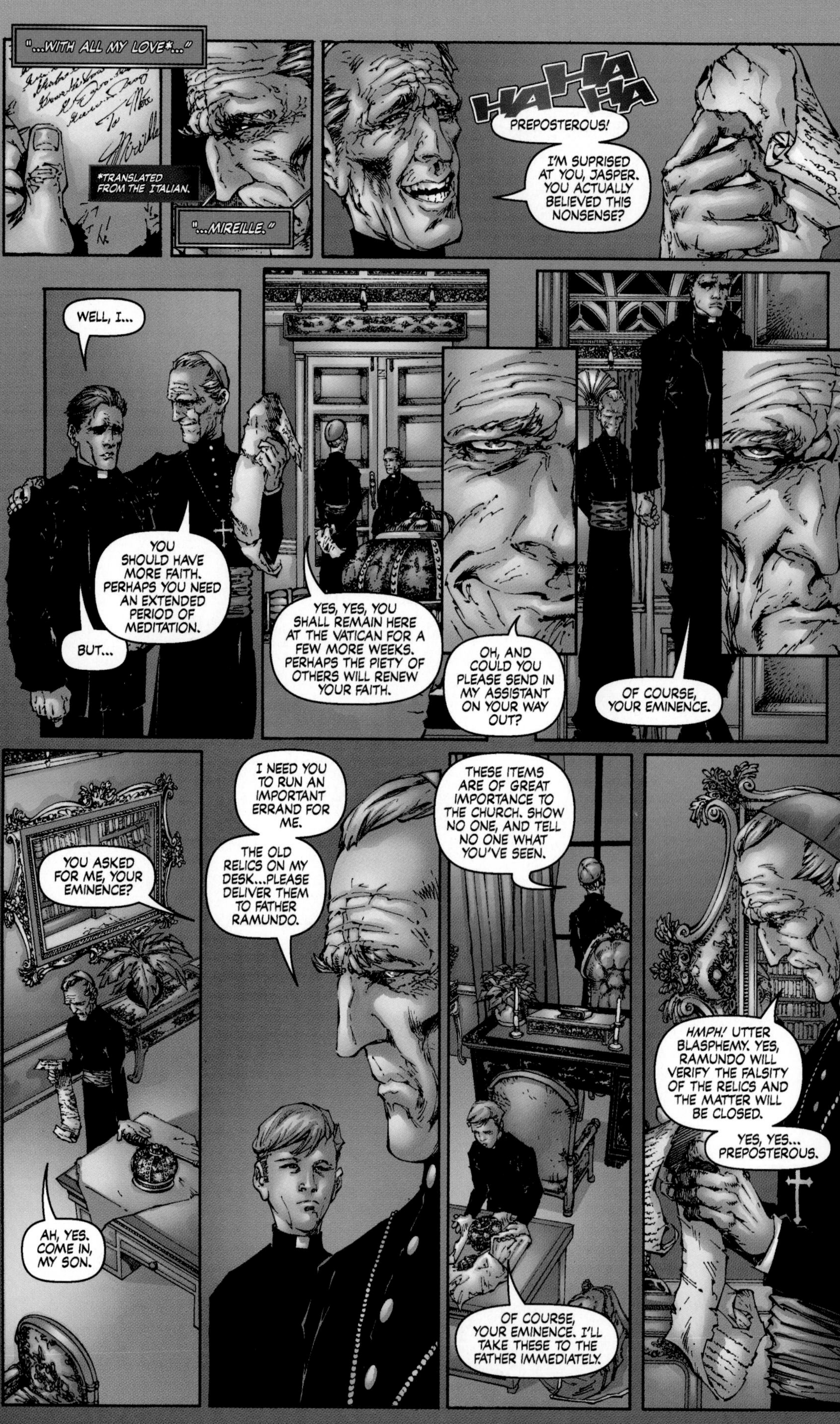

"...WITH ALL MY LOVE*..."
*TRANSLATED FROM THE ITALIAN.
"...MIREILLE."
HA HA HA
PREPOSTEROUS!
I'M SUPRISED AT YOU, JASPER. YOU ACTUALLY BELIEVED THIS NONSENSE?
WELL, I...
YOU SHOULD HAVE MORE FAITH. PERHAPS YOU NEED AN EXTENDED PERIOD OF MEDITATION.
BUT...
YES, YES, YOU SHALL REMAIN HERE AT THE VATICAN FOR A FEW MORE WEEKS. PERHAPS THE PIETY OF OTHERS WILL RENEW YOUR FAITH.
OH, AND COULD YOU PLEASE SEND IN MY ASSISTANT ON YOUR WAY OUT?
OF COURSE, YOUR EMINENCE.
YOU ASKED FOR ME, YOUR EMINENCE?
AH, YES. COME IN, MY SON.
I NEED YOU TO RUN AN IMPORTANT ERRAND FOR ME.
THE OLD RELICS ON MY DESK...PLEASE DELIVER THEM TO FATHER RAMUNDO.
THESE ITEMS ARE OF GREAT IMPORTANCE TO THE CHURCH. SHOW NO ONE, AND TELL NO ONE WHAT YOU'VE SEEN.
OF COURSE, YOUR EMINENCE. I'LL TAKE THESE TO THE FATHER IMMEDIATELY.
HMPH! UTTER BLASPHEMY. YES, RAMUNDO WILL VERIFY THE FALSITY OF THE RELICS AND THE MATTER WILL BE CLOSED.
YES, YES... PREPOSTEROUS.

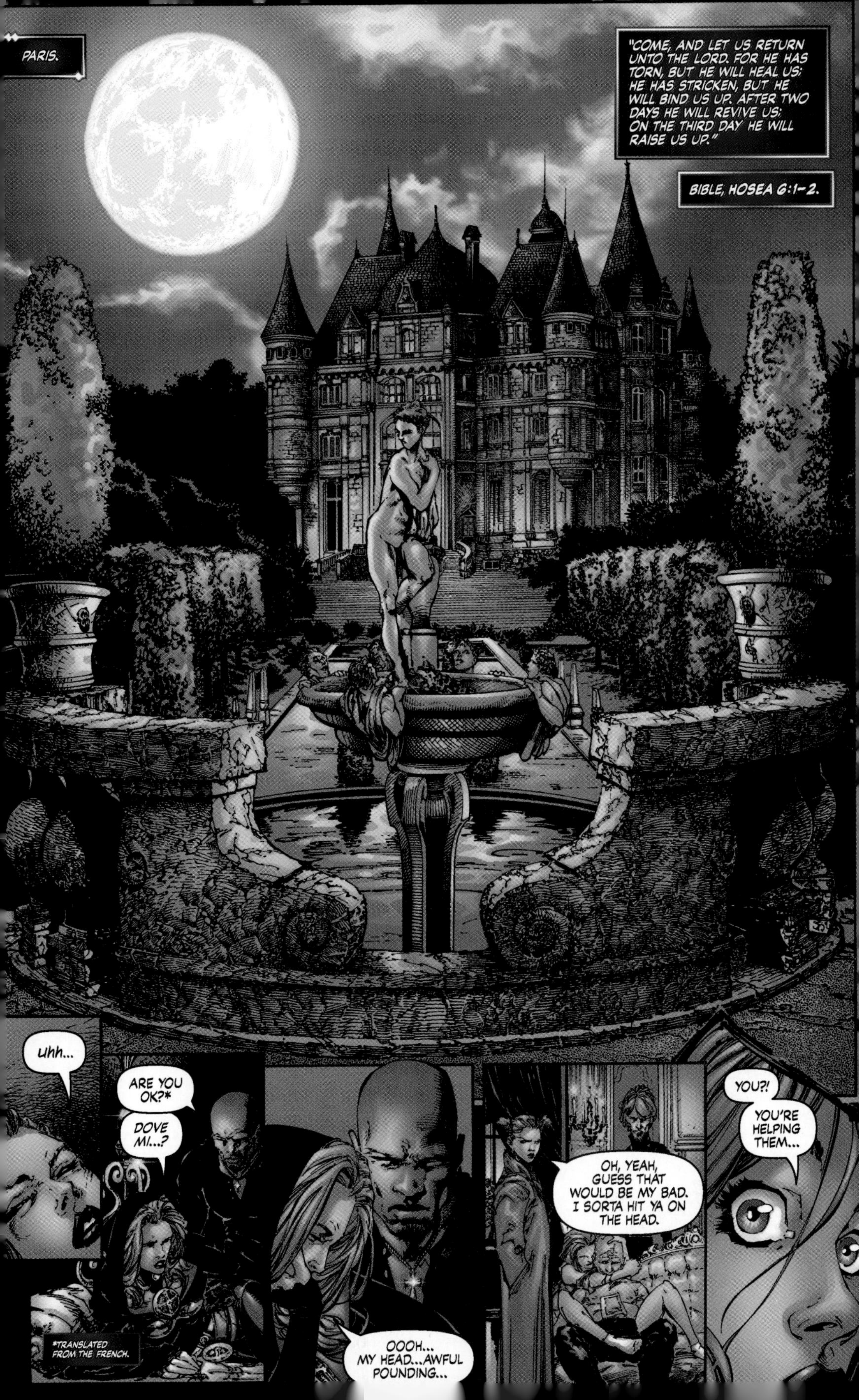

PARIS.
"COME, AND LET US RETURN UNTO THE LORD. FOR HE HAS TORN, BUT HE WILL HEAL US: HE HAS STRICKEN, BUT HE WILL BIND US UP. AFTER TWO DAYS HE WILL REVIVE US: ON THE THIRD DAY HE WILL RAISE US UP."
BIBLE, HOSEA 6:1-2.
uhh...
ARE YOU OK?*
DOVE MI...?
*TRANSLATED FROM THE FRENCH.
OOOH... MY HEAD...AWFUL POUNDING...
OH, YEAH, GUESS THAT WOULD BE MY BAD. I SORTA HIT YA ON THE HEAD.
YOU?!
YOU'RE HELPING THEM...

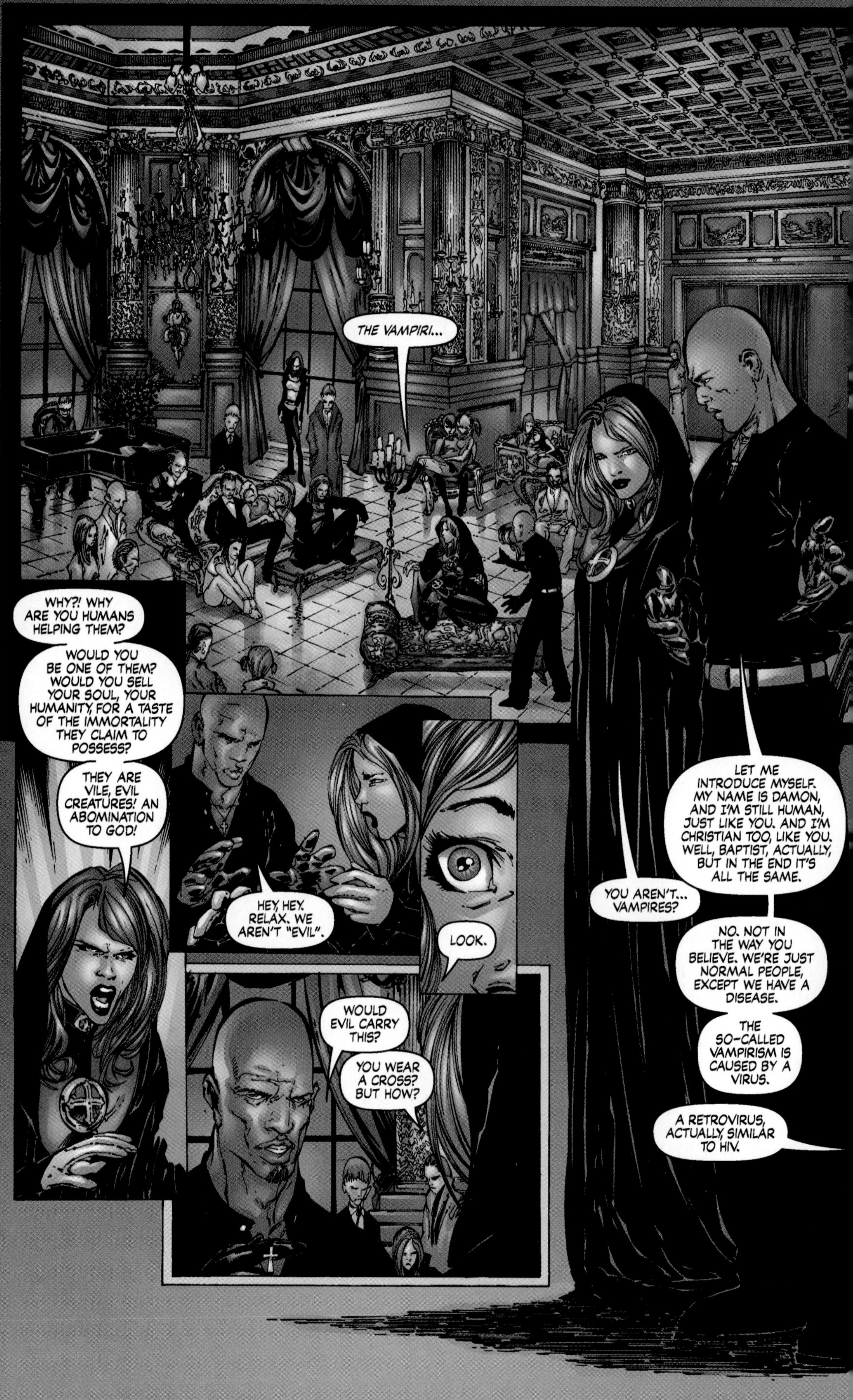
THE VAMPIRI...
WHY?! WHY ARE YOU HUMANS HELPING THEM?
WOULD YOU BE ONE OF THEM? WOULD YOU SELL YOUR SOUL, YOUR HUMANITY, FOR A TASTE OF THE IMMORTALITY THEY CLAIM TO POSSESS?
THEY ARE VILE, EVIL CREATURES! AN ABOMINATION TO GOD!
HEY, HEY. RELAX. WE AREN'T "EVIL".
LOOK.
WOULD EVIL CARRY THIS?
YOU WEAR A CROSS? BUT HOW?
LET ME INTRODUCE MYSELF. MY NAME IS DAMON, AND I'M STILL HUMAN, JUST LIKE YOU. AND I'M CHRISTIAN TOO, LIKE YOU. WELL, BAPTIST, ACTUALLY, BUT IN THE END IT'S ALL THE SAME.
YOU AREN'T... VAMPIRES?
NO. NOT IN THE WAY YOU BELIEVE. WE'RE JUST NORMAL PEOPLE, EXCEPT WE HAVE A DISEASE.
THE SO-CALLED VAMPIRISM IS CAUSED BY A VIRUS.
A RETROVIRUS, ACTUALLY, SIMILAR TO HIV.

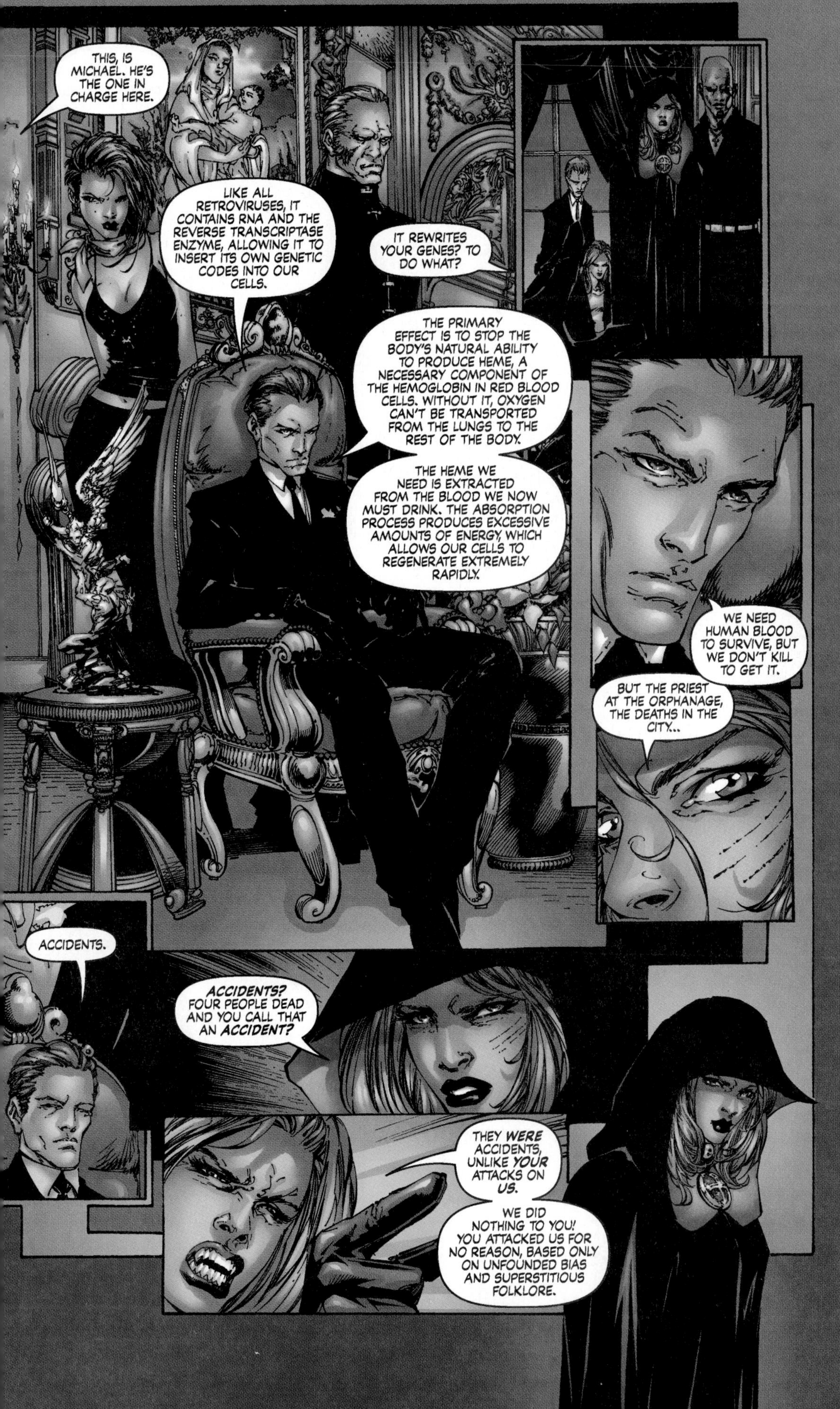
THIS, IS MICHAEL. HE'S THE ONE IN CHARGE HERE.
LIKE ALL RETROVIRUSES, IT CONTAINS RNA AND THE REVERSE TRANSCRIPTASE ENZYME, ALLOWING IT TO INSERT ITS OWN GENETIC CODES INTO OUR CELLS.
IT REWRITES YOUR GENES? TO DO WHAT?
THE PRIMARY EFFECT IS TO STOP THE BODY'S NATURAL ABILITY TO PRODUCE HEME, A NECESSARY COMPONENT OF THE HEMOGLOBIN IN RED BLOOD CELLS. WITHOUT IT, OXYGEN CAN'T BE TRANSPORTED FROM THE LUNGS TO THE REST OF THE BODY.
THE HEME WE NEED IS EXTRACTED FROM THE BLOOD WE NOW MUST DRINK. THE ABSORPTION PROCESS PRODUCES EXCESSIVE AMOUNTS OF ENERGY, WHICH ALLOWS OUR CELLS TO REGENERATE EXTREMELY RAPIDLY.
WE NEED HUMAN BLOOD TO SURVIVE, BUT WE DON'T KILL TO GET IT.
BUT THE PRIEST AT THE ORPHANAGE, THE DEATHS IN THE CITY..
ACCIDENTS.
ACCIDENTS? FOUR PEOPLE DEAD AND YOU CALL THAT AN ACCIDENT?
THEY WERE ACCIDENTS, UNLIKE YOUR ATTACKS ON US.
WE DID NOTHING TO YOU! YOU ATTACKED US FOR NO REASON, BASED ONLY ON UNFOUNDED BIAS AND SUPERSTITIOUS FOLKLORE.

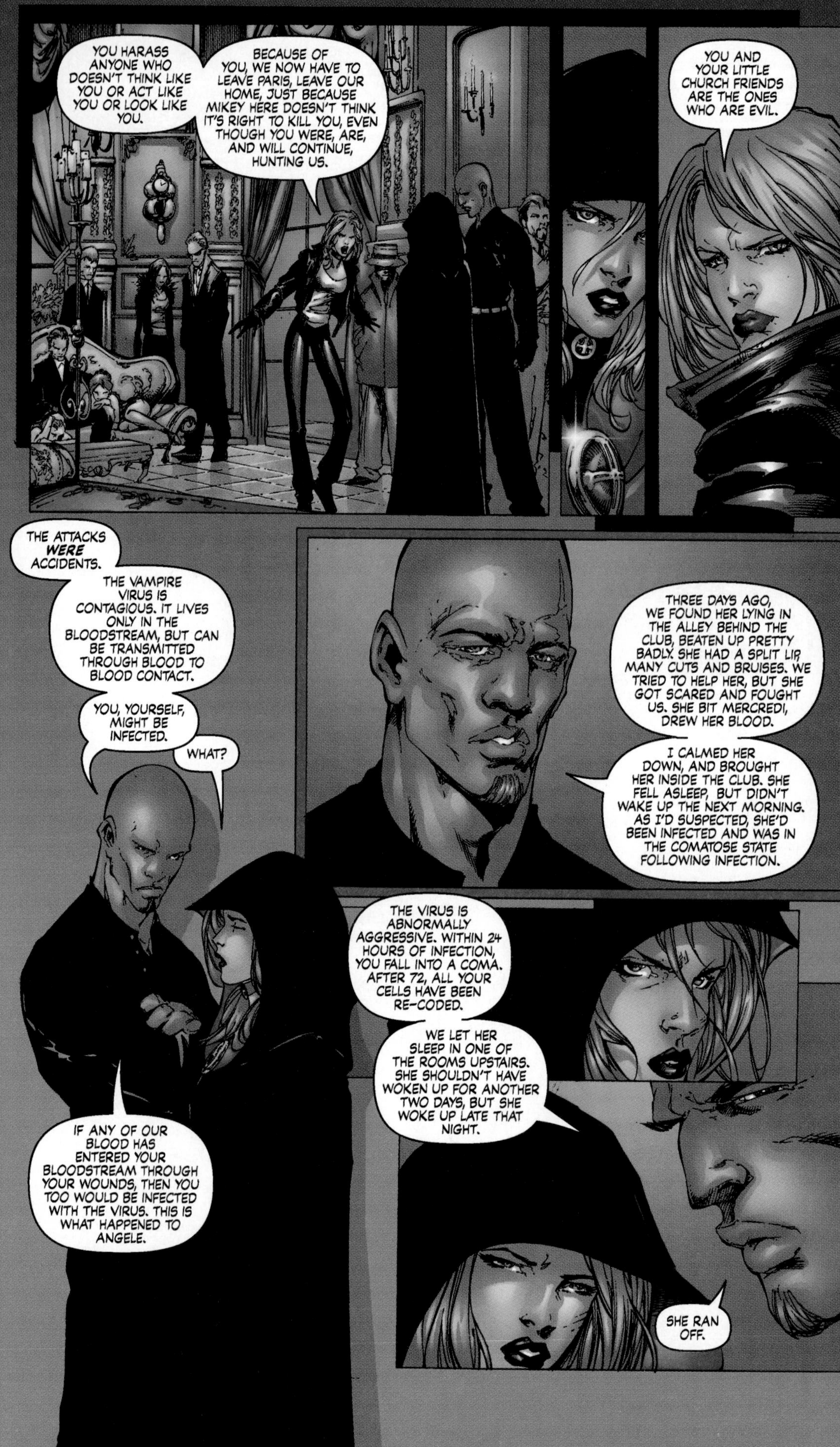
YOU HARASS ANYONE WHO DOESN'T THINK LIKE YOU OR ACT LIKE YOU OR LOOK LIKE YOU.
BECAUSE OF YOU, WE NOW HAVE TO LEAVE PARIS, LEAVE OUR HOME, JUST BECAUSE MIKEY HERE DOESN'T THINK IT'S RIGHT TO KILL YOU, EVEN THOUGH YOU WERE, ARE, AND WILL CONTINUE, HUNTING US.
YOU AND YOUR LITTLE CHURCH FRIENDS ARE THE ONES WHO ARE EVIL.
THE ATTACKS *WERE* ACCIDENTS.
THE VAMPIRE VIRUS IS CONTAGIOUS. IT LIVES ONLY IN THE BLOODSTREAM, BUT CAN BE TRANSMITTED THROUGH BLOOD TO BLOOD CONTACT.
YOU, YOURSELF, MIGHT BE INFECTED.
WHAT?
THREE DAYS AGO, WE FOUND HER LYING IN THE ALLEY BEHIND THE CLUB, BEATEN UP PRETTY BADLY. SHE HAD A SPLIT LIP, MANY CUTS AND BRUISES. WE TRIED TO HELP HER, BUT SHE GOT SCARED AND FOUGHT US. SHE BIT MERCREDI, DREW HER BLOOD.
I CALMED HER DOWN, AND BROUGHT HER INSIDE THE CLUB. SHE FELL ASLEEP, BUT DIDN'T WAKE UP THE NEXT MORNING. AS I'D SUSPECTED, SHE'D BEEN INFECTED AND WAS IN THE COMATOSE STATE FOLLOWING INFECTION.
THE VIRUS IS ABNORMALLY AGGRESSIVE. WITHIN 24 HOURS OF INFECTION, YOU FALL INTO A COMA. AFTER 72, ALL YOUR CELLS HAVE BEEN RE-CODED.
WE LET HER SLEEP IN ONE OF THE ROOMS UPSTAIRS. SHE SHOULDN'T HAVE WOKEN UP FOR ANOTHER TWO DAYS, BUT SHE WOKE UP LATE THAT NIGHT.
IF ANY OF OUR BLOOD HAS ENTERED YOUR BLOODSTREAM THROUGH YOUR WOUNDS, THEN YOU TOO WOULD BE INFECTED WITH THE VIRUS. THIS IS WHAT HAPPENED TO ANGELE.
SHE RAN OFF.

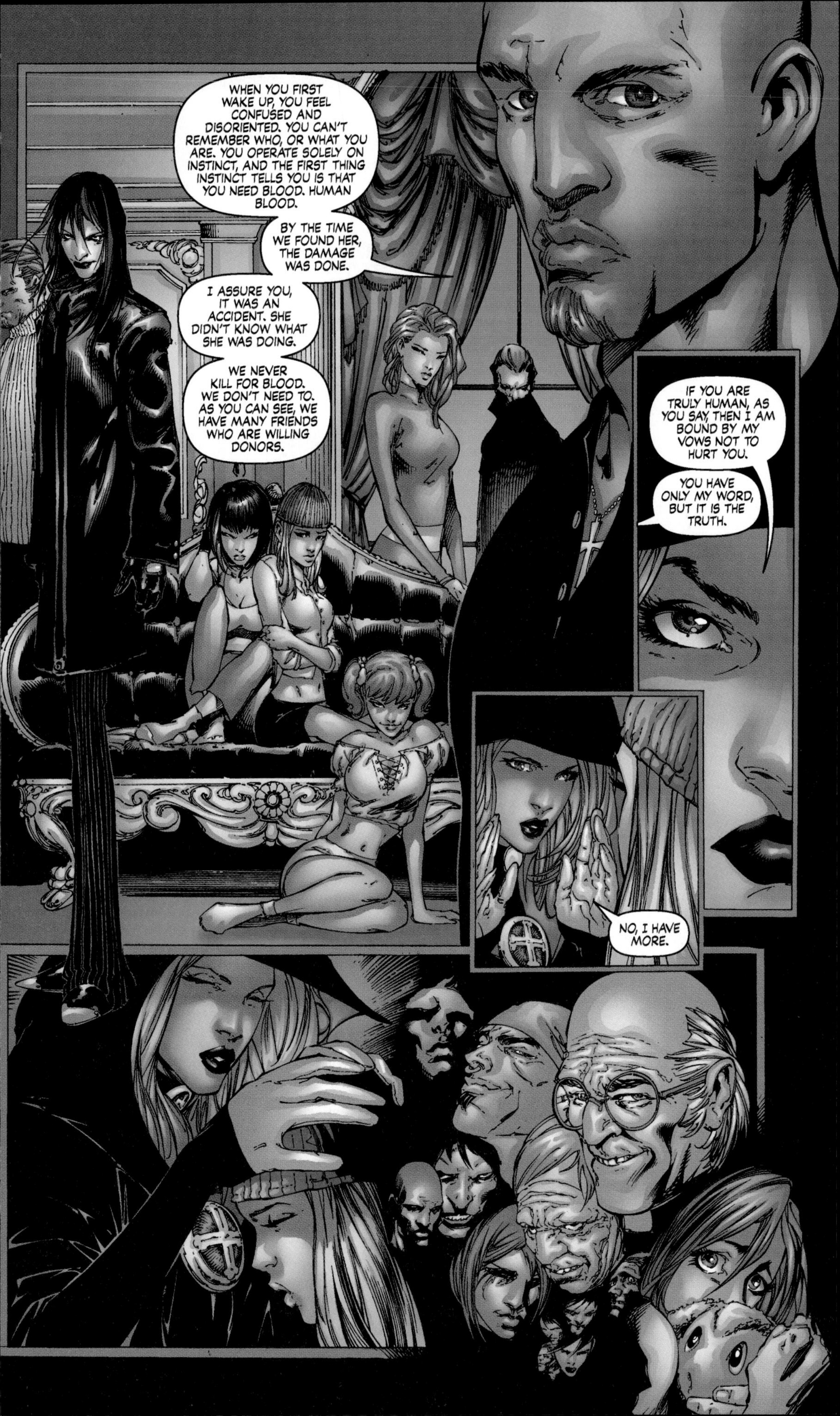
WHEN YOU FIRST WAKE UP, YOU FEEL CONFUSED AND DISORIENTED. YOU CAN'T REMEMBER WHO, OR WHAT YOU ARE. YOU OPERATE SOLELY ON INSTINCT, AND THE FIRST THING INSTINCT TELLS YOU IS THAT YOU NEED BLOOD. HUMAN BLOOD.
BY THE TIME WE FOUND HER, THE DAMAGE WAS DONE.
I ASSURE YOU, IT WAS AN ACCIDENT. SHE DIDN'T KNOW WHAT SHE WAS DOING.
WE NEVER KILL FOR BLOOD. WE DON'T NEED TO. AS YOU CAN SEE, WE HAVE MANY FRIENDS WHO ARE WILLING DONORS.
IF YOU ARE TRULY HUMAN, AS YOU SAY, THEN I AM BOUND BY MY VOWS NOT TO HURT YOU.
YOU HAVE ONLY MY WORD, BUT IT IS THE TRUTH.
NO, I HAVE MORE.

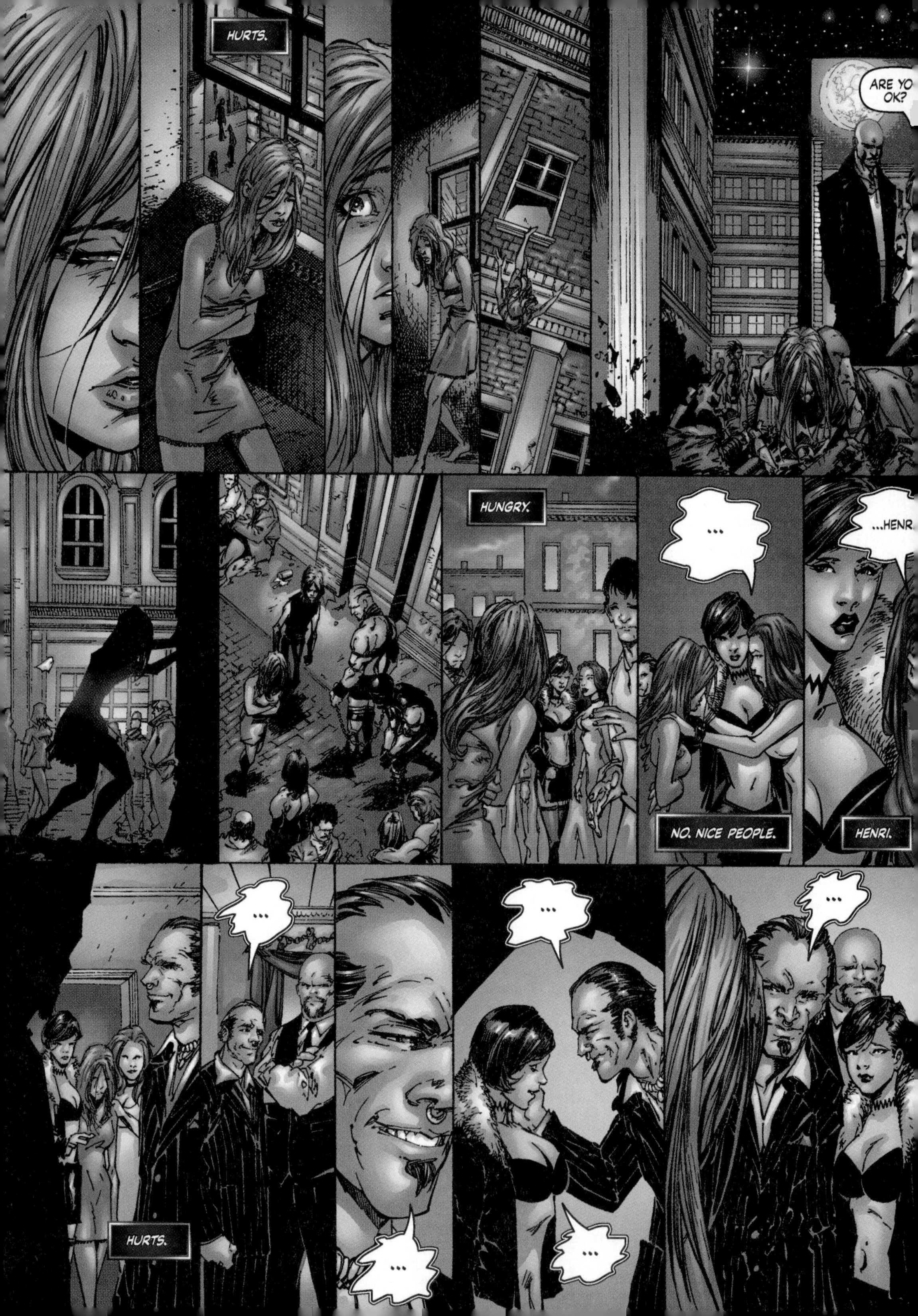
HURTS.
ARE YO OK?
HUNGRY.
...
NO. NICE PEOPLE.
...HENR.
HENRI.
...
HURTS.
...
...
...
...

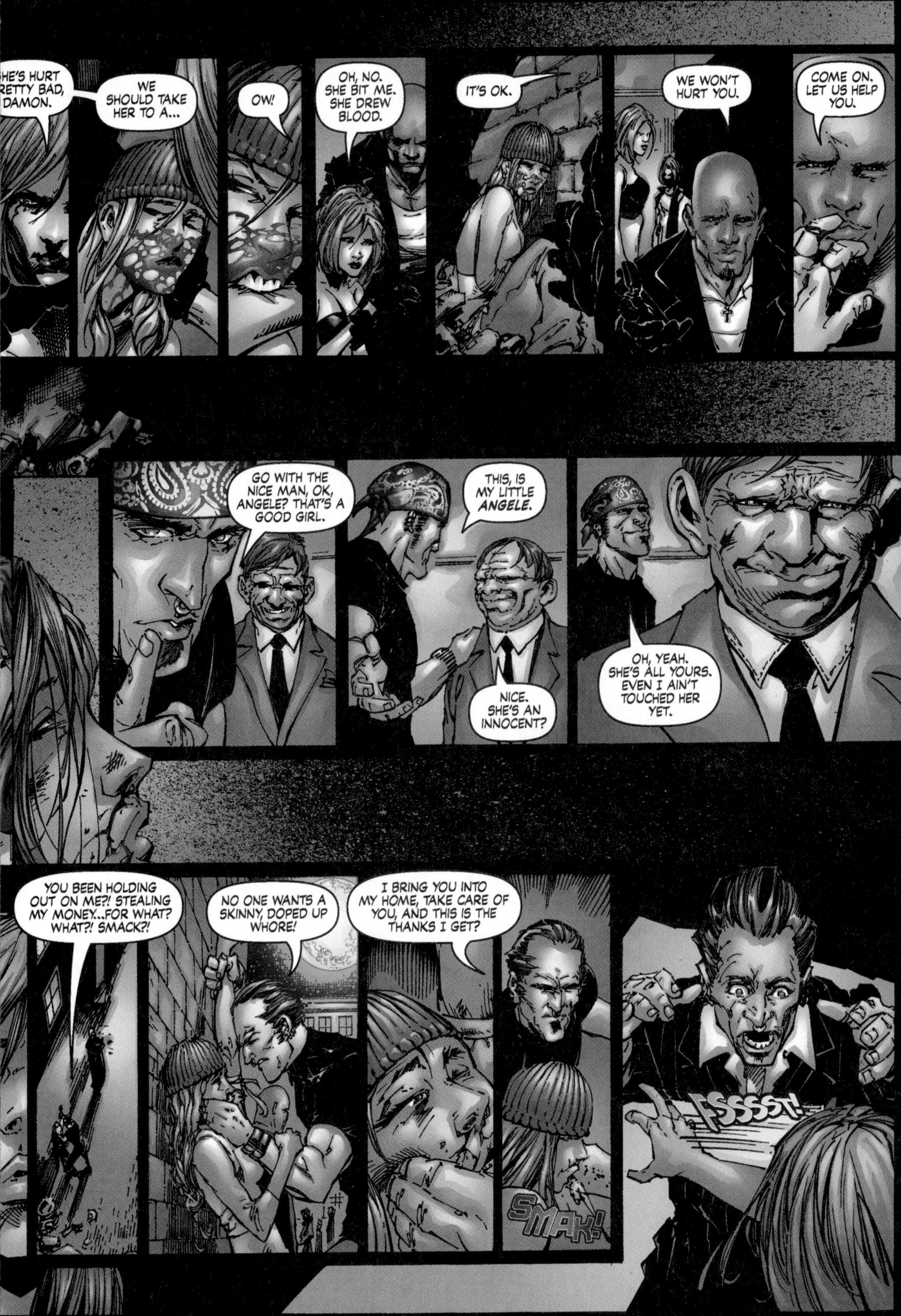

HE'S HURT
RETTY BAD,
DAMON.
WE SHOULD TAKE HER TO A...
OW!
OH, NO. SHE BIT ME. SHE DREW BLOOD.
IT'S OK.
WE WON'T HURT YOU.
COME ON. LET US HELP YOU.
GO WITH THE NICE MAN, OK, ANGELE? THAT'S A GOOD GIRL.
THIS, IS MY LITTLE ANGELE.
NICE. SHE'S AN INNOCENT?
OH, YEAH. SHE'S ALL YOURS. EVEN I AIN'T TOUCHED HER YET.
YOU BEEN HOLDING OUT ON ME?! STEALING MY MONEY...FOR WHAT? WHAT?! SMACK?!
NO ONE WANTS A SKINNY, DOPED UP WHORE!
I BRING YOU INTO MY HOME, TAKE CARE OF YOU, AND THIS IS THE THANKS I GET?
SMAK!
FSSSST!

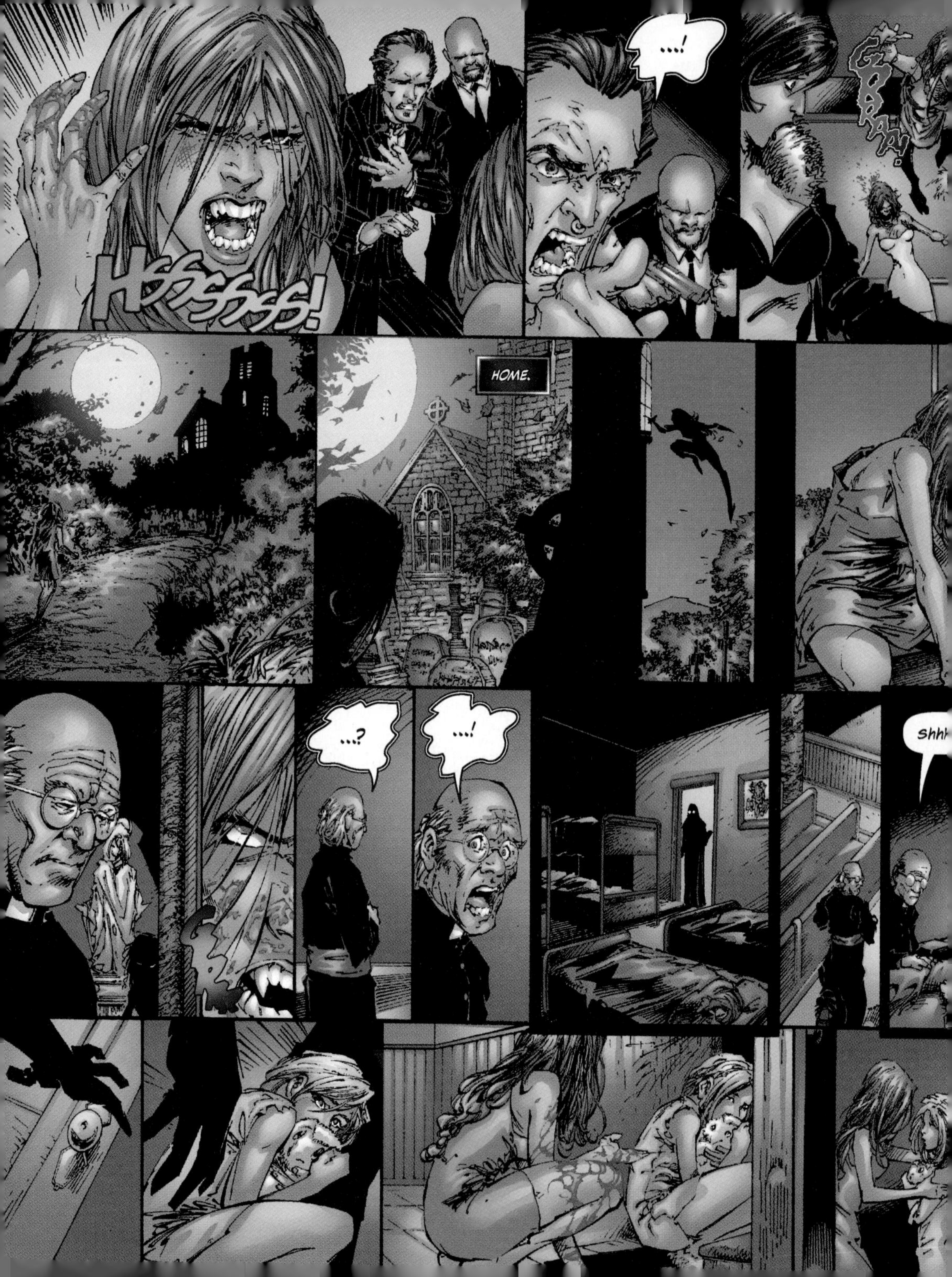
HSSSSS!
...!
HOME.
...?
...!
Shh

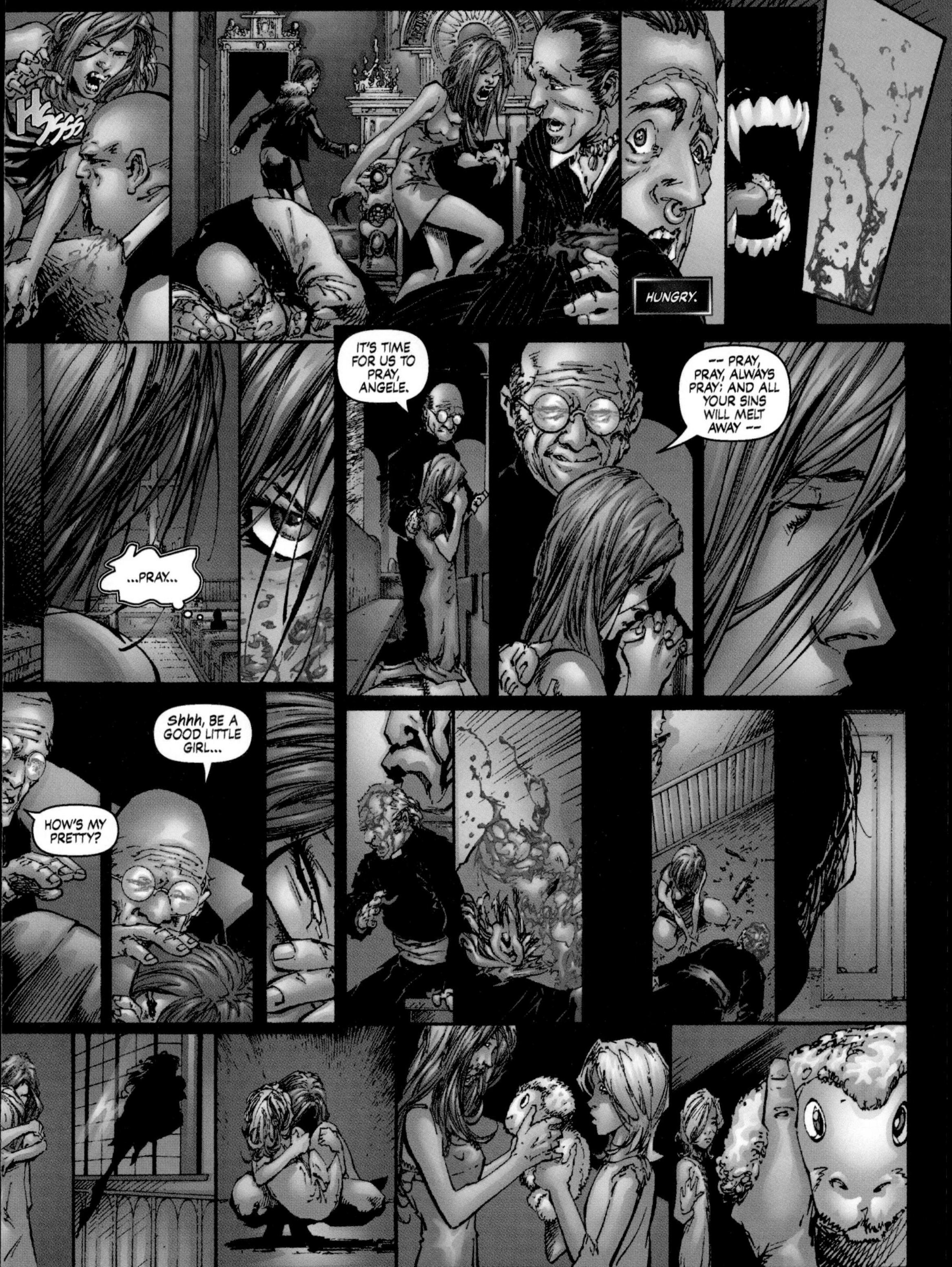
HSSSS
HUNGRY.
...PRAY...
IT'S TIME FOR US TO PRAY, ANGELE.
-- PRAY, PRAY, ALWAYS PRAY; AND ALL YOUR SINS WILL MELT AWAY --
HOW'S MY PRETTY?
Shhh, BE A GOOD LITTLE GIRL...

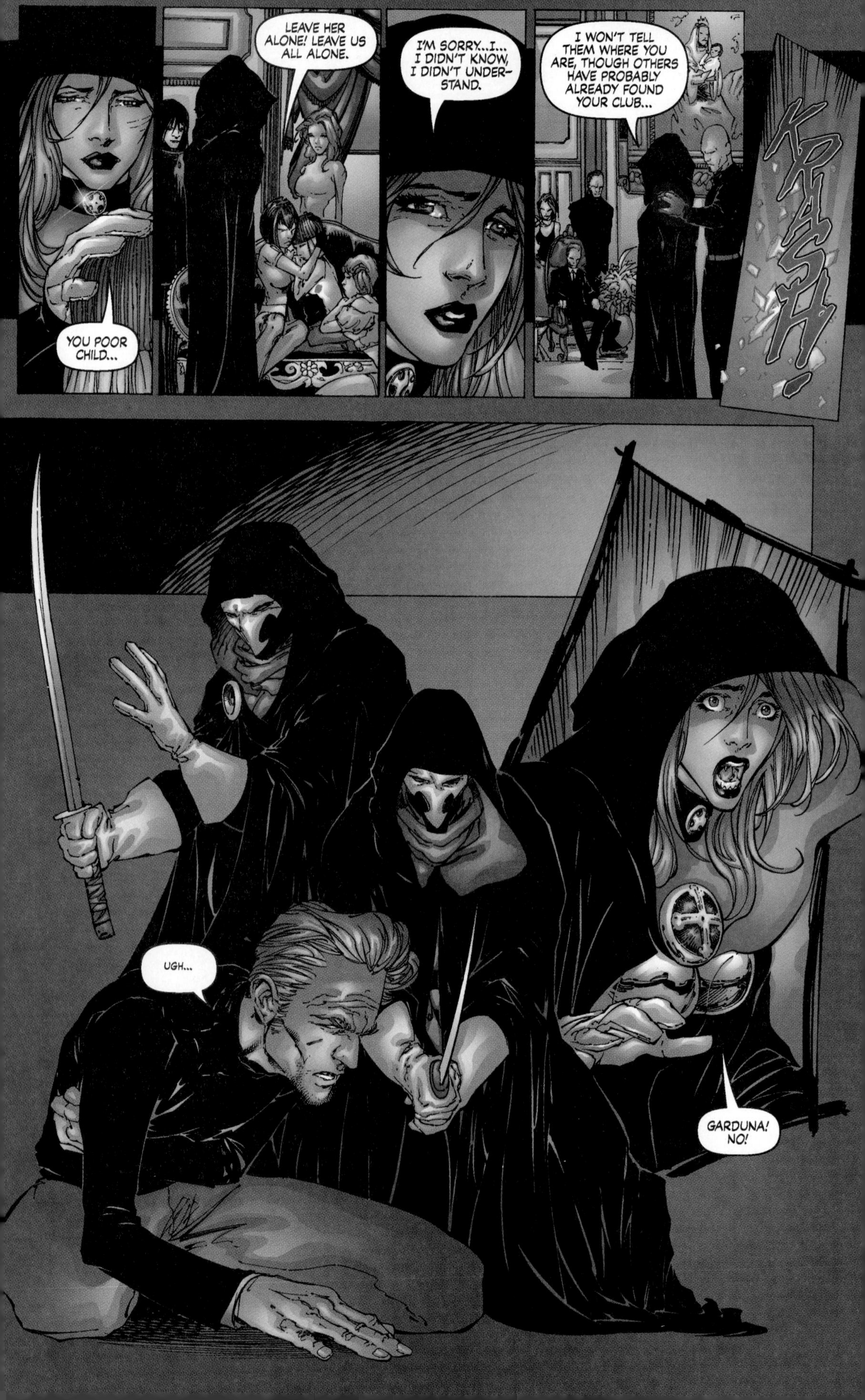
YOU POOR CHILD...
LEAVE HER ALONE! LEAVE US ALL ALONE.
I'M SORRY...I... I DIDN'T KNOW, I DIDN'T UNDER-STAND.
I WON'T TELL THEM WHERE YOU ARE, THOUGH OTHERS HAVE PROBABLY ALREADY FOUND YOUR CLUB...
KRASH!
UGH...
GARDUNA! NO!

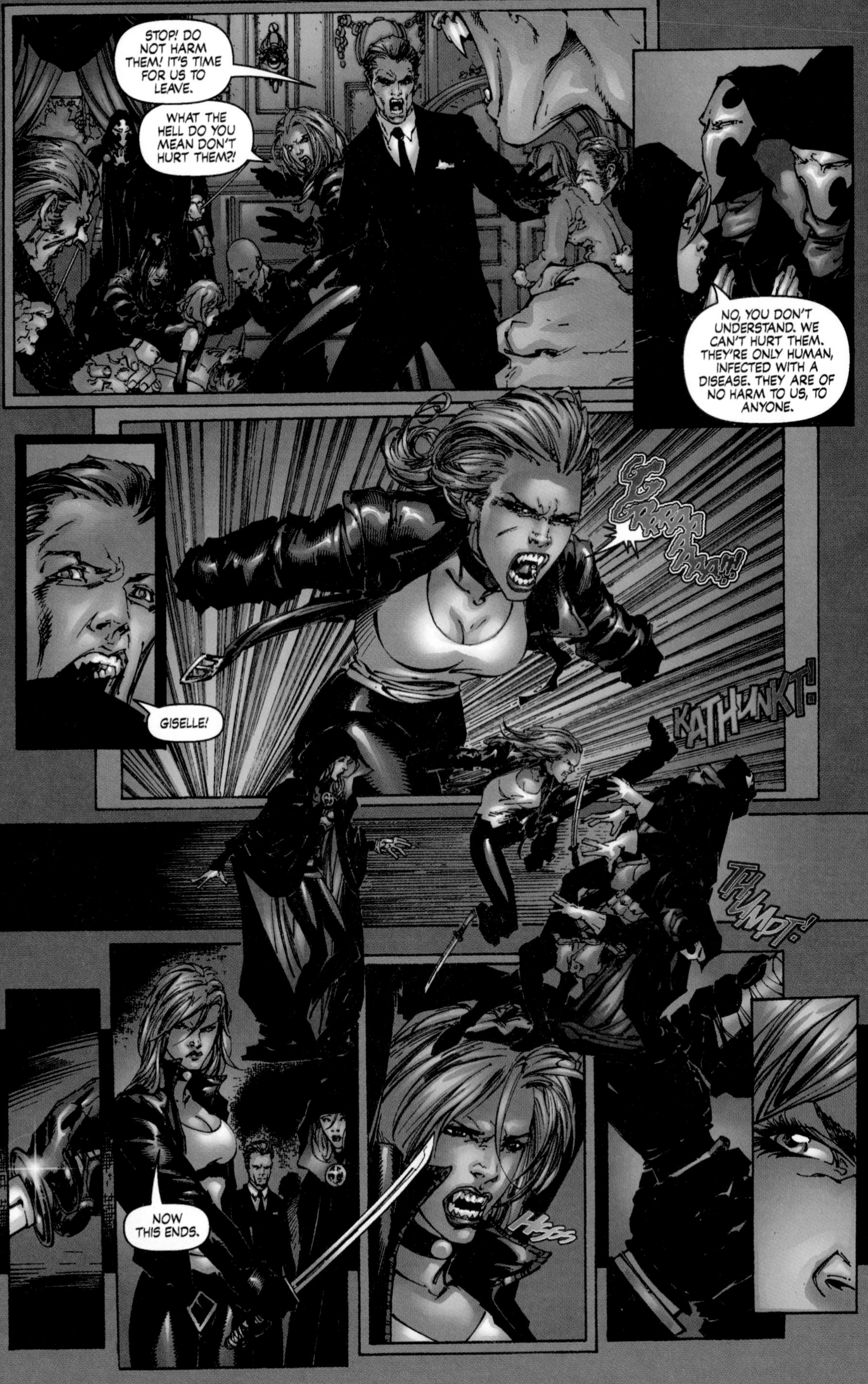
STOP! DO NOT HARM THEM! IT'S TIME FOR US TO LEAVE.
WHAT THE HELL DO YOU MEAN DON'T HURT THEM?!
NO, YOU DON'T UNDERSTAND. WE CAN'T HURT THEM. THEY'RE ONLY HUMAN, INFECTED WITH A DISEASE. THEY ARE OF NO HARM TO US, TO ANYONE.
GISELLE!
KATHUNKT!
THUMPT!
NOW THIS ENDS.
HSSS

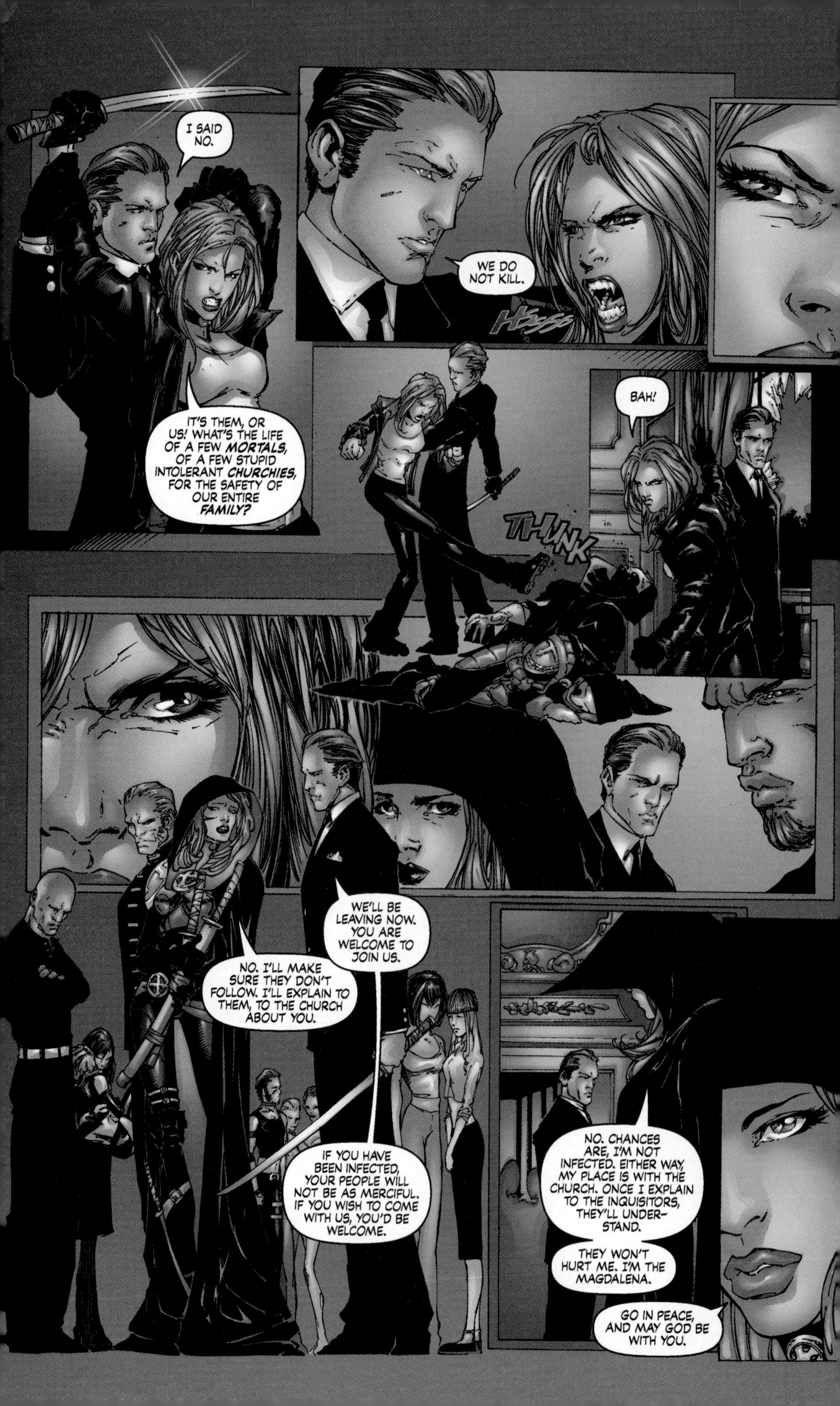
I SAID NO.
IT'S THEM, OR US! WHAT'S THE LIFE OF A FEW *MORTALS,* OF A FEW STUPID INTOLERANT *CHURCHIES,* FOR THE SAFETY OF OUR ENTIRE *FAMILY?*
WE DO NOT KILL.
HSSSS
BAH!
THUNK
WE'LL BE LEAVING NOW. YOU ARE WELCOME TO JOIN US.
NO. I'LL MAKE SURE THEY DON'T FOLLOW. I'LL EXPLAIN TO THEM, TO THE CHURCH ABOUT YOU.
IF YOU HAVE BEEN INFECTED, YOUR PEOPLE WILL NOT BE AS MERCIFUL. IF YOU WISH TO COME WITH US, YOU'D BE WELCOME.
NO. CHANCES ARE, I'M NOT INFECTED. EITHER WAY, MY PLACE IS WITH THE CHURCH. ONCE I EXPLAIN TO THE INQUISITORS, THEY'LL UNDER-STAND.
THEY WON'T HURT ME. I'M THE MAGDALENA.
GO IN PEACE, AND MAY GOD BE WITH YOU.

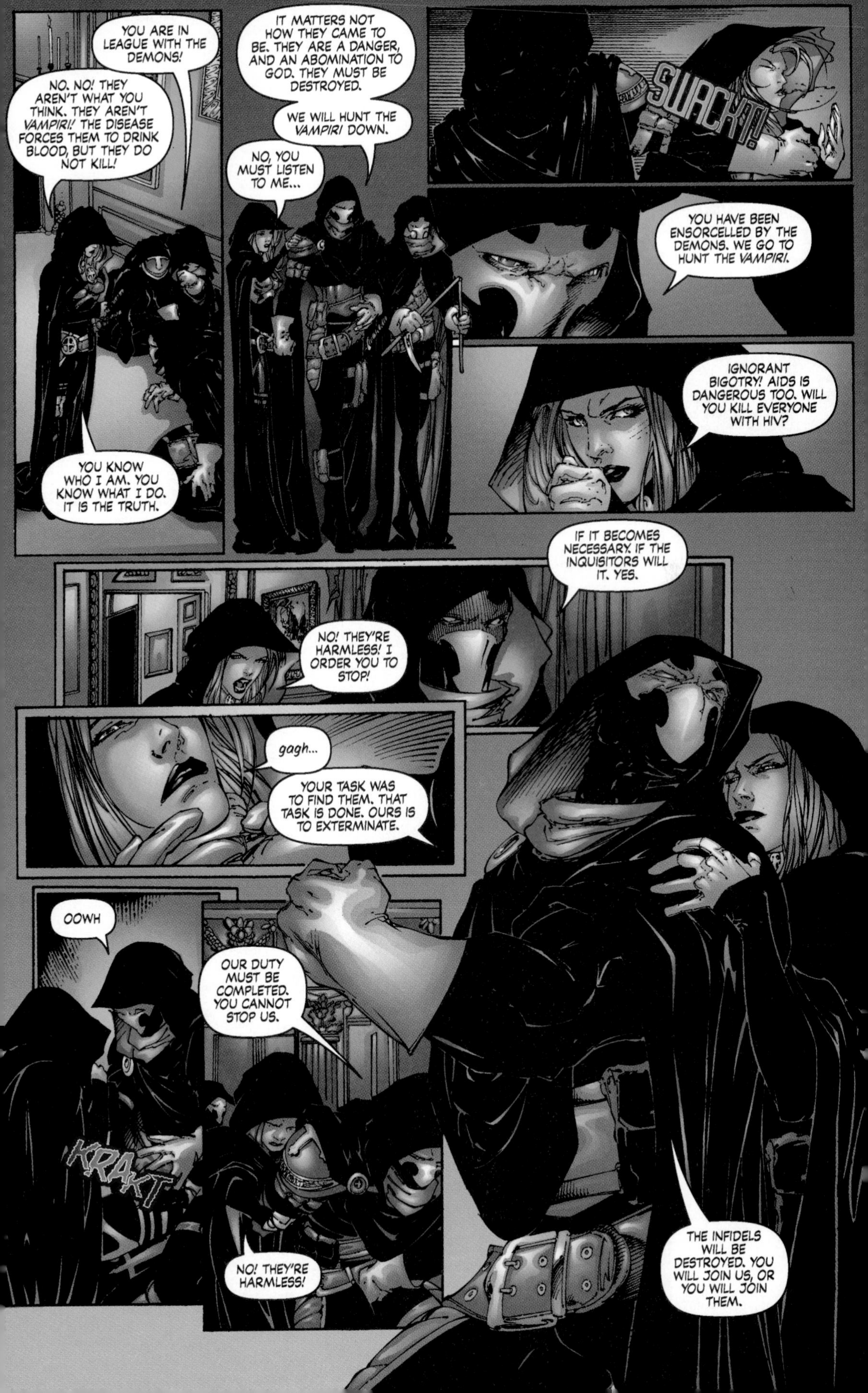
YOU ARE IN LEAGUE WITH THE DEMONS!
NO. NO! THEY AREN'T WHAT YOU THINK. THEY AREN'T VAMPIRI! THE DISEASE FORCES THEM TO DRINK BLOOD, BUT THEY DO NOT KILL!
YOU KNOW WHO I AM. YOU KNOW WHAT I DO. IT IS THE TRUTH.
IT MATTERS NOT HOW THEY CAME TO BE. THEY ARE A DANGER, AND AN ABOMINATION TO GOD. THEY MUST BE DESTROYED.
WE WILL HUNT THE VAMPIRI DOWN.
NO, YOU MUST LISTEN TO ME...
SWACK!!
YOU HAVE BEEN ENSORCELLED BY THE DEMONS. WE GO TO HUNT THE VAMPIRI.
IGNORANT BIGOTRY! AIDS IS DANGEROUS TOO. WILL YOU KILL EVERYONE WITH HIV?
IF IT BECOMES NECESSARY. IF THE INQUISITORS WILL IT. YES.
NO! THEY'RE HARMLESS! I ORDER YOU TO STOP!
gagh...
YOUR TASK WAS TO FIND THEM. THAT TASK IS DONE. OURS IS TO EXTERMINATE.
OOWH
OUR DUTY MUST BE COMPLETED. YOU CANNOT STOP US.
KRAKT
NO! THEY'RE HARMLESS!
THE INFIDELS WILL BE DESTROYED. YOU WILL JOIN US, OR YOU WILL JOIN THEM.

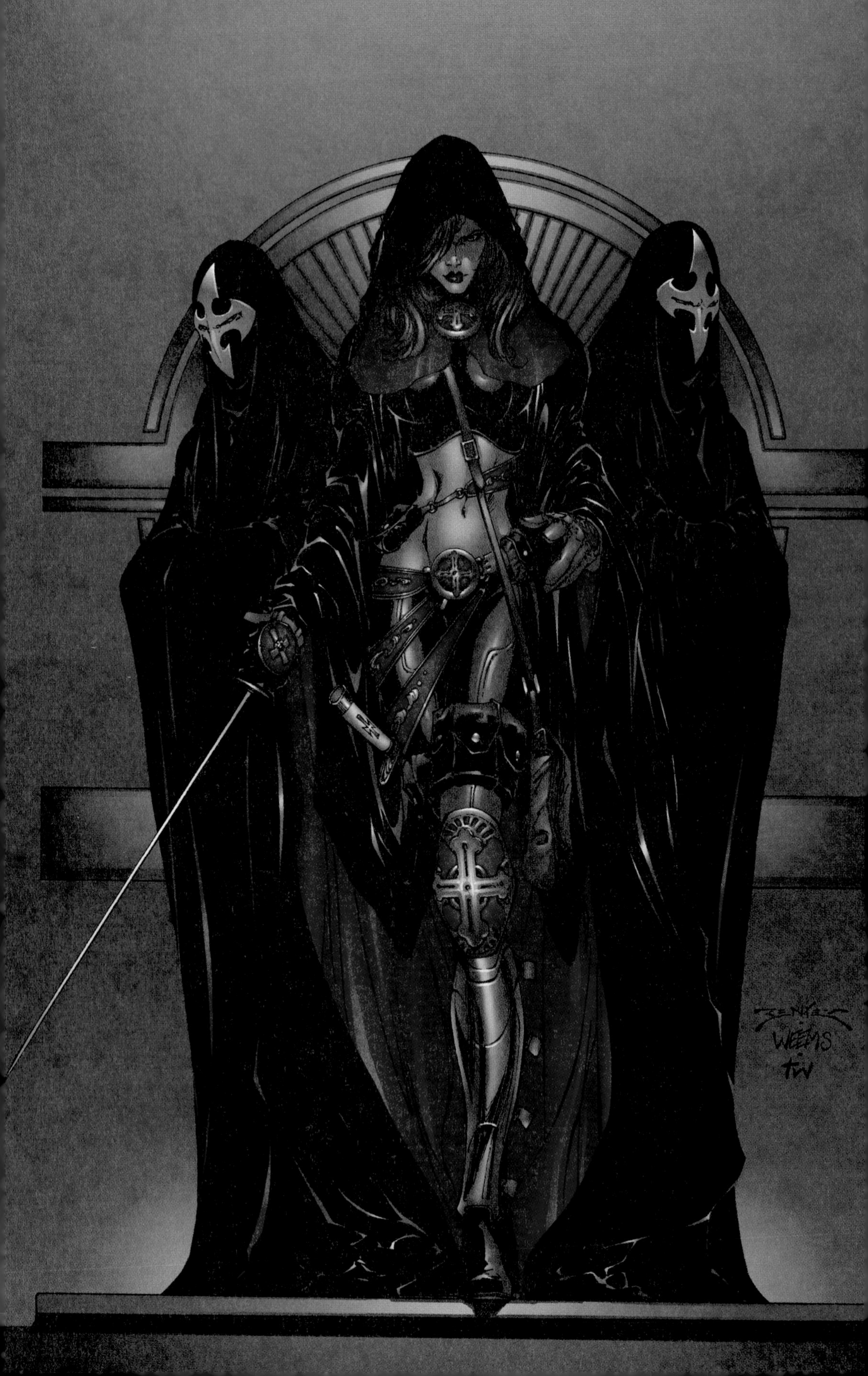

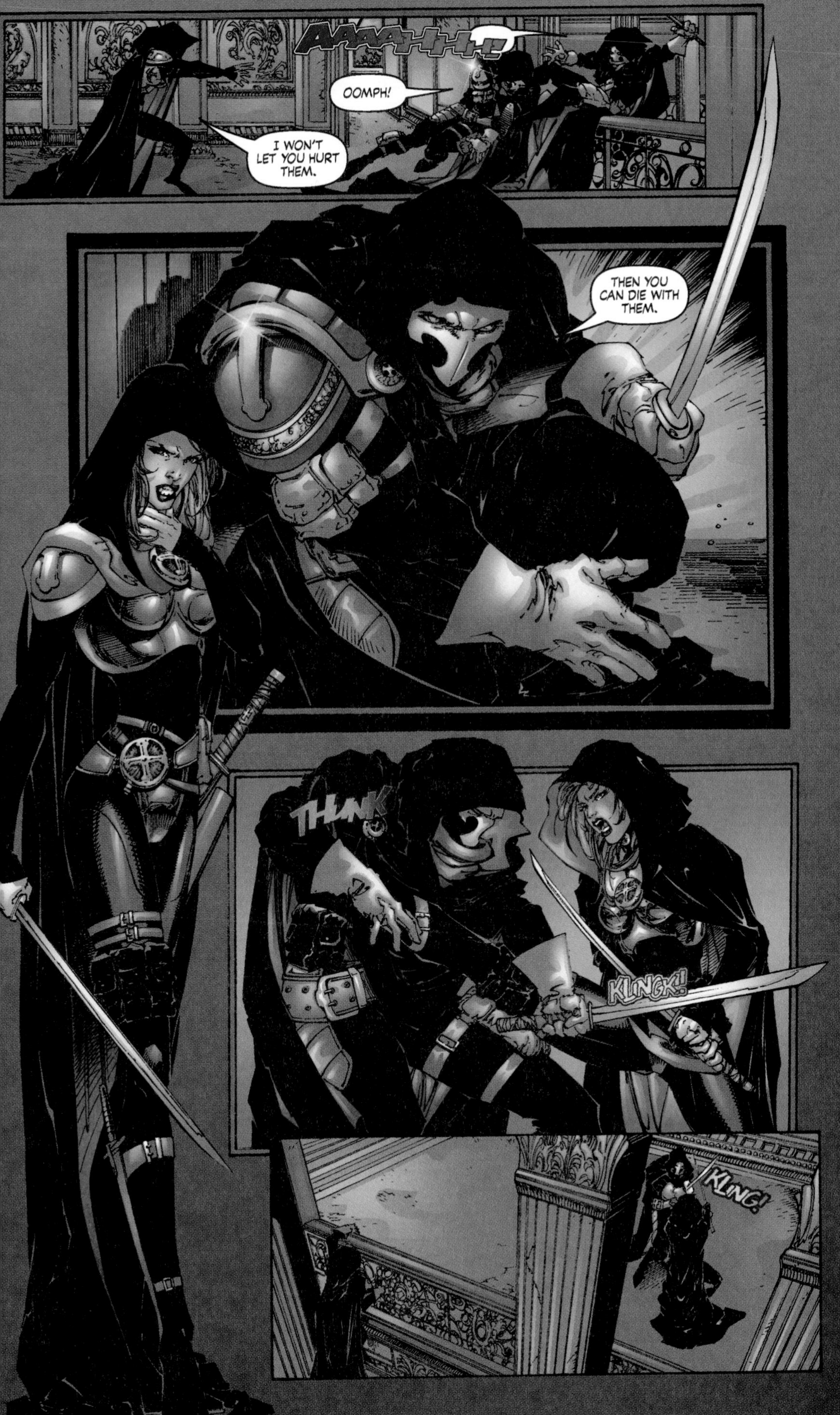
AAAAHHHH!
OOMPH!
I WON'T LET YOU HURT THEM.
THEN YOU CAN DIE WITH THEM.
THUNK
KLINGK!
KLING!

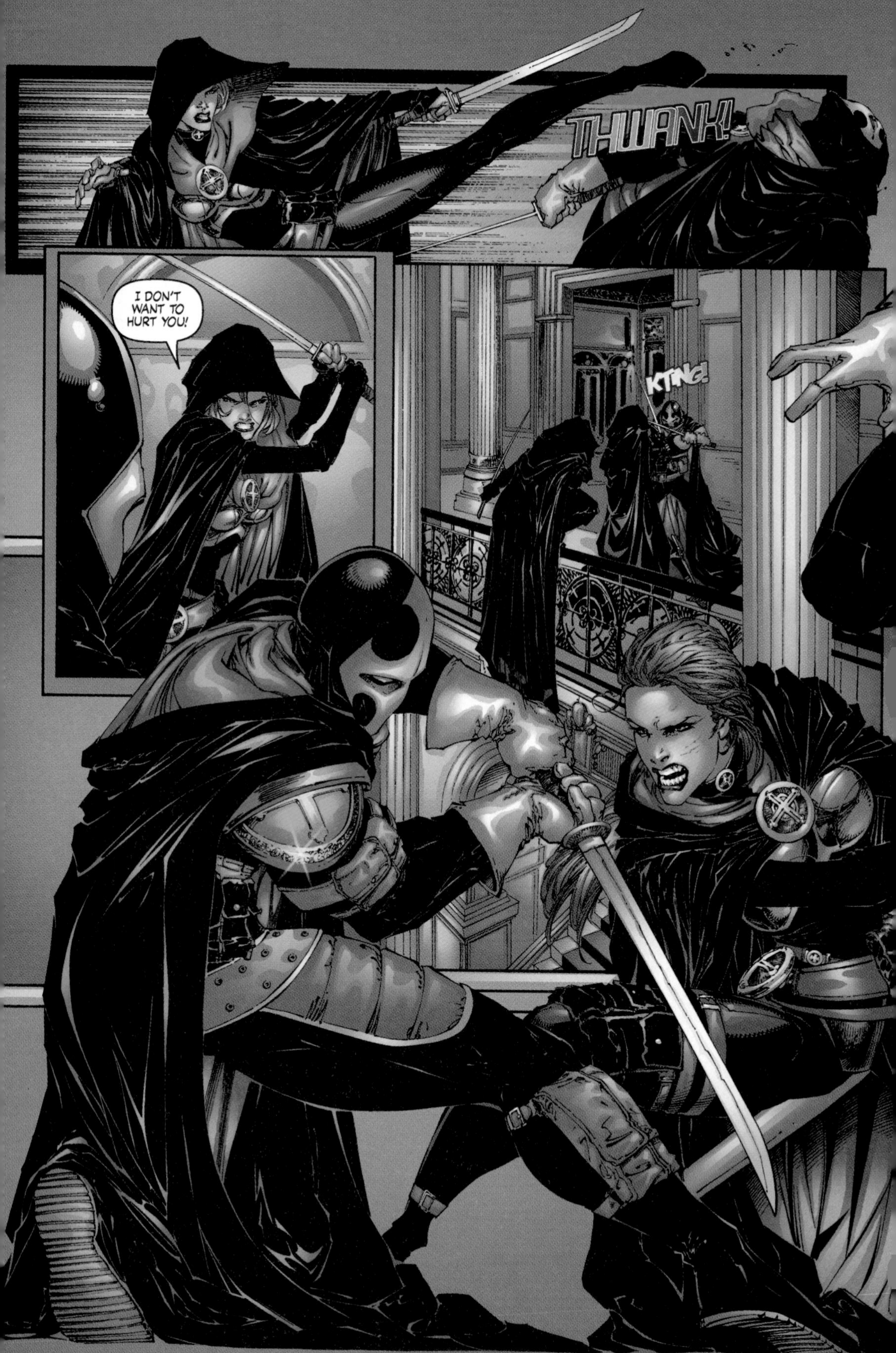
THWANK!
I DON'T WANT TO HURT YOU!
KTING!

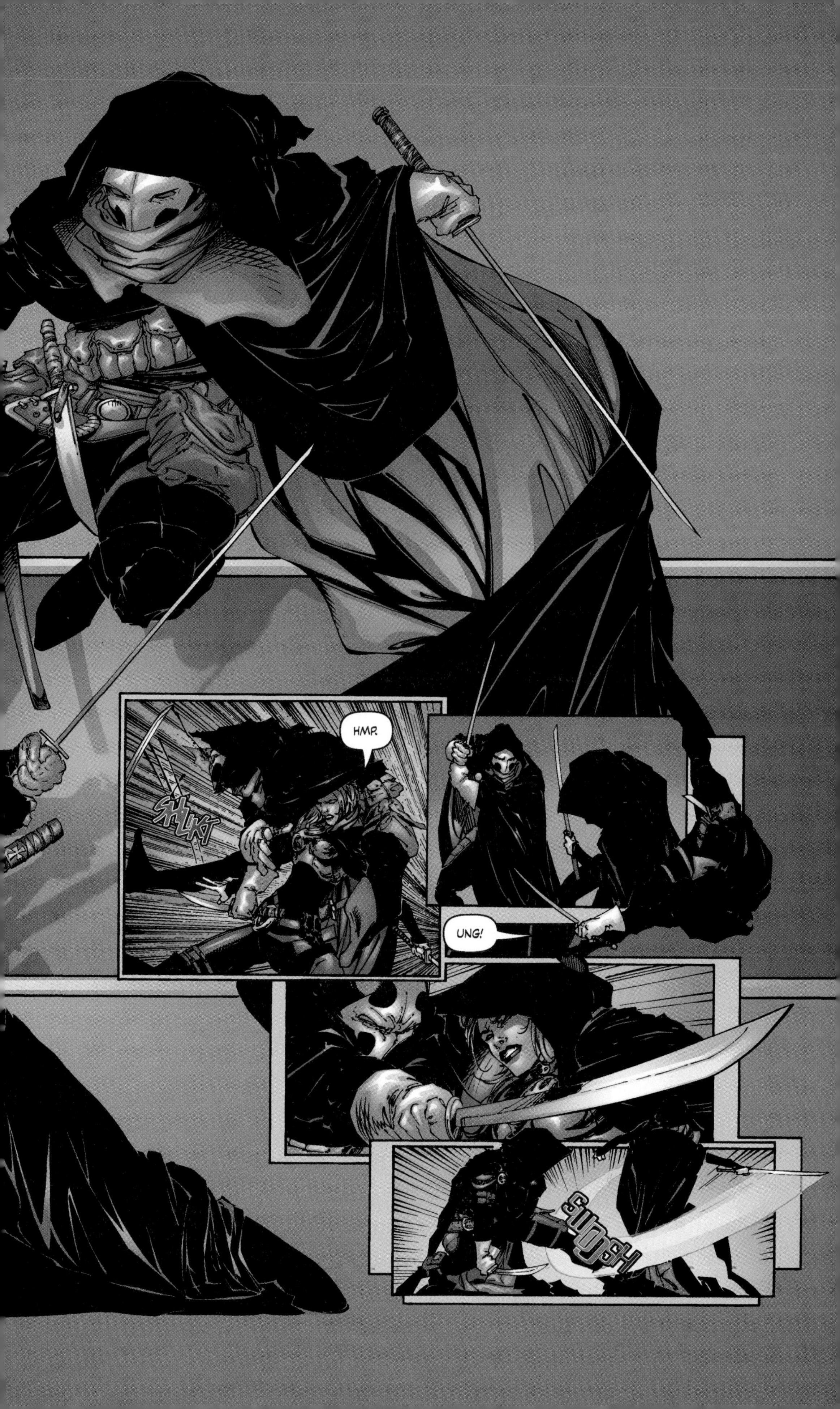
HMR.
SHLUKT
UNG!
SWOSH

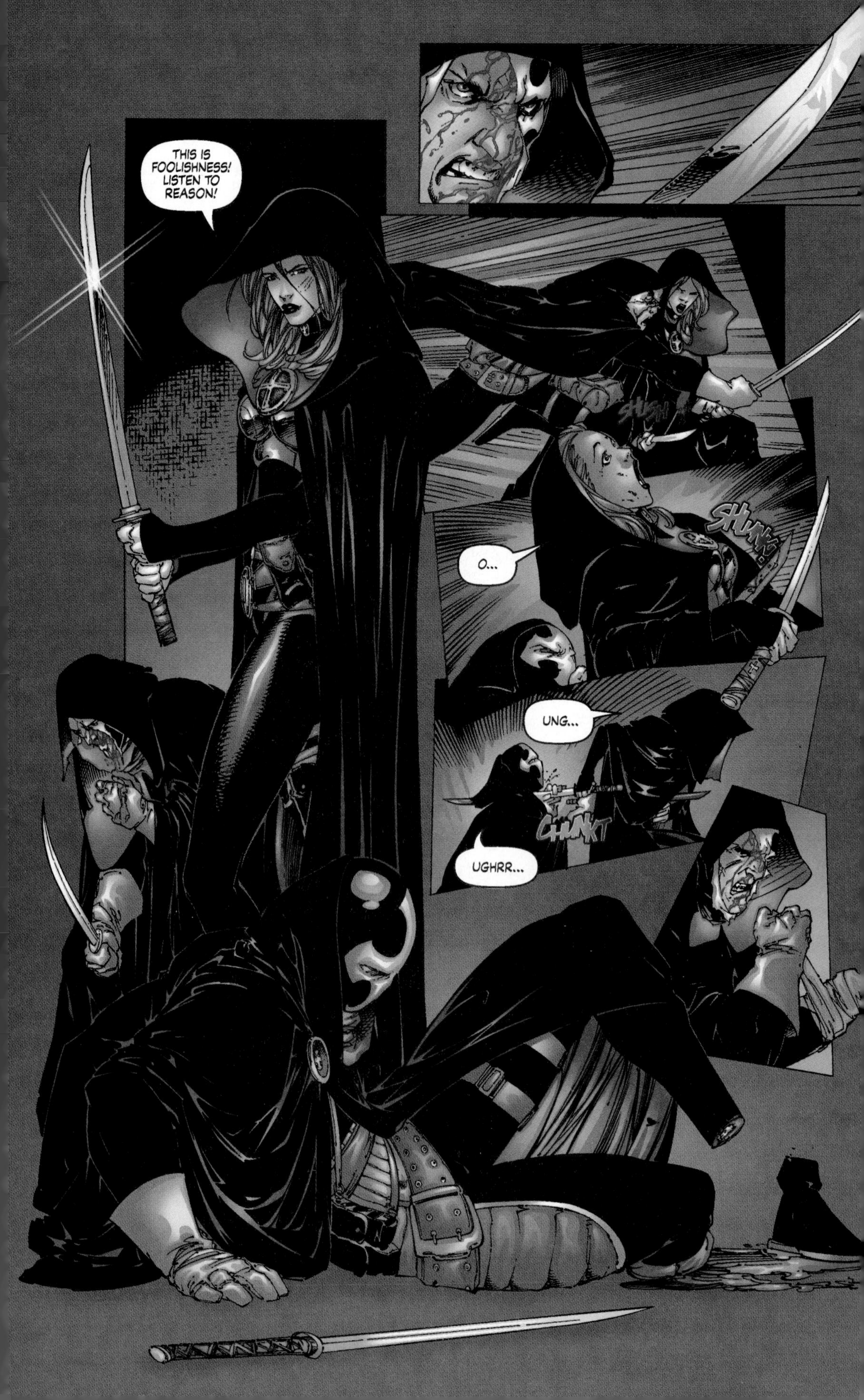

THIS IS FOOLISHNESS! LISTEN TO REASON!
SHUSH
O...
SHUNK
UNG...
CHUNKT
UGHRR...

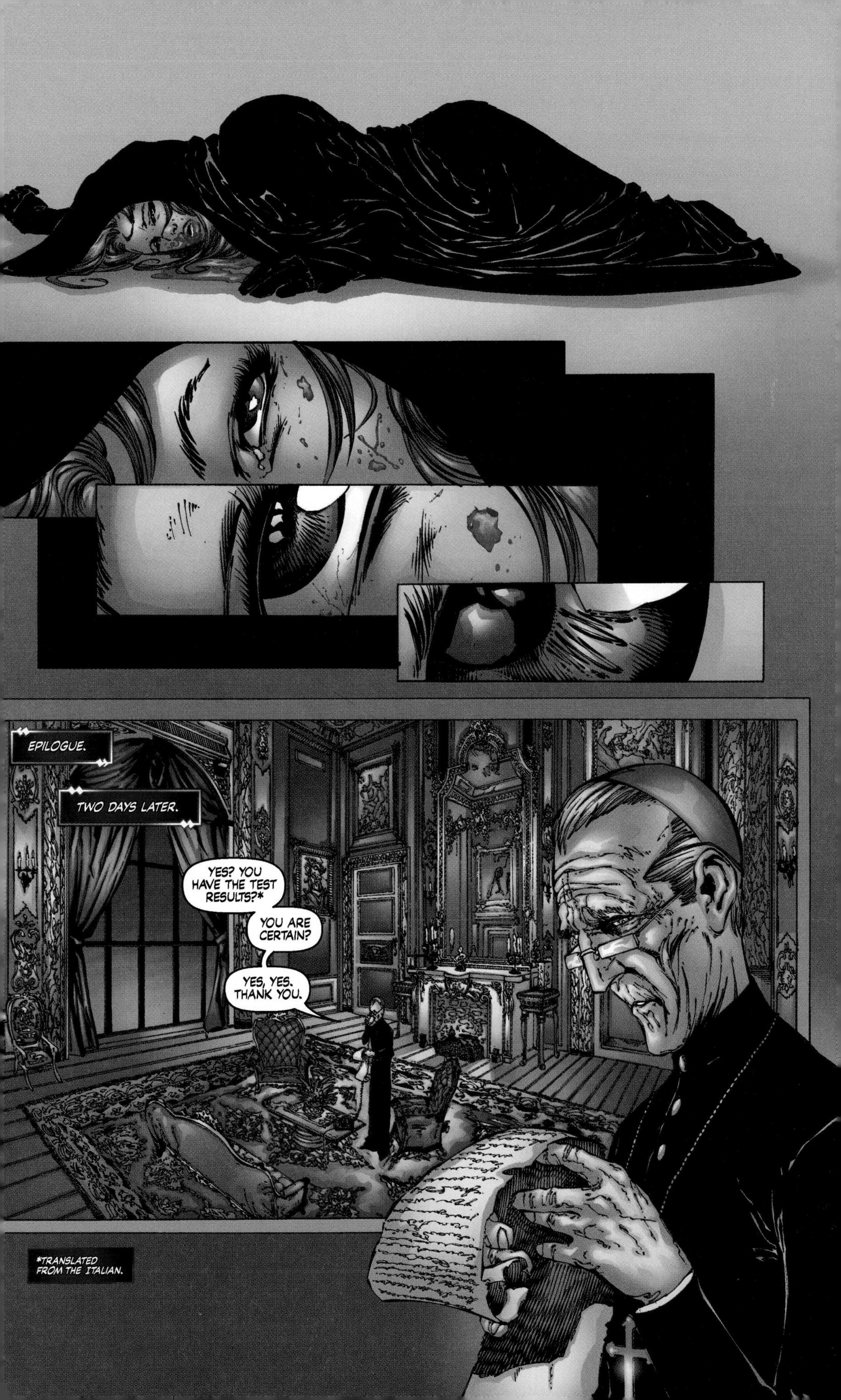
EPILOGUE.
TWO DAYS LATER.
YES? YOU HAVE THE TEST RESULTS?*
YOU ARE CERTAIN?
YES, YES. THANK YOU.
*TRANSLATED FROM THE ITALIAN.

FRANCE, 1244.

"THE STORY BEGINS WITH A YOUNG MAN NAMED JESUS."

"JESUS, OF COURSE, WAS NO SON OF GOD, BUT A MAN. A PROPHET, AND A KING, BUT NO DIVINITY."

"JESUS WAS THE HEIR TO THE DAVIDIC LINE, AND THUS THE TRUE KING OF ISRAEL, AND MANY BELIEVED HIM TO BE THE MESSIAH DESTINED TO THROW OUT THE ROMANS AND THE CORRUPT JEWS IN POWER, AND BRING PEACE AND PROSPERITY TO JUDEA."

"AND SO HE WAS BETROTHED AT AN EARLY AGE TO MARY, OF THE ROYAL HOUSE OF BENJAMIN, DESCENDED FROM SAUL, FIRST KING OF THE JEWS."

SALOME. I AM ENTRUSTING YOU WITH A MOST IMPORTANT MISSION.

YOU HAVE FAMILY TO THE NORTH. RETURN THERE, AND TAKE THESE WITH YOU. KEEP THEM SAFE.

BUT WHAT ABOUT YOU? WILL YOU NOT TRY TO ESCAPE?

I WILL NOT LEAVE.

"BUT THE KINGSHIP WAS NOT TO BE. JESUS WAS KILLED, AND MARY SPIRITED AWAY THE BODY AND BURIED IT WITH HONOR, TELLING OTHERS A TALL TALE OF ANGELS AND RESURRECTION. WHO COULD'VE FORESEEN THE CONSEQUENCES OF SUCH A FABRICATION?"

"MARY FLED TO EGYPT, WHERE SHE GAVE BIRTH TO HER ONLY CHILD, A DAUGHTER, SARAH, FROM WHOM WE ARE DESCENDED."

NOW GO. MAY THE LORD PROTECT YOU.

WORRY NOT, CHILD. THE LORD WILL LOOK AFTER ME.

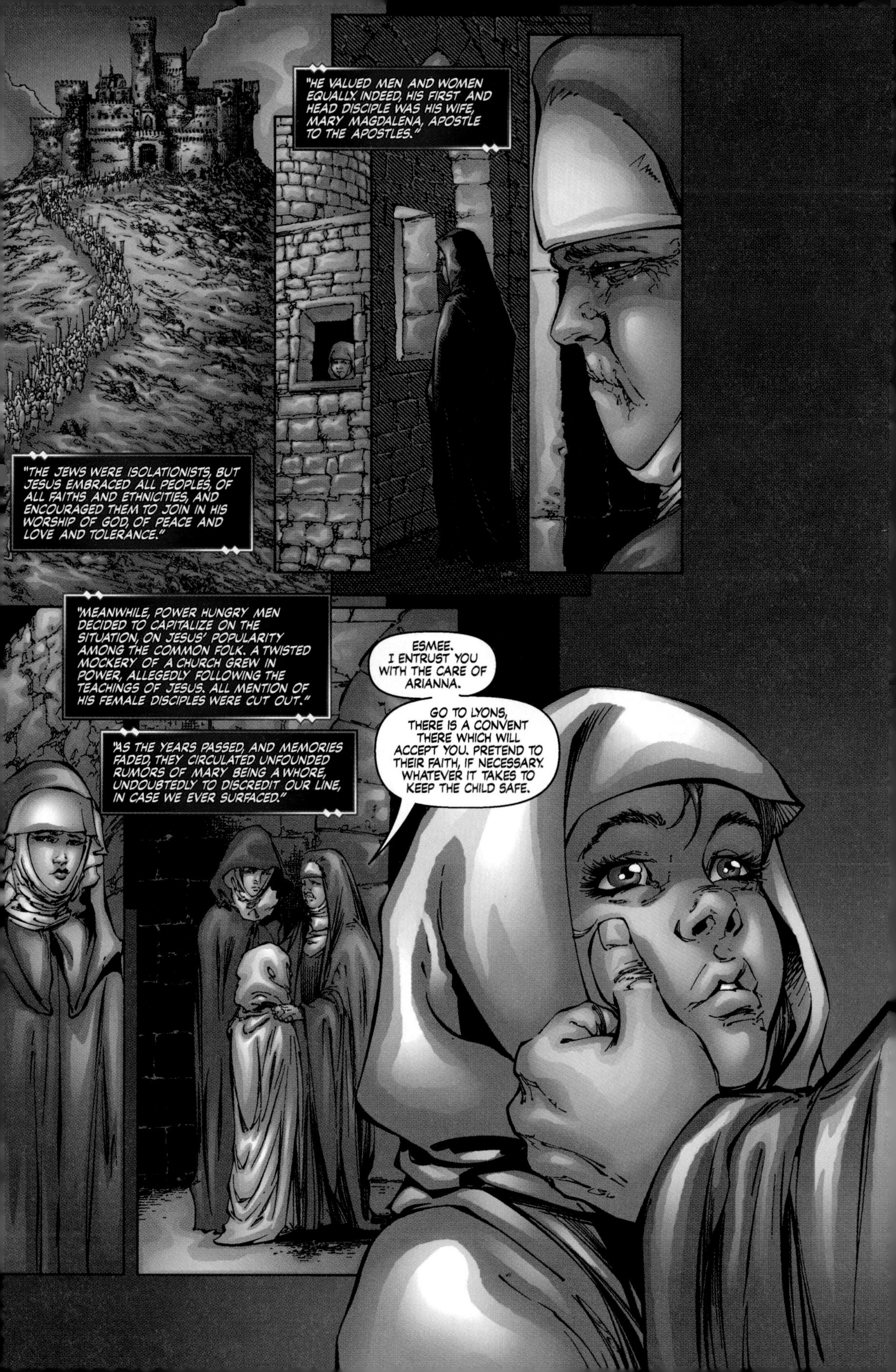
"HE VALUED MEN AND WOMEN EQUALLY. INDEED, HIS FIRST AND HEAD DISCIPLE WAS HIS WIFE, MARY MAGDALENA, APOSTLE TO THE APOSTLES."
"THE JEWS WERE ISOLATIONISTS, BUT JESUS EMBRACED ALL PEOPLES, OF ALL FAITHS AND ETHNICITIES, AND ENCOURAGED THEM TO JOIN IN HIS WORSHIP OF GOD, OF PEACE AND LOVE AND TOLERANCE."
"MEANWHILE, POWER HUNGRY MEN DECIDED TO CAPITALIZE ON THE SITUATION, ON JESUS' POPULARITY AMONG THE COMMON FOLK. A TWISTED MOCKERY OF A CHURCH GREW IN POWER, ALLEGEDLY FOLLOWING THE TEACHINGS OF JESUS. ALL MENTION OF HIS FEMALE DISCIPLES WERE CUT OUT."
"AS THE YEARS PASSED, AND MEMORIES FADED, THEY CIRCULATED UNFOUNDED RUMORS OF MARY BEING A WHORE, UNDOUBTEDLY TO DISCREDIT OUR LINE, IN CASE WE EVER SURFACED."
ESMEE. I ENTRUST YOU WITH THE CARE OF ARIANNA.
GO TO LYONS, THERE IS A CONVENT THERE WHICH WILL ACCEPT YOU. PRETEND TO THEIR FAITH, IF NECESSARY. WHATEVER IT TAKES TO KEEP THE CHILD SAFE.

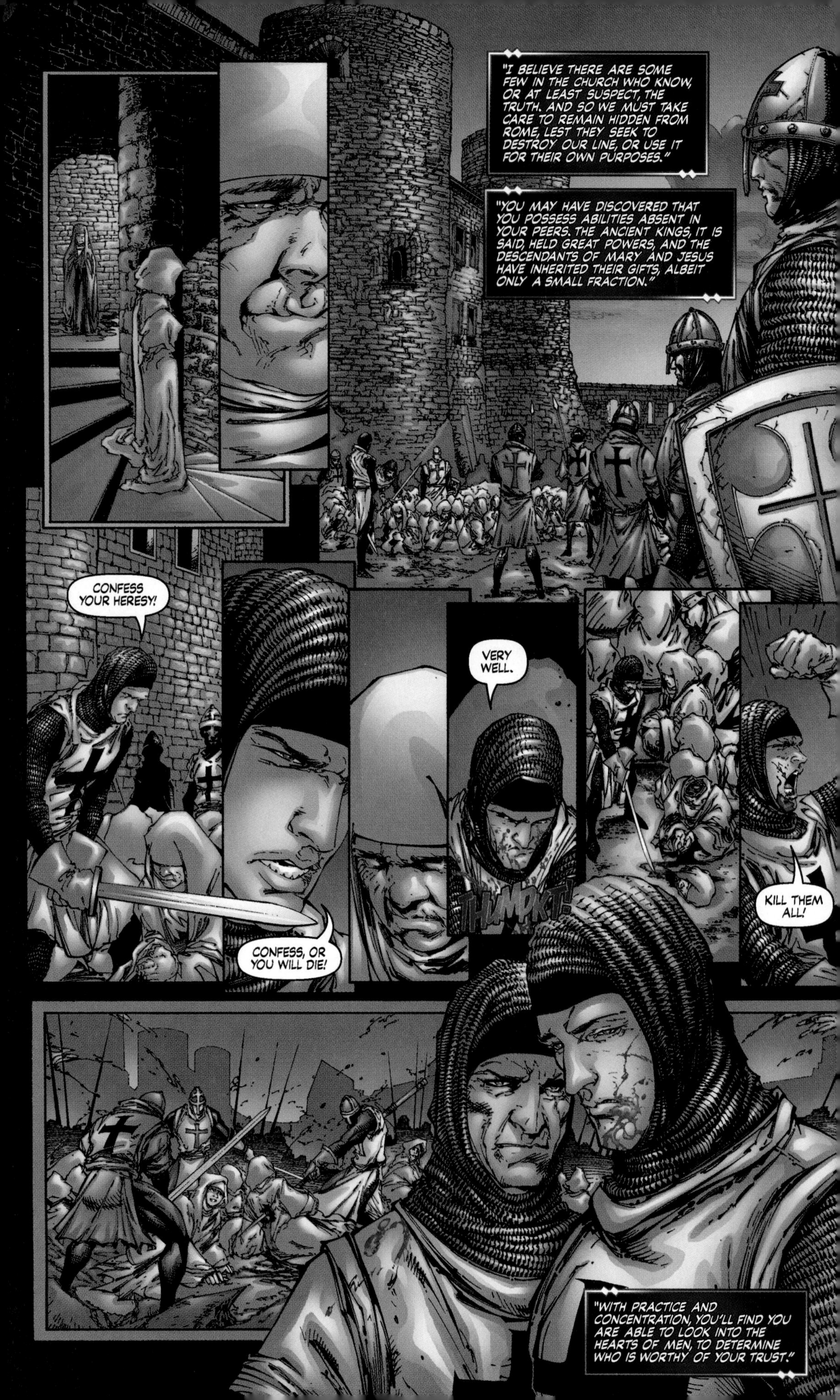
"I BELIEVE THERE ARE SOME FEW IN THE CHURCH WHO KNOW, OR AT LEAST SUSPECT, THE TRUTH. AND SO WE MUST TAKE CARE TO REMAIN HIDDEN FROM ROME, LEST THEY SEEK TO DESTROY OUR LINE, OR USE IT FOR THEIR OWN PURPOSES."
"YOU MAY HAVE DISCOVERED THAT YOU POSSESS ABILITIES ABSENT IN YOUR PEERS. THE ANCIENT KINGS, IT IS SAID, HELD GREAT POWERS, AND THE DESCENDANTS OF MARY AND JESUS HAVE INHERITED THEIR GIFTS, ALBEIT ONLY A SMALL FRACTION."
CONFESS YOUR HERESY!
CONFESS, OR YOU WILL DIE!
VERY WELL.
THUMPKT!
KILL THEM ALL!
"WITH PRACTICE AND CONCENTRATION, YOU'LL FIND YOU ARE ABLE TO LOOK INTO THE HEARTS OF MEN, TO DETERMINE WHO IS WORTHY OF YOUR TRUST."

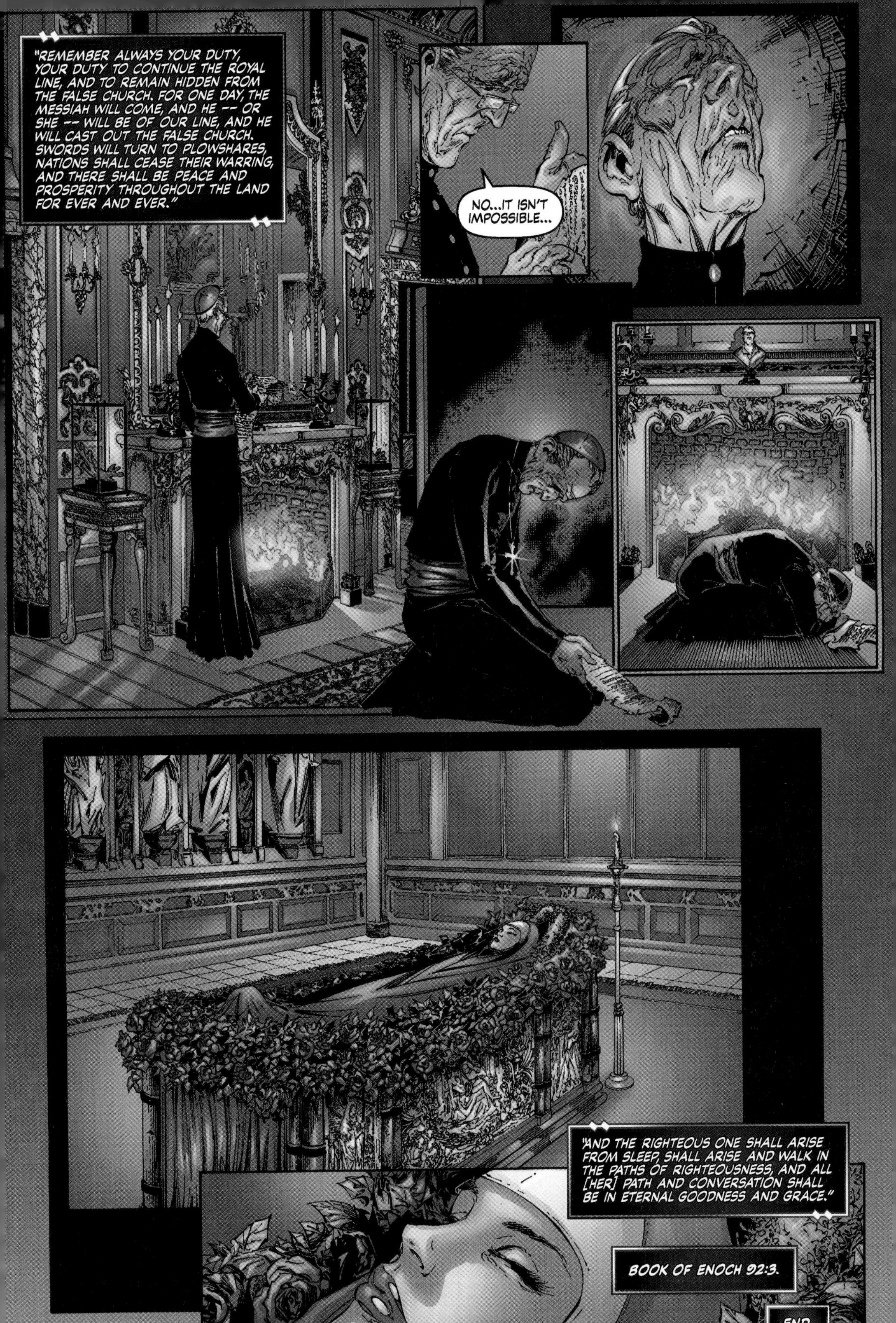
"REMEMBER ALWAYS YOUR DUTY, YOUR DUTY TO CONTINUE THE ROYAL LINE, AND TO REMAIN HIDDEN FROM THE FALSE CHURCH. FOR ONE DAY, THE MESSIAH WILL COME, AND HE -- OR SHE -- WILL BE OF OUR LINE, AND HE WILL CAST OUT THE FALSE CHURCH. SWORDS WILL TURN TO PLOWSHARES, NATIONS SHALL CEASE THEIR WARRING, AND THERE SHALL BE PEACE AND PROSPERITY THROUGHOUT THE LAND FOR EVER AND EVER."
NO...IT ISN'T IMPOSSIBLE...
"AND THE RIGHTEOUS ONE SHALL ARISE FROM SLEEP, SHALL ARISE AND WALK IN THE PATHS OF RIGHTEOUSNESS, AND ALL [HER] PATH AND CONVERSATION SHALL BE IN ETERNAL GOODNESS AND GRACE."
BOOK OF ENOCH 92:3.
END.

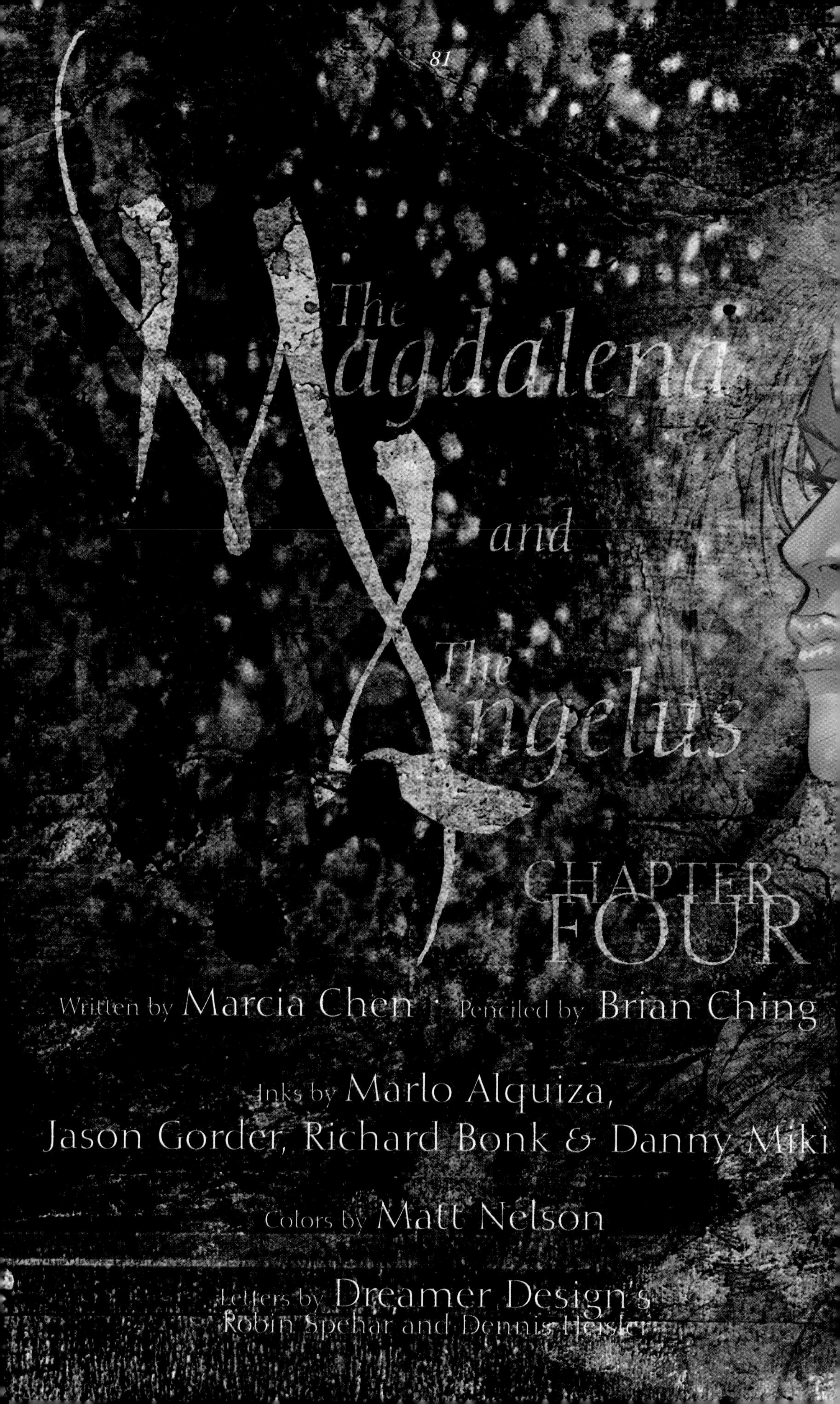
The Magdalena and The Angelus
CHAPTER FOUR
Written by Marcia Chen · Penciled by Brian Ching
Inks by Marlo Alquiza, Jason Gorder, Richard Bonk & Danny Miki
Colors by Matt Nelson
Letters by Dreamer Design's Robin Spehar and Dennis Heisler

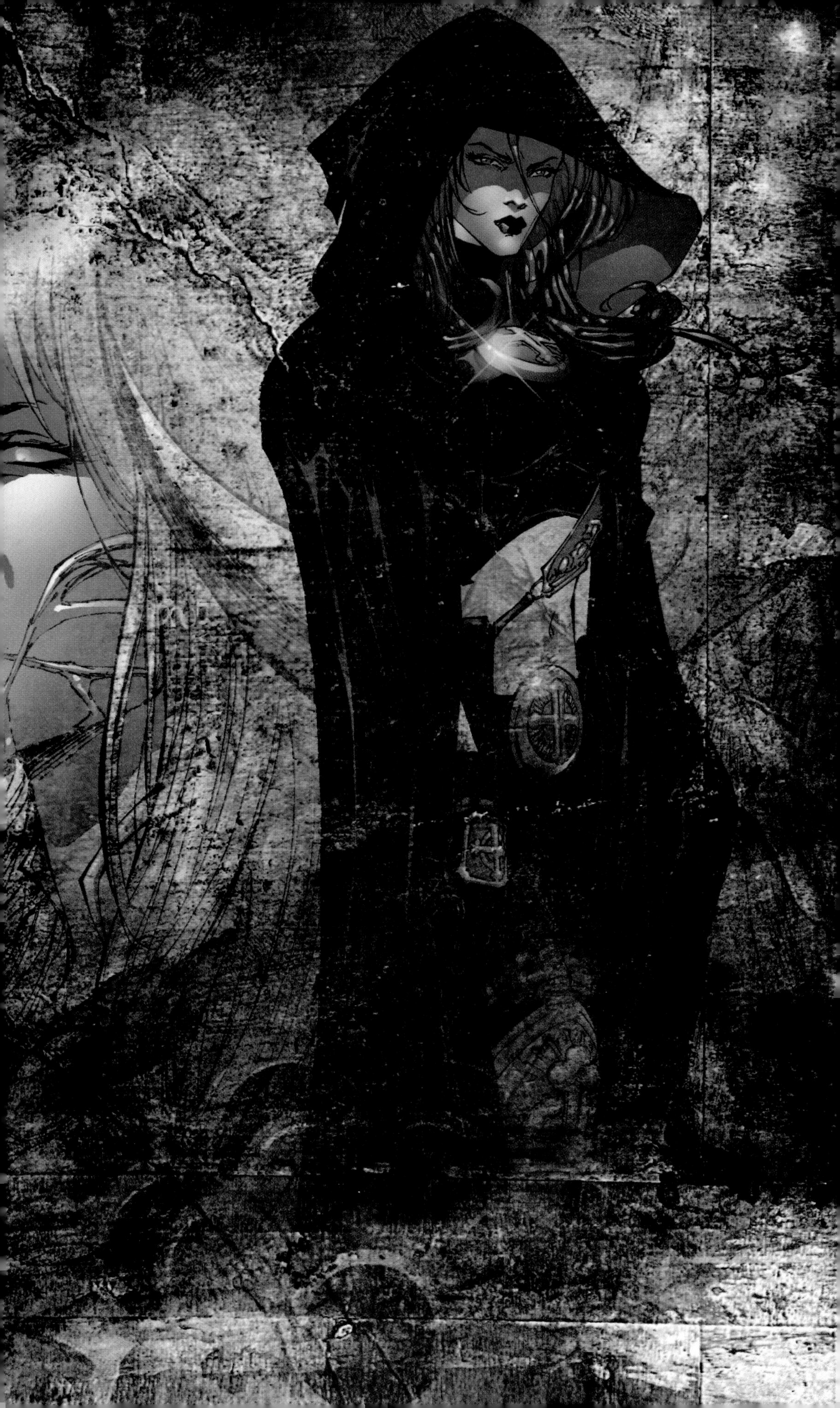

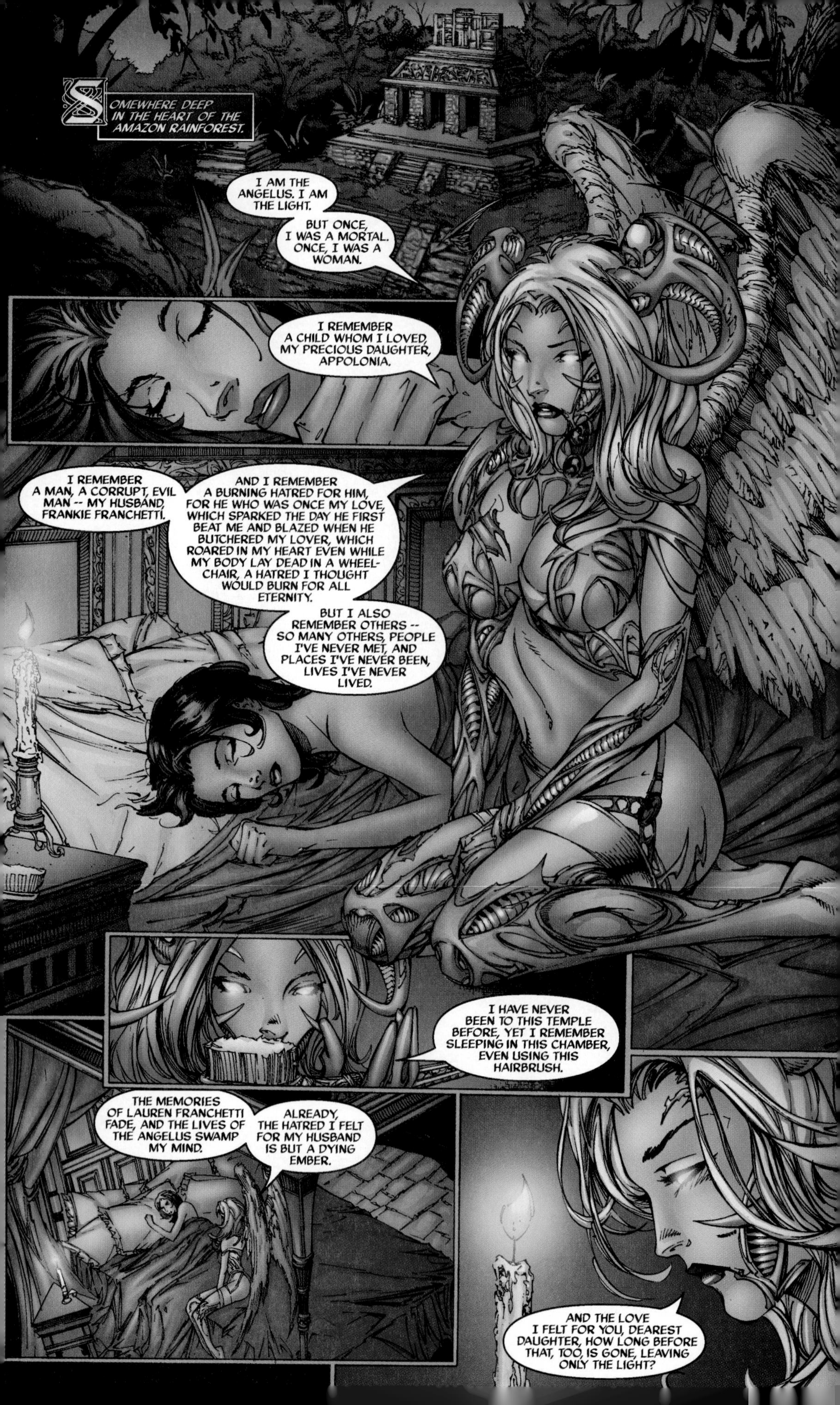
SOMEWHERE DEEP IN THE HEART OF THE AMAZON RAINFOREST.
I AM THE ANGELUS. I AM THE LIGHT.
BUT ONCE, I WAS A MORTAL. ONCE, I WAS A WOMAN.
I REMEMBER A CHILD WHOM I LOVED, MY PRECIOUS DAUGHTER, APPOLONIA.
I REMEMBER A MAN, A CORRUPT, EVIL MAN -- MY HUSBAND, FRANKIE FRANCHETTI.
AND I REMEMBER A BURNING HATRED FOR HIM, FOR HE WHO WAS ONCE MY LOVE, WHICH SPARKED THE DAY HE FIRST BEAT ME AND BLAZED WHEN HE BUTCHERED MY LOVER, WHICH ROARED IN MY HEART EVEN WHILE MY BODY LAY DEAD IN A WHEEL-CHAIR, A HATRED I THOUGHT WOULD BURN FOR ALL ETERNITY.
BUT I ALSO REMEMBER OTHERS -- SO MANY OTHERS, PEOPLE I'VE NEVER MET, AND PLACES I'VE NEVER BEEN, LIVES I'VE NEVER LIVED.
I HAVE NEVER BEEN TO THIS TEMPLE BEFORE, YET I REMEMBER SLEEPING IN THIS CHAMBER, EVEN USING THIS HAIRBRUSH.
THE MEMORIES OF LAUREN FRANCHETTI FADE, AND THE LIVES OF THE ANGELUS SWAMP MY MIND.
ALREADY, THE HATRED I FELT FOR MY HUSBAND IS BUT A DYING EMBER.
AND THE LOVE I FELT FOR YOU, DEAREST DAUGHTER, HOW LONG BEFORE THAT, TOO, IS GONE, LEAVING ONLY THE LIGHT?

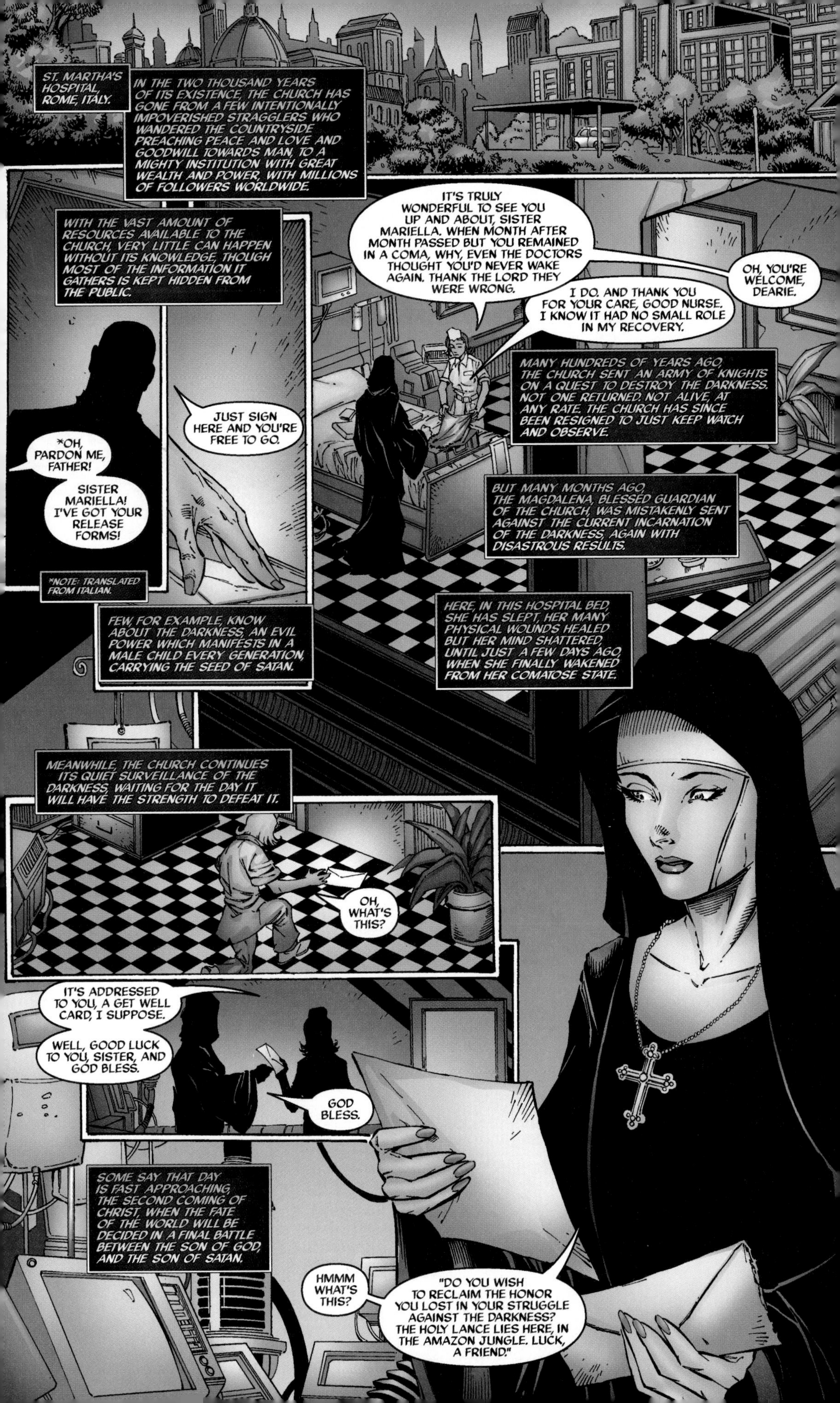
ST. MARTHA'S HOSPITAL, ROME, ITALY.
IN THE TWO THOUSAND YEARS OF ITS EXISTENCE, THE CHURCH HAS GONE FROM A FEW INTENTIONALLY IMPOVERISHED STRAGGLERS WHO WANDERED THE COUNTRYSIDE PREACHING PEACE AND LOVE AND GOODWILL TOWARDS MAN, TO A MIGHTY INSTITUTION WITH GREAT WEALTH AND POWER, WITH MILLIONS OF FOLLOWERS WORLDWIDE.
WITH THE VAST AMOUNT OF RESOURCES AVAILABLE TO THE CHURCH, VERY LITTLE CAN HAPPEN WITHOUT ITS KNOWLEDGE, THOUGH MOST OF THE INFORMATION IT GATHERS IS KEPT HIDDEN FROM THE PUBLIC.
*OH, PARDON ME, FATHER!
SISTER MARIELLA! I'VE GOT YOUR RELEASE FORMS!
JUST SIGN HERE AND YOU'RE FREE TO GO.
*NOTE: TRANSLATED FROM ITALIAN.
FEW, FOR EXAMPLE, KNOW ABOUT THE DARKNESS, AN EVIL POWER WHICH MANIFESTS IN A MALE CHILD EVERY GENERATION, CARRYING THE SEED OF SATAN.
IT'S TRULY WONDERFUL TO SEE YOU UP AND ABOUT, SISTER MARIELLA. WHEN MONTH AFTER MONTH PASSED BUT YOU REMAINED IN A COMA, WHY, EVEN THE DOCTORS THOUGHT YOU'D NEVER WAKE AGAIN. THANK THE LORD THEY WERE WRONG.
I DO. AND THANK YOU FOR YOUR CARE, GOOD NURSE. I KNOW IT HAD NO SMALL ROLE IN MY RECOVERY.
OH, YOU'RE WELCOME, DEARIE.
MANY HUNDREDS OF YEARS AGO, THE CHURCH SENT AN ARMY OF KNIGHTS ON A QUEST TO DESTROY THE DARKNESS. NOT ONE RETURNED. NOT ALIVE, AT ANY RATE. THE CHURCH HAS SINCE BEEN RESIGNED TO JUST KEEP WATCH AND OBSERVE.
BUT MANY MONTHS AGO, THE MAGDALENA, BLESSED GUARDIAN OF THE CHURCH, WAS MISTAKENLY SENT AGAINST THE CURRENT INCARNATION OF THE DARKNESS, AGAIN WITH DISASTROUS RESULTS.
HERE, IN THIS HOSPITAL BED, SHE HAS SLEPT, HER MANY PHYSICAL WOUNDS HEALED BUT HER MIND SHATTERED, UNTIL JUST A FEW DAYS AGO, WHEN SHE FINALLY WAKENED FROM HER COMATOSE STATE.
MEANWHILE, THE CHURCH CONTINUES ITS QUIET SURVEILLANCE OF THE DARKNESS, WAITING FOR THE DAY IT WILL HAVE THE STRENGTH TO DEFEAT IT.
OH, WHAT'S THIS?
IT'S ADDRESSED TO YOU, A GET WELL CARD, I SUPPOSE.
WELL, GOOD LUCK TO YOU, SISTER, AND GOD BLESS.
GOD BLESS.
SOME SAY THAT DAY IS FAST APPROACHING, THE SECOND COMING OF CHRIST, WHEN THE FATE OF THE WORLD WILL BE DECIDED IN A FINAL BATTLE BETWEEN THE SON OF GOD AND THE SON OF SATAN.
HMMM WHAT'S THIS?
"DO YOU WISH TO RECLAIM THE HONOR YOU LOST IN YOUR STRUGGLE AGAINST THE DARKNESS? THE HOLY LANCE LIES HERE, IN THE AMAZON JUNGLE. LUCK, A FRIEND."

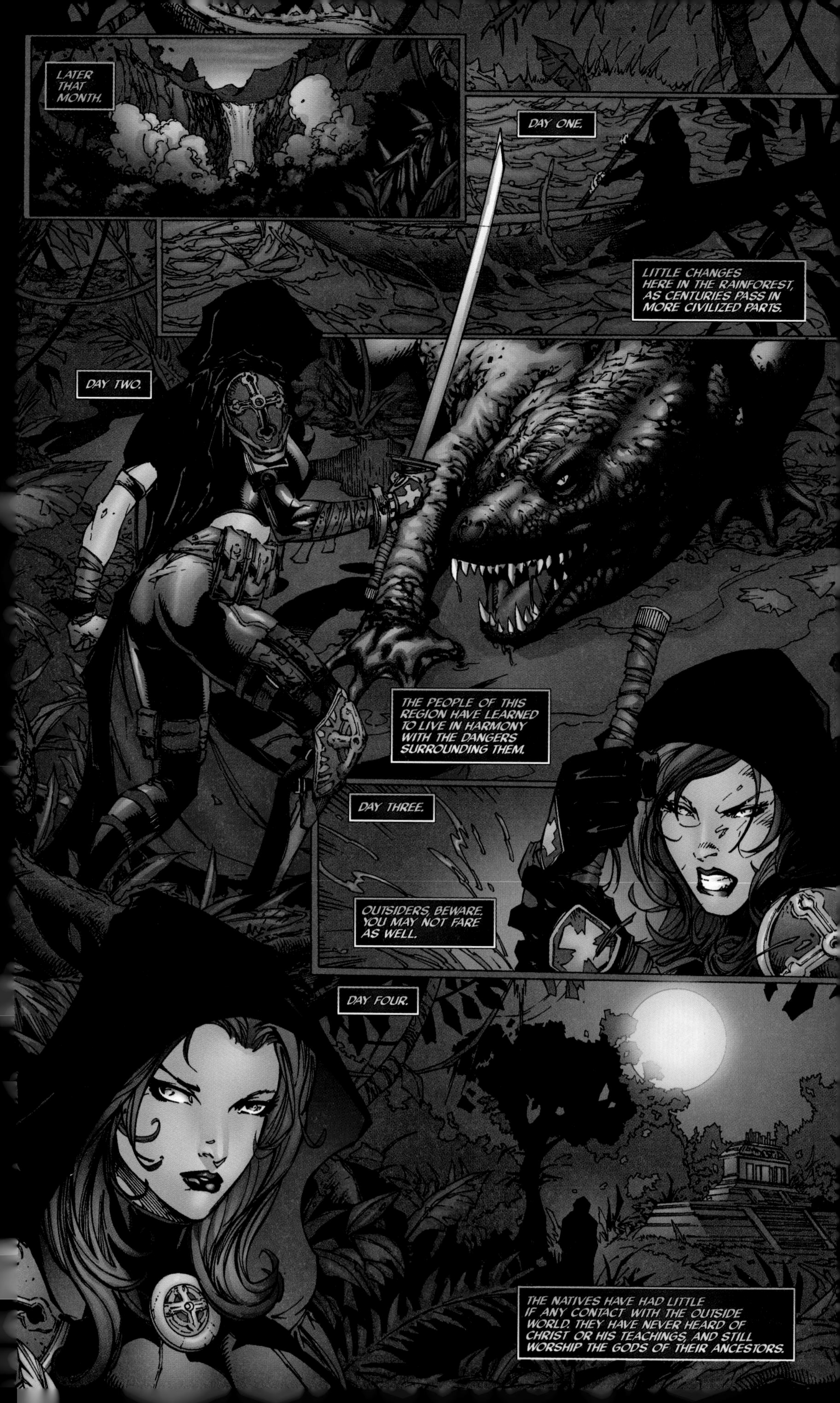

LATER THAT MONTH.
DAY ONE.
LITTLE CHANGES HERE IN THE RAINFOREST, AS CENTURIES PASS IN MORE CIVILIZED PARTS.
DAY TWO.
THE PEOPLE OF THIS REGION HAVE LEARNED TO LIVE IN HARMONY WITH THE DANGERS SURROUNDING THEM.
DAY THREE.
OUTSIDERS, BEWARE. YOU MAY NOT FARE AS WELL.
DAY FOUR.
THE NATIVES HAVE HAD LITTLE IF ANY CONTACT WITH THE OUTSIDE WORLD. THEY HAVE NEVER HEARD OF CHRIST OR HIS TEACHINGS, AND STILL WORSHIP THE GODS OF THEIR ANCESTORS.

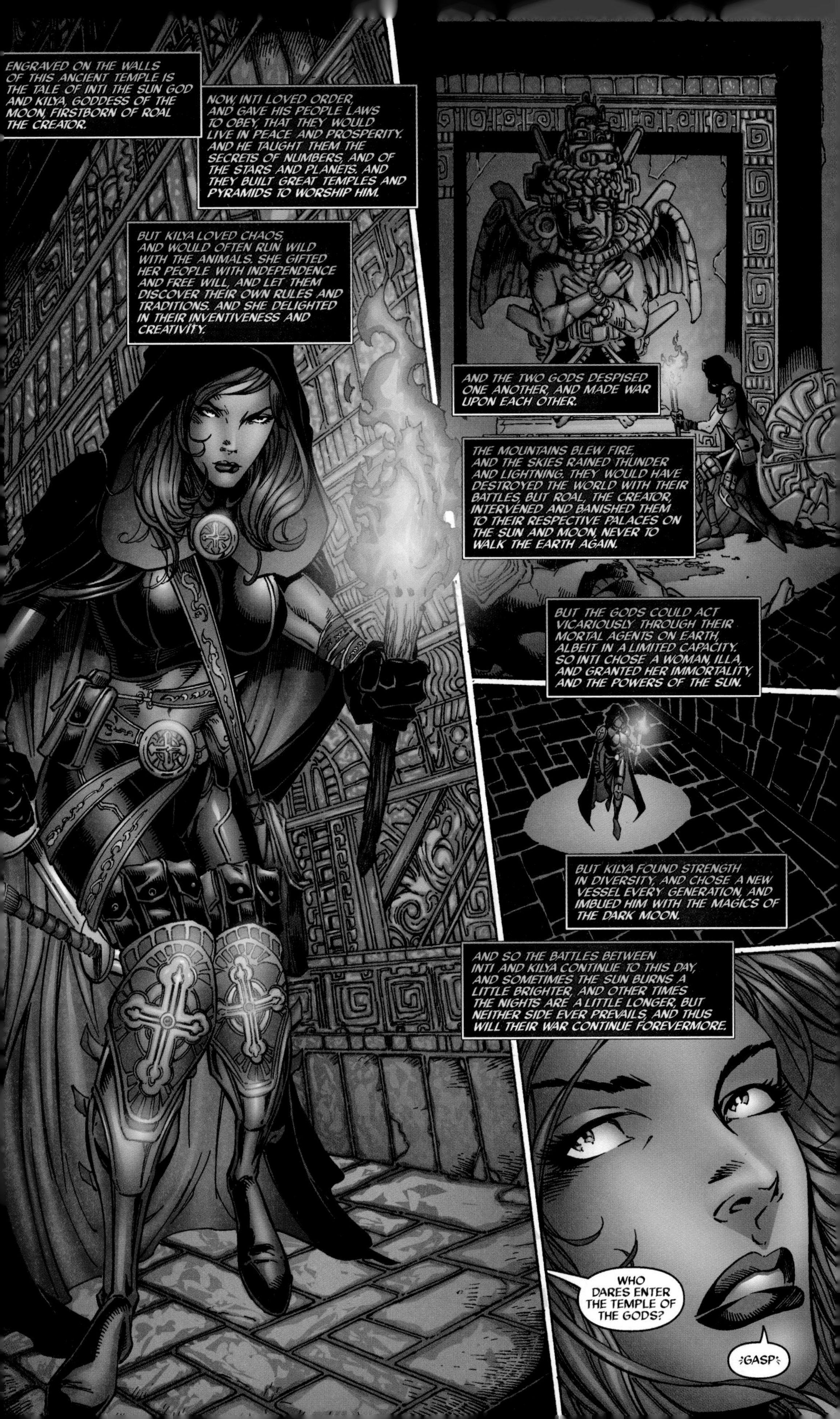

ENGRAVED ON THE WALLS OF THIS ANCIENT TEMPLE IS THE TALE OF INTI THE SUN GOD AND KILYA, GODDESS OF THE MOON, FIRSTBORN OF ROAL THE CREATOR.
NOW, INTI LOVED ORDER, AND GAVE HIS PEOPLE LAWS TO OBEY, THAT THEY WOULD LIVE IN PEACE AND PROSPERITY. AND HE TAUGHT THEM THE SECRETS OF NUMBERS, AND OF THE STARS AND PLANETS. AND THEY BUILT GREAT TEMPLES AND PYRAMIDS TO WORSHIP HIM.
BUT KILYA LOVED CHAOS, AND WOULD OFTEN RUN WILD WITH THE ANIMALS. SHE GIFTED HER PEOPLE WITH INDEPENDENCE AND FREE WILL, AND LET THEM DISCOVER THEIR OWN RULES AND TRADITIONS. AND SHE DELIGHTED IN THEIR INVENTIVENESS AND CREATIVITY.
AND THE TWO GODS DESPISED ONE ANOTHER, AND MADE WAR UPON EACH OTHER.
THE MOUNTAINS BLEW FIRE, AND THE SKIES RAINED THUNDER AND LIGHTNING. THEY WOULD HAVE DESTROYED THE WORLD WITH THEIR BATTLES, BUT ROAL, THE CREATOR, INTERVENED AND BANISHED THEM TO THEIR RESPECTIVE PALACES ON THE SUN AND MOON, NEVER TO WALK THE EARTH AGAIN.
BUT THE GODS COULD ACT VICARIOUSLY THROUGH THEIR MORTAL AGENTS ON EARTH, ALBEIT IN A LIMITED CAPACITY. SO INTI CHOSE A WOMAN, ILLA, AND GRANTED HER IMMORTALITY, AND THE POWERS OF THE SUN.
BUT KILYA FOUND STRENGTH IN DIVERSITY, AND CHOSE A NEW VESSEL EVERY GENERATION, AND IMBUED HIM WITH THE MAGICS OF THE DARK MOON.
AND SO THE BATTLES BETWEEN INTI AND KILYA CONTINUE TO THIS DAY, AND SOMETIMES THE SUN BURNS A LITTLE BRIGHTER, AND OTHER TIMES THE NIGHTS ARE A LITTLE LONGER, BUT NEITHER SIDE EVER PREVAILS, AND THUS WILL THEIR WAR CONTINUE FOREVERMORE.
WHO DARES ENTER THE TEMPLE OF THE GODS?
GASP

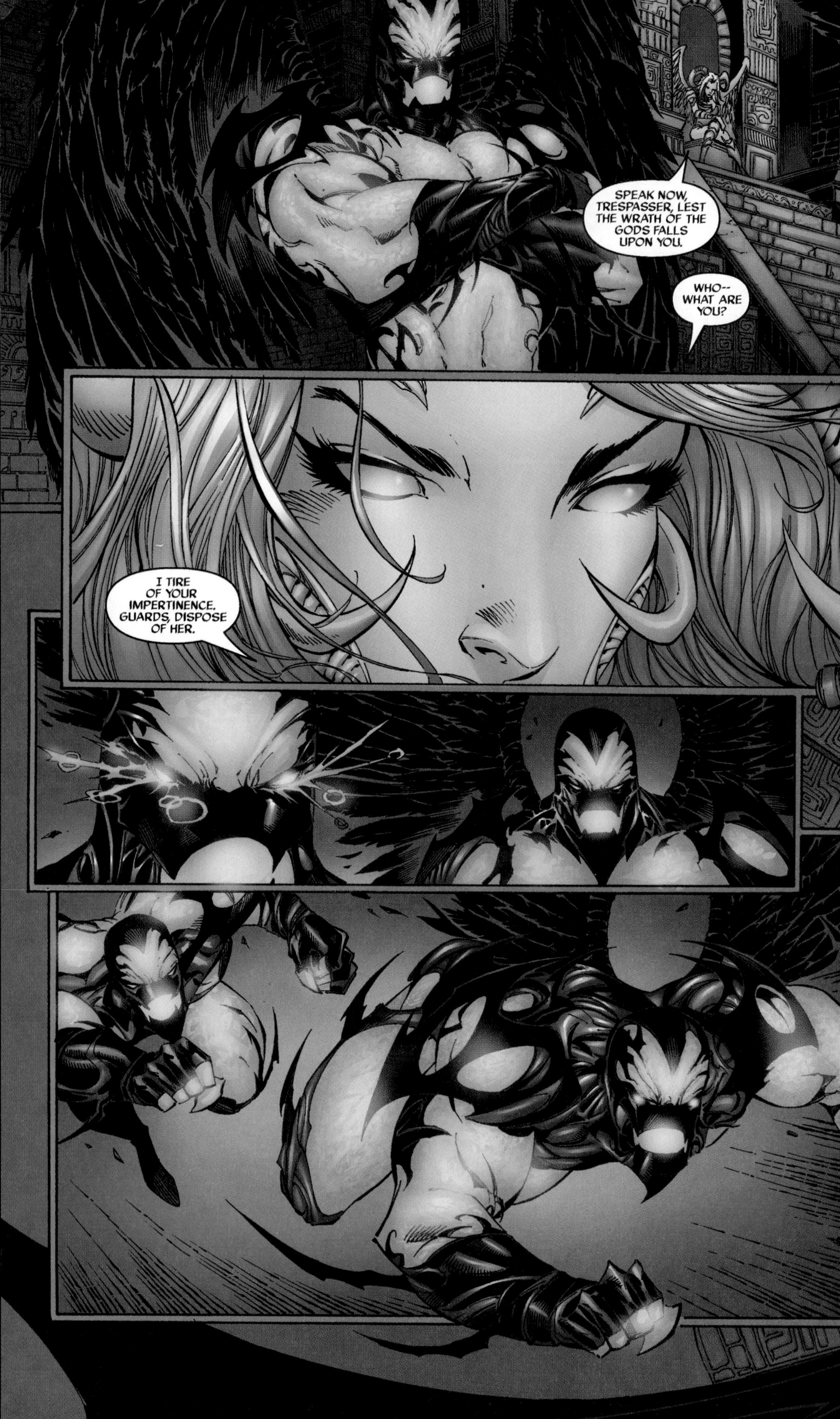
SPEAK NOW, TRESPASSER, LEST THE WRATH OF THE GODS FALLS UPON YOU.
WHO-- WHAT ARE YOU?
I TIRE OF YOUR IMPERTINENCE. GUARDS, DISPOSE OF HER.

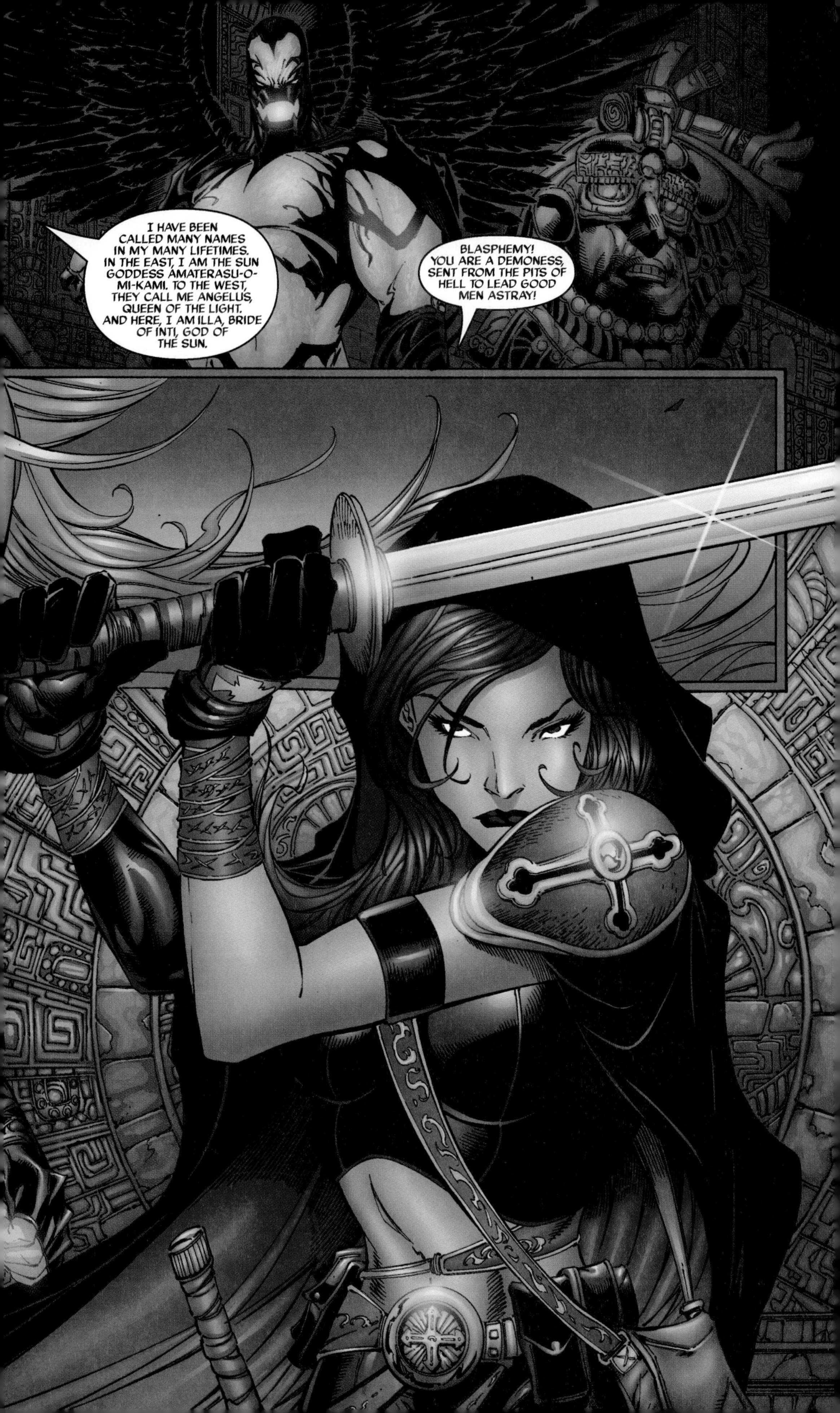
I HAVE BEEN CALLED MANY NAMES IN MY MANY LIFETIMES. IN THE EAST, I AM THE SUN GODDESS AMATERASU-O-MI-KAMI. TO THE WEST, THEY CALL ME ANGELUS, QUEEN OF THE LIGHT. AND HERE, I AM ILLA, BRIDE OF INTI, GOD OF THE SUN.
BLASPHEMY! YOU ARE A DEMONESS, SENT FROM THE PITS OF HELL TO LEAD GOOD MEN ASTRAY!

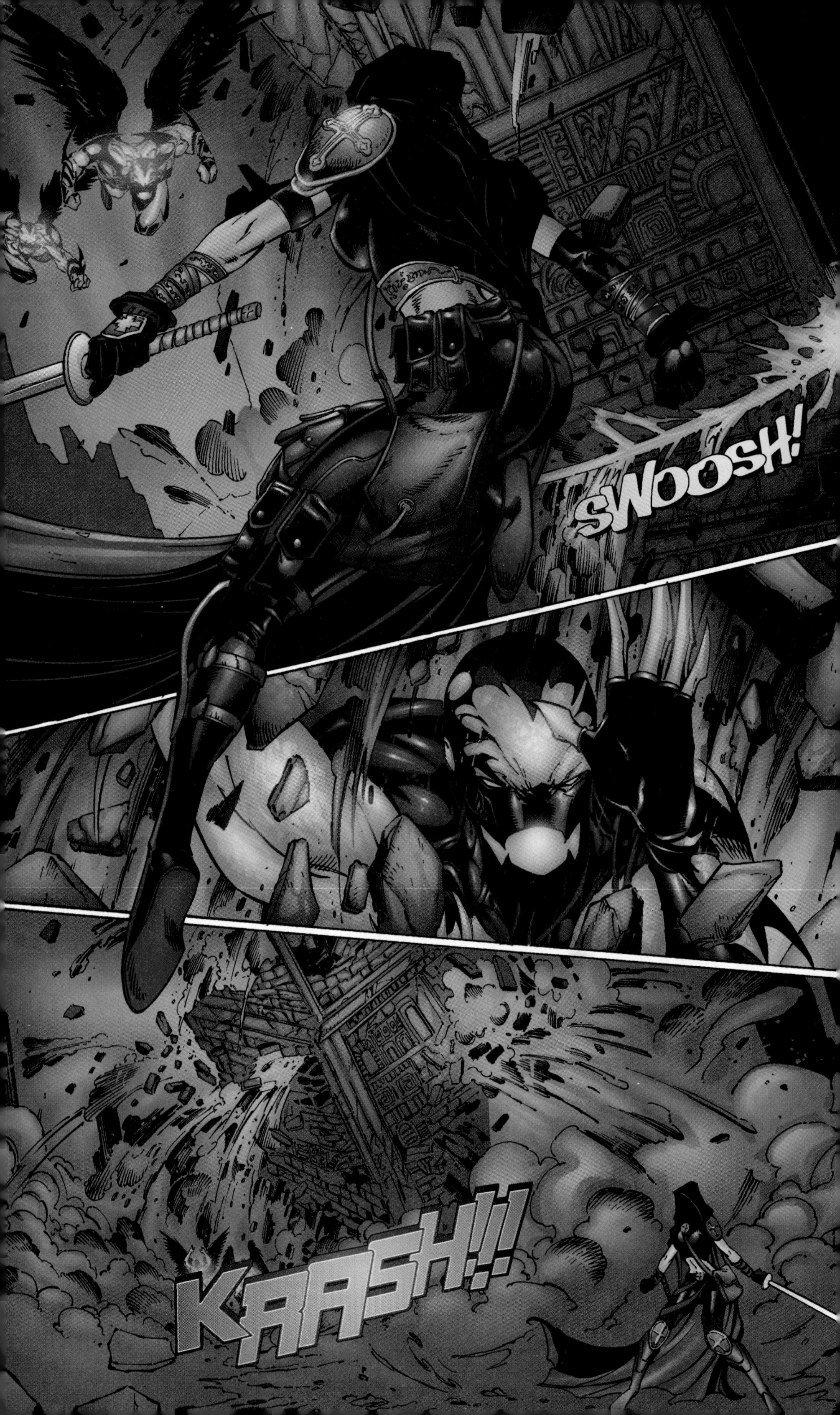

SWOOSH!
KRASH!!!

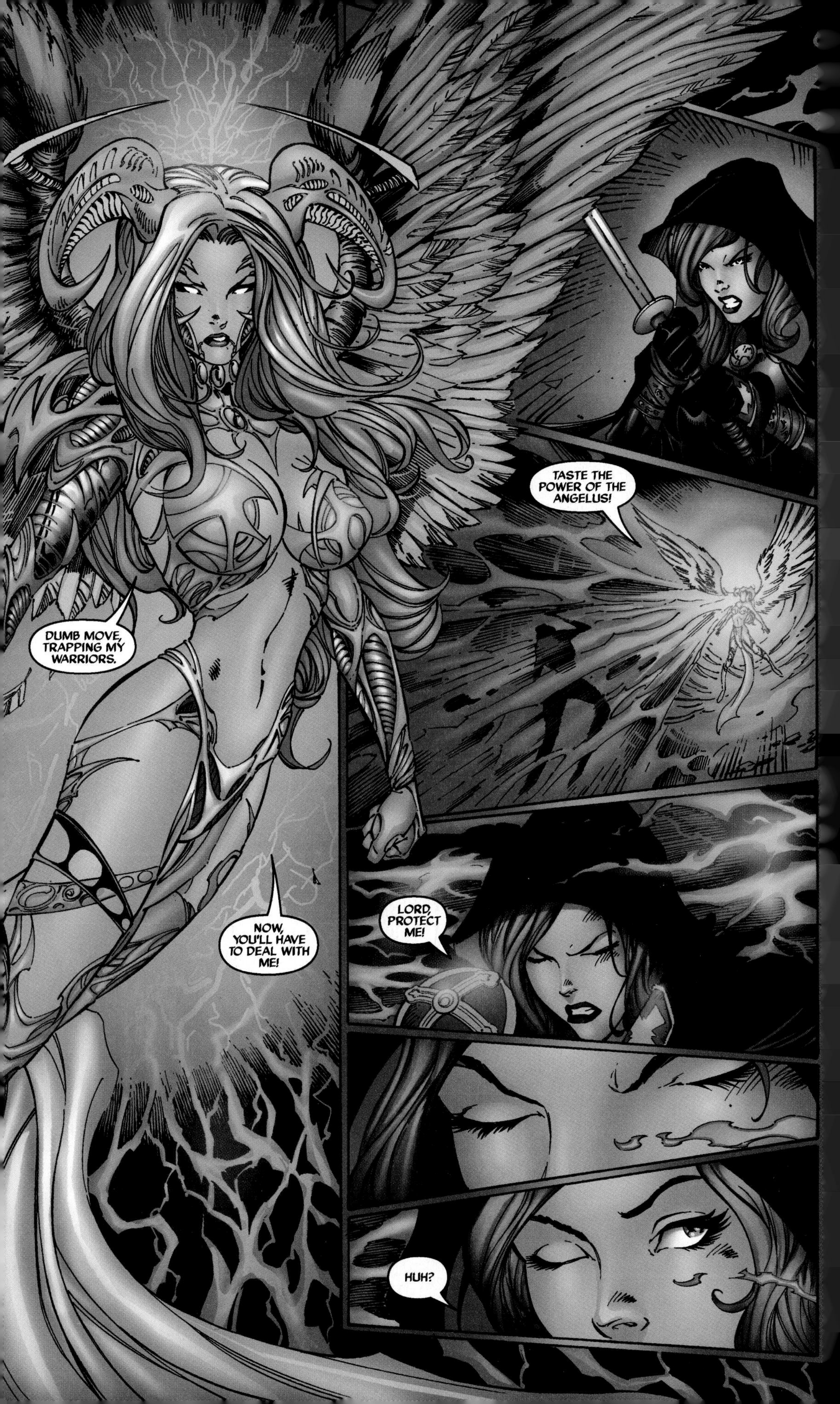
DUMB MOVE, TRAPPING MY WARRIORS.
NOW, YOU'LL HAVE TO DEAL WITH ME!
TASTE THE POWER OF THE ANGELUS!
LORD, PROTECT ME!
HUH?

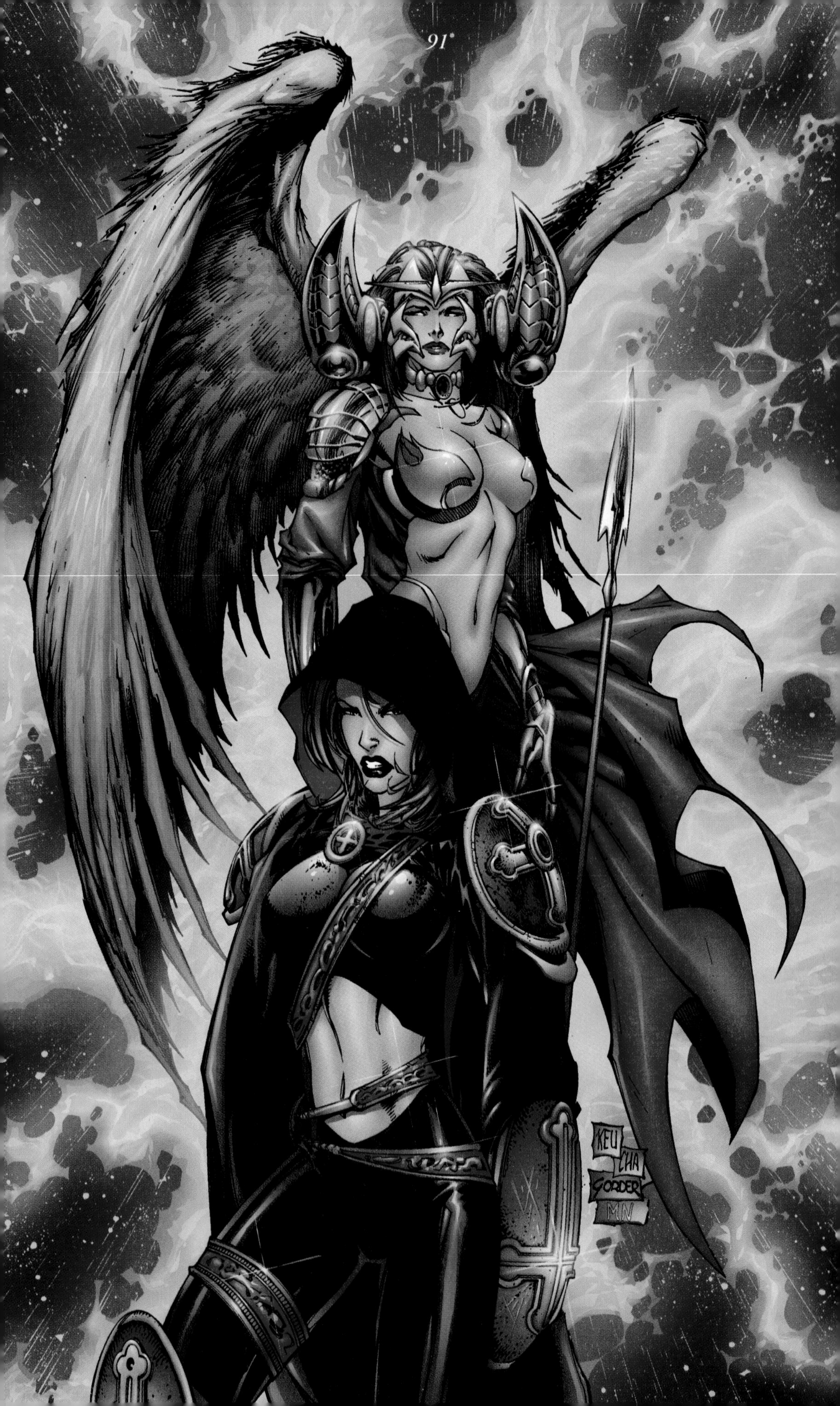
KEU
CHA
GORDER
MN

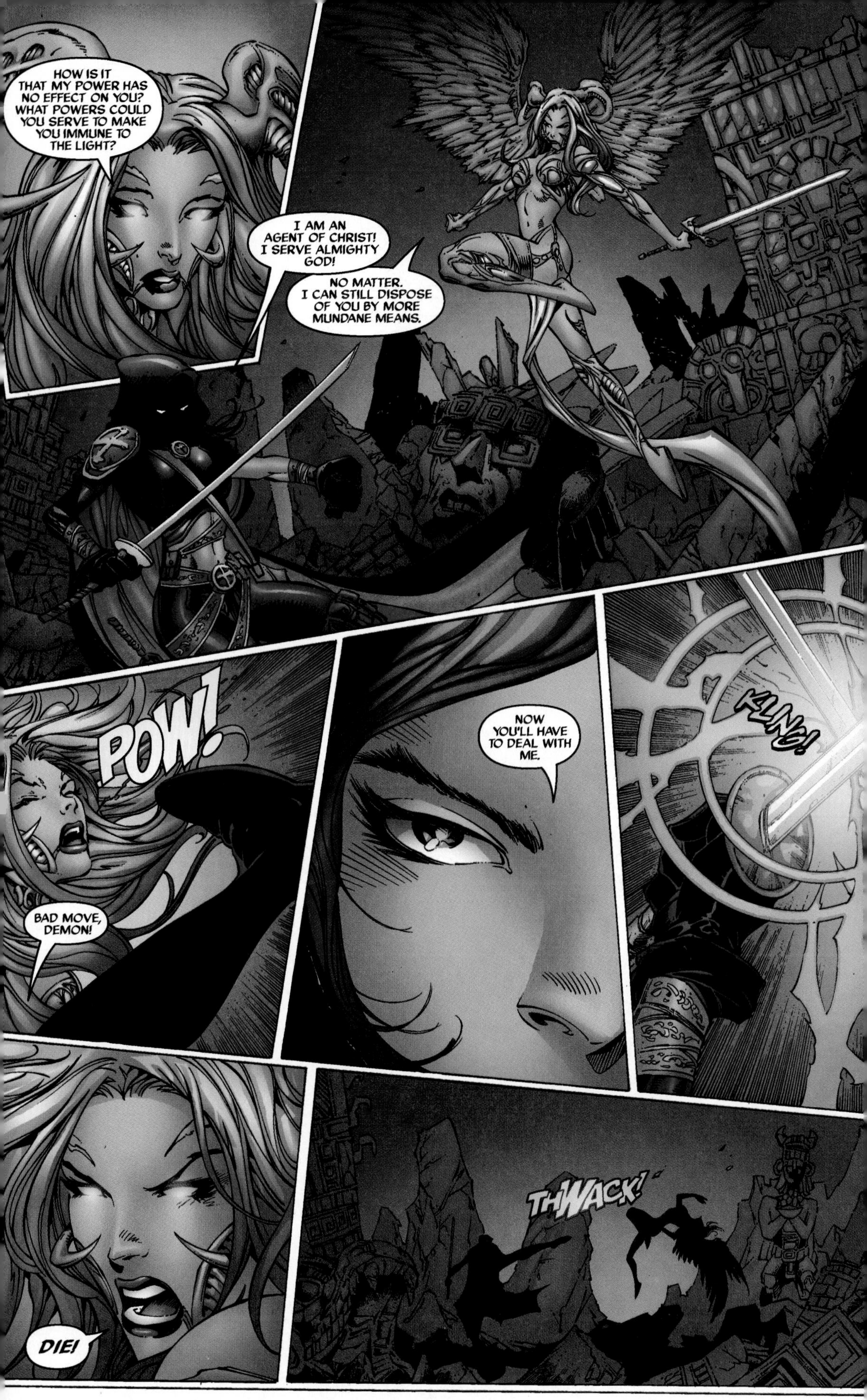
HOW IS IT THAT MY POWER HAS NO EFFECT ON YOU? WHAT POWERS COULD YOU SERVE TO MAKE YOU IMMUNE TO THE LIGHT?
I AM AN AGENT OF CHRIST! I SERVE ALMIGHTY GOD!
NO MATTER. I CAN STILL DISPOSE OF YOU BY MORE MUNDANE MEANS.
POW!
BAD MOVE, DEMON!
NOW YOU'LL HAVE TO DEAL WITH ME.
KLING!
DIE!
THWACK!

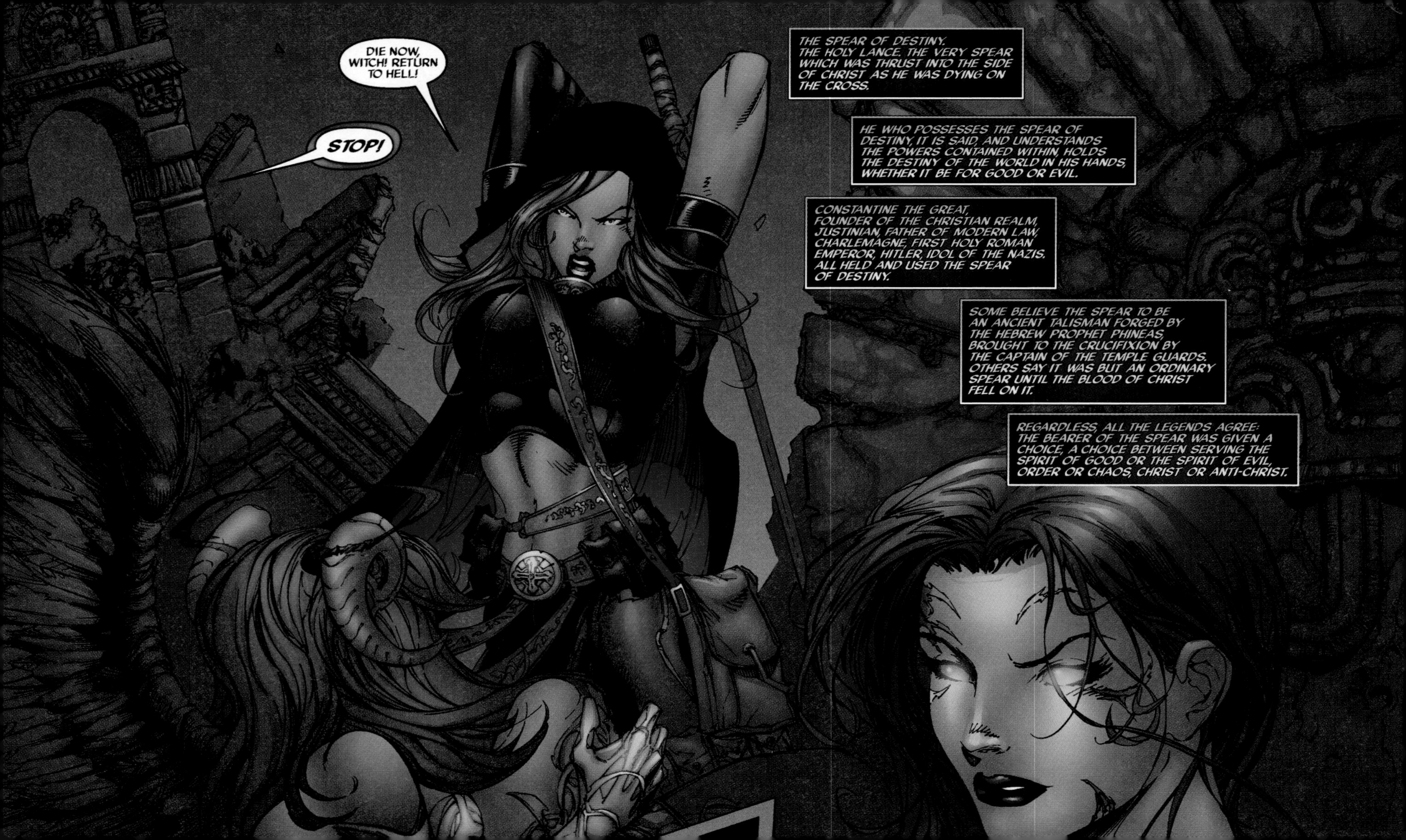
DIE NOW, WITCH! RETURN TO HELL!
STOP!
THE SPEAR OF DESTINY. THE HOLY LANCE. THE VERY SPEAR WHICH WAS THRUST INTO THE SIDE OF CHRIST AS HE WAS DYING ON THE CROSS.
HE WHO POSSESSES THE SPEAR OF DESTINY, IT IS SAID, AND UNDERSTANDS THE POWERS CONTAINED WITHIN, HOLDS THE DESTINY OF THE WORLD IN HIS HANDS, WHETHER IT BE FOR GOOD OR EVIL.
CONSTANTINE THE GREAT, FOUNDER OF THE CHRISTIAN REALM, JUSTINIAN, FATHER OF MODERN LAW, CHARLEMAGNE, FIRST HOLY ROMAN EMPEROR, HITLER, IDOL OF THE NAZIS. ALL HELD AND USED THE SPEAR OF DESTINY.
SOME BELIEVE THE SPEAR TO BE AN ANCIENT TALISMAN FORGED BY THE HEBREW PROPHET PHINEAS, BROUGHT TO THE CRUCIFIXION BY THE CAPTAIN OF THE TEMPLE GUARDS. OTHERS SAY IT WAS BUT AN ORDINARY SPEAR UNTIL THE BLOOD OF CHRIST FELL ON IT.
REGARDLESS, ALL THE LEGENDS AGREE: THE BEARER OF THE SPEAR WAS GIVEN A CHOICE, A CHOICE BETWEEN SERVING THE SPIRIT OF GOOD OR THE SPIRIT OF EVIL, ORDER OR CHAOS, CHRIST OR ANTI-CHRIST.

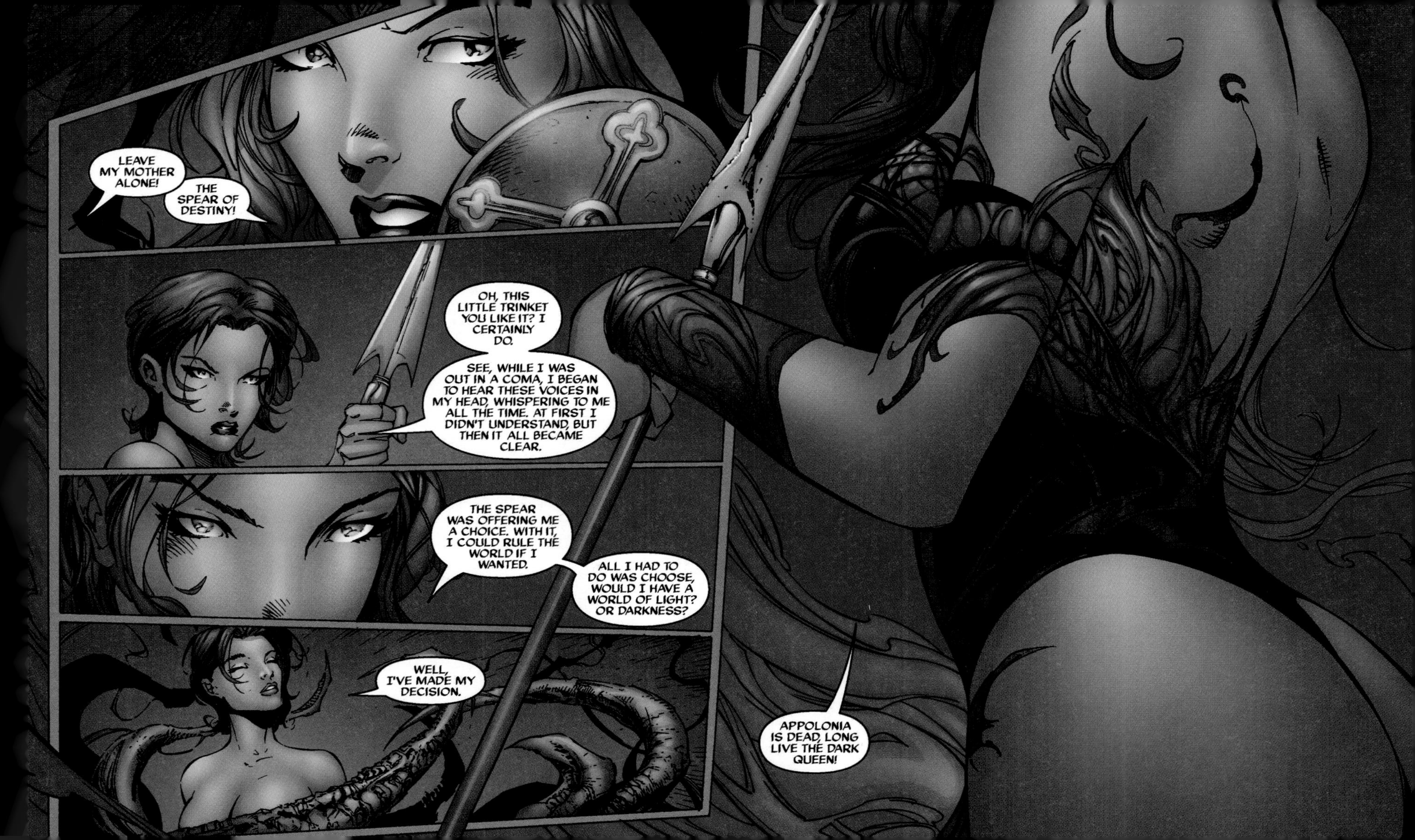
LEAVE MY MOTHER ALONE!
THE SPEAR OF DESTINY!
OH, THIS LITTLE TRINKET YOU LIKE IT? I CERTAINLY DO.
SEE, WHILE I WAS OUT IN A COMA, I BEGAN TO HEAR THESE VOICES IN MY HEAD, WHISPERING TO ME ALL THE TIME. AT FIRST I DIDN'T UNDERSTAND, BUT THEN IT ALL BECAME CLEAR.
THE SPEAR WAS OFFERING ME A CHOICE. WITH IT, I COULD RULE THE WORLD IF I WANTED.
ALL I HAD TO DO WAS CHOOSE, WOULD I HAVE A WORLD OF LIGHT? OR DARKNESS?
WELL, I'VE MADE MY DECISION.
APPOLONIA IS DEAD, LONG LIVE THE DARK QUEEN!

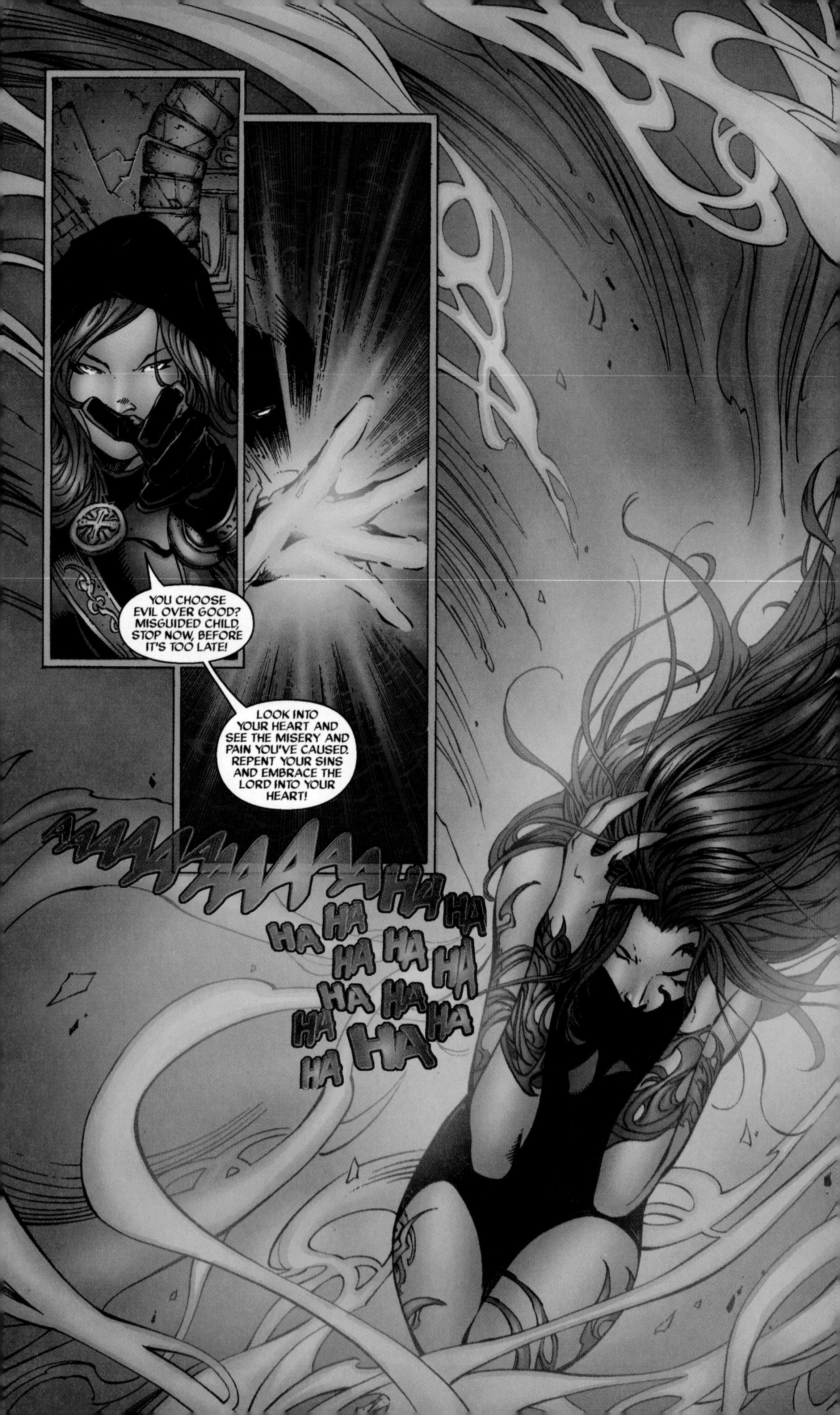
YOU CHOOSE EVIL OVER GOOD? MISGUIDED CHILD, STOP NOW, BEFORE IT'S TOO LATE!
LOOK INTO YOUR HEART AND SEE THE MISERY AND PAIN YOU'VE CAUSED. REPENT YOUR SINS AND EMBRACE THE LORD INTO YOUR HEART!
AAAAAAAAAAAAAAAAHA HA HA HA HA HA HA HA HA HA HA HA HA HA HA

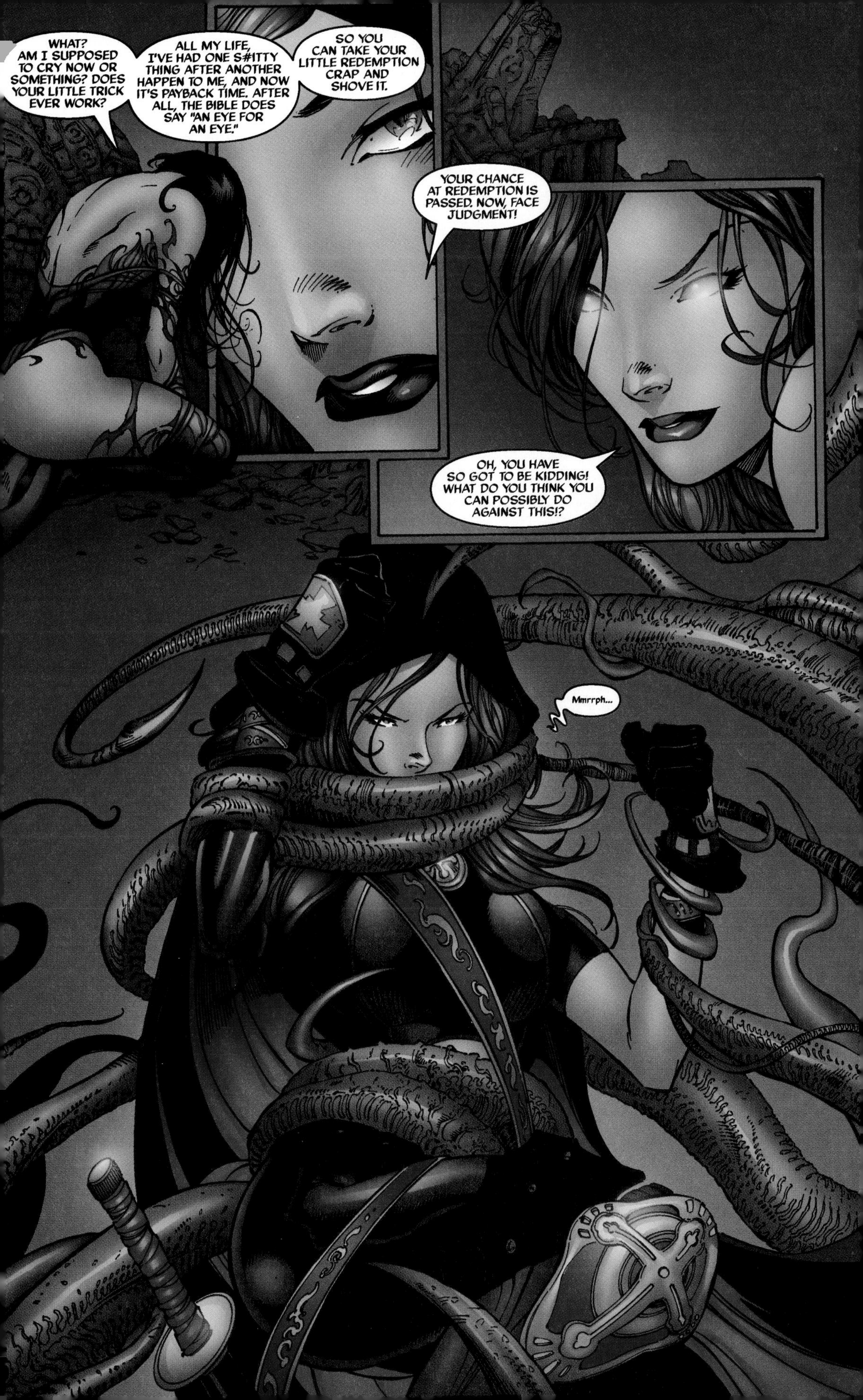
WHAT? AM I SUPPOSED TO CRY NOW OR SOMETHING? DOES YOUR LITTLE TRICK EVER WORK?
ALL MY LIFE, I'VE HAD ONE S#ITTY THING AFTER ANOTHER HAPPEN TO ME, AND NOW IT'S PAYBACK TIME. AFTER ALL, THE BIBLE DOES SAY "AN EYE FOR AN EYE."
SO YOU CAN TAKE YOUR LITTLE REDEMPTION CRAP AND SHOVE IT.
YOUR CHANCE AT REDEMPTION IS PASSED. NOW, FACE JUDGMENT!
OH, YOU HAVE SO GOT TO BE KIDDING! WHAT DO YOU THINK YOU CAN POSSIBLY DO AGAINST THIS!?
Mmrrph...

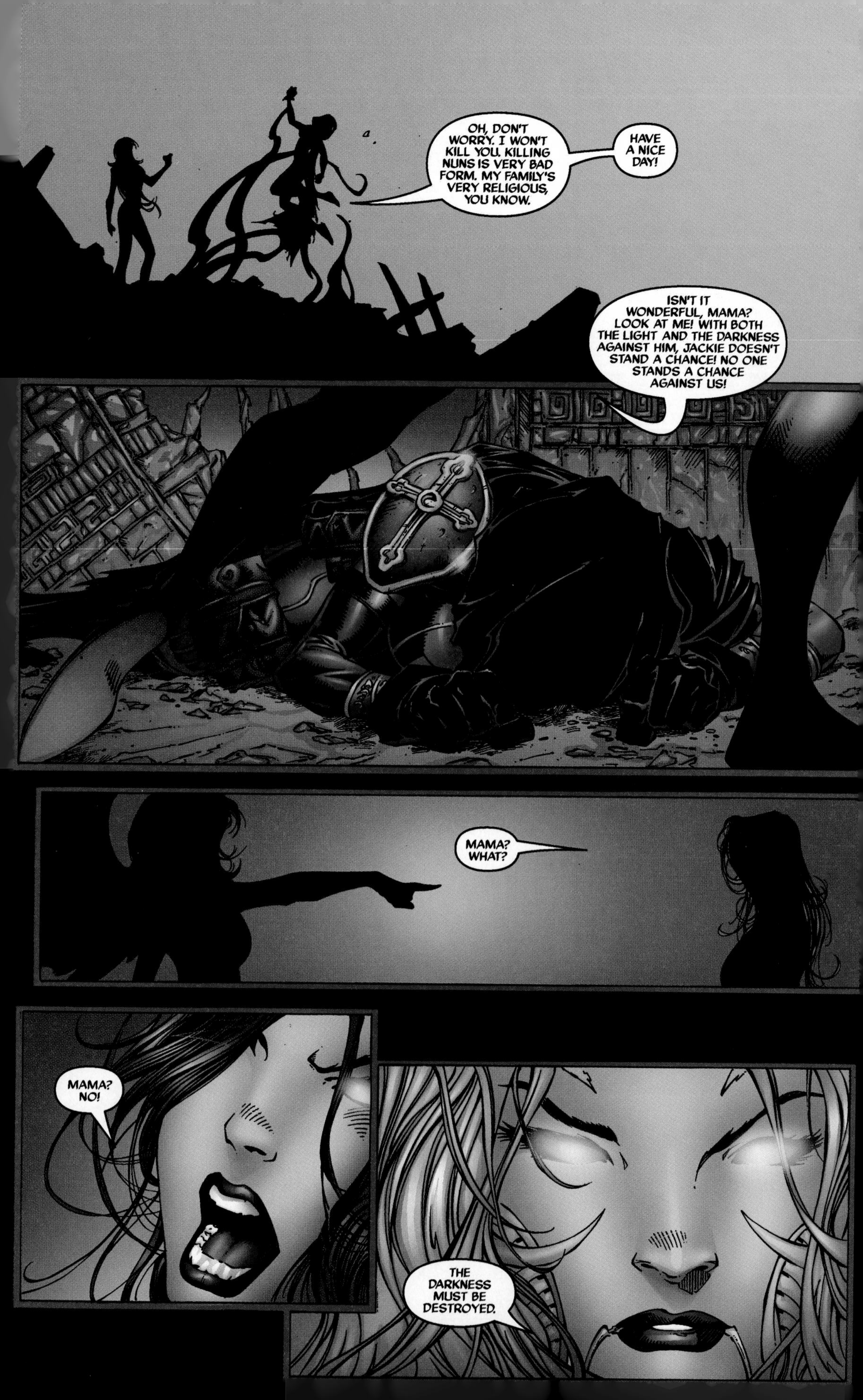
OH, DON'T WORRY. I WON'T KILL YOU. KILLING NUNS IS VERY BAD FORM. MY FAMILY'S VERY RELIGIOUS, YOU KNOW.
HAVE A NICE DAY!
ISN'T IT WONDERFUL, MAMA? LOOK AT ME! WITH BOTH THE LIGHT AND THE DARKNESS AGAINST HIM, JACKIE DOESN'T STAND A CHANCE! NO ONE STANDS A CHANCE AGAINST US!
MAMA? WHAT?
MAMA? NO!
THE DARKNESS MUST BE DESTROYED.

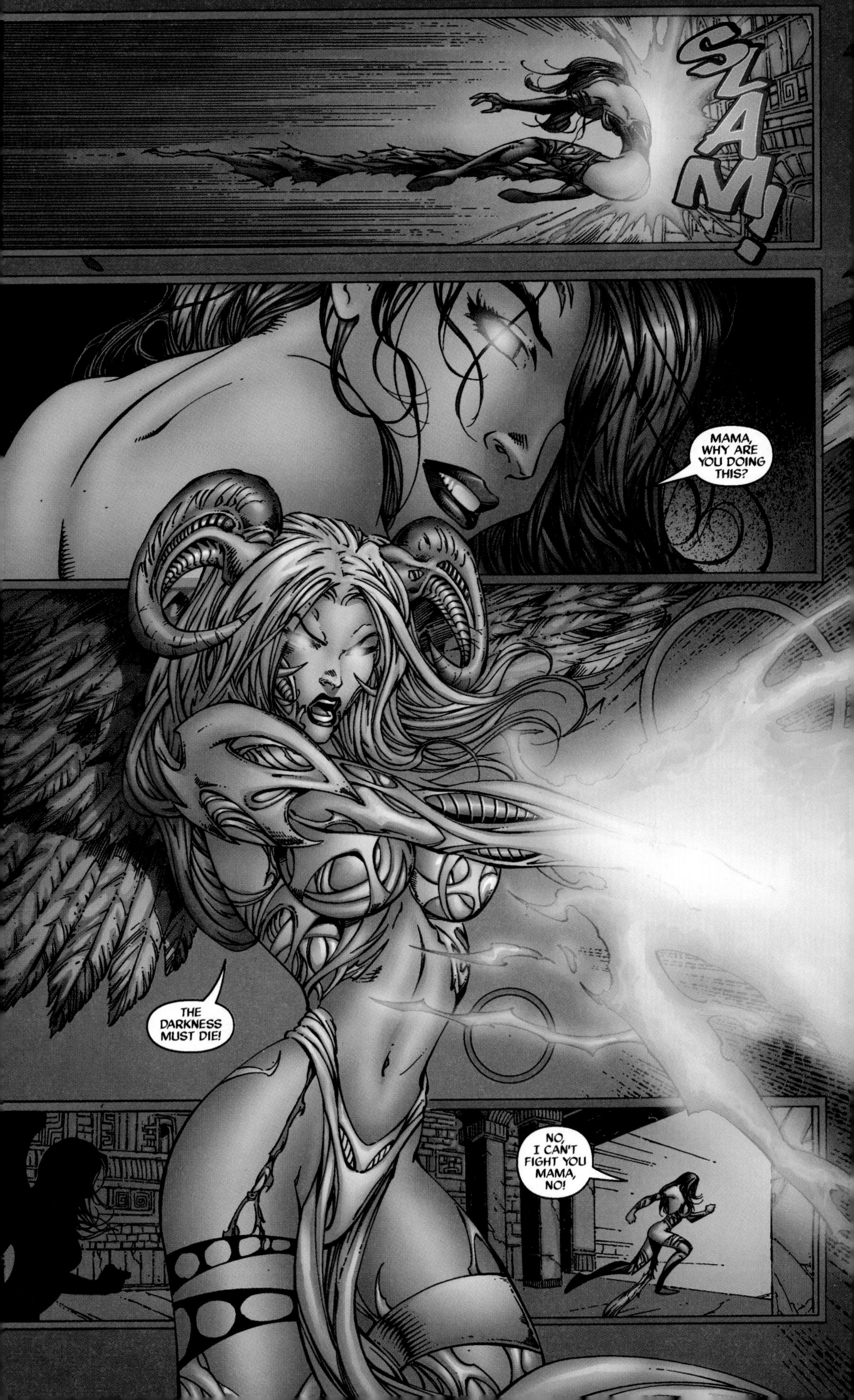
SLAM!
MAMA, WHY ARE YOU DOING THIS?
THE DARKNESS MUST DIE!
NO, I CAN'T FIGHT YOU MAMA, NO!

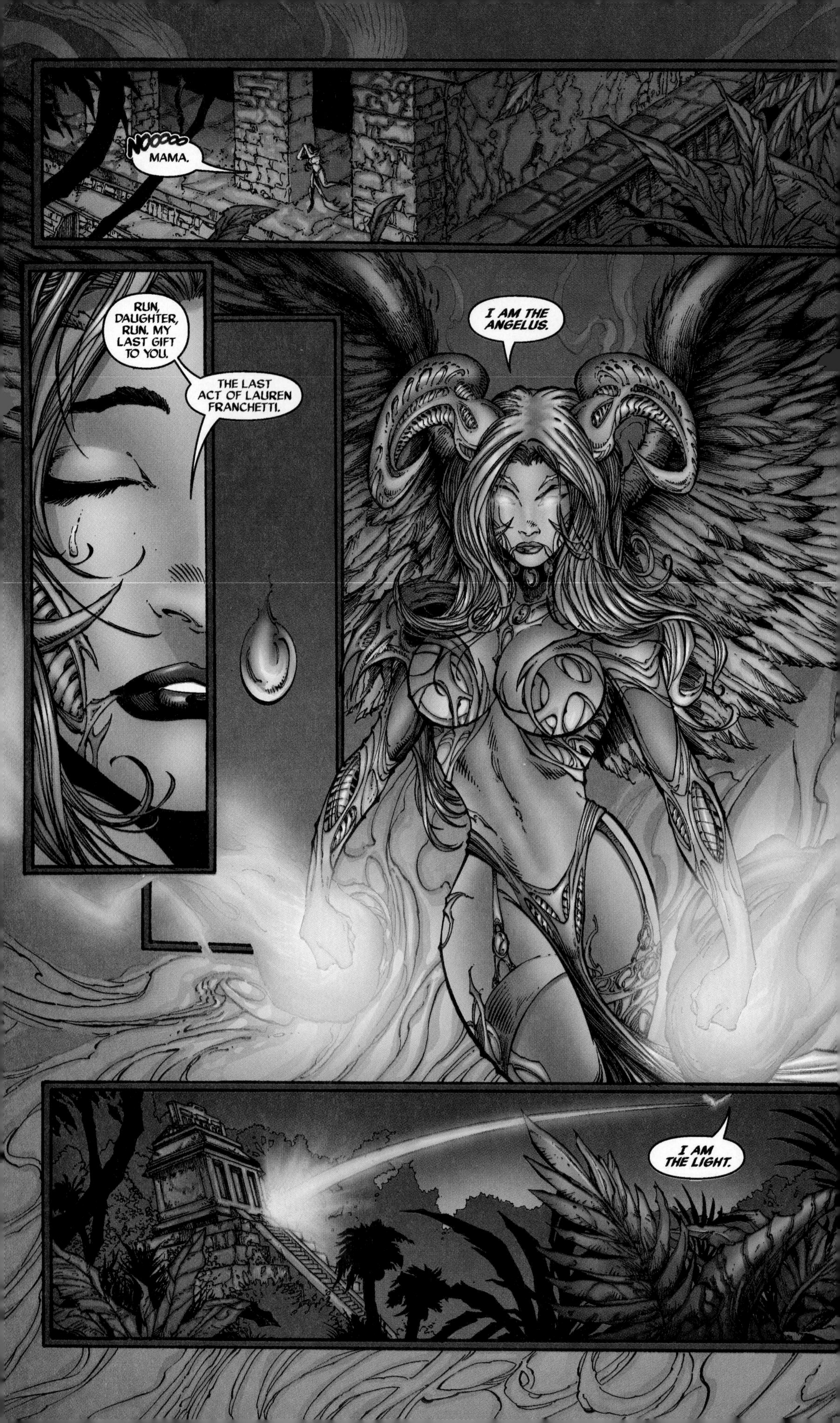
NOOOOO
MAMA.
RUN, DAUGHTER, RUN. MY LAST GIFT TO YOU.
THE LAST ACT OF LAUREN FRANCHETTI.
I AM THE ANGELUS.
I AM THE LIGHT.

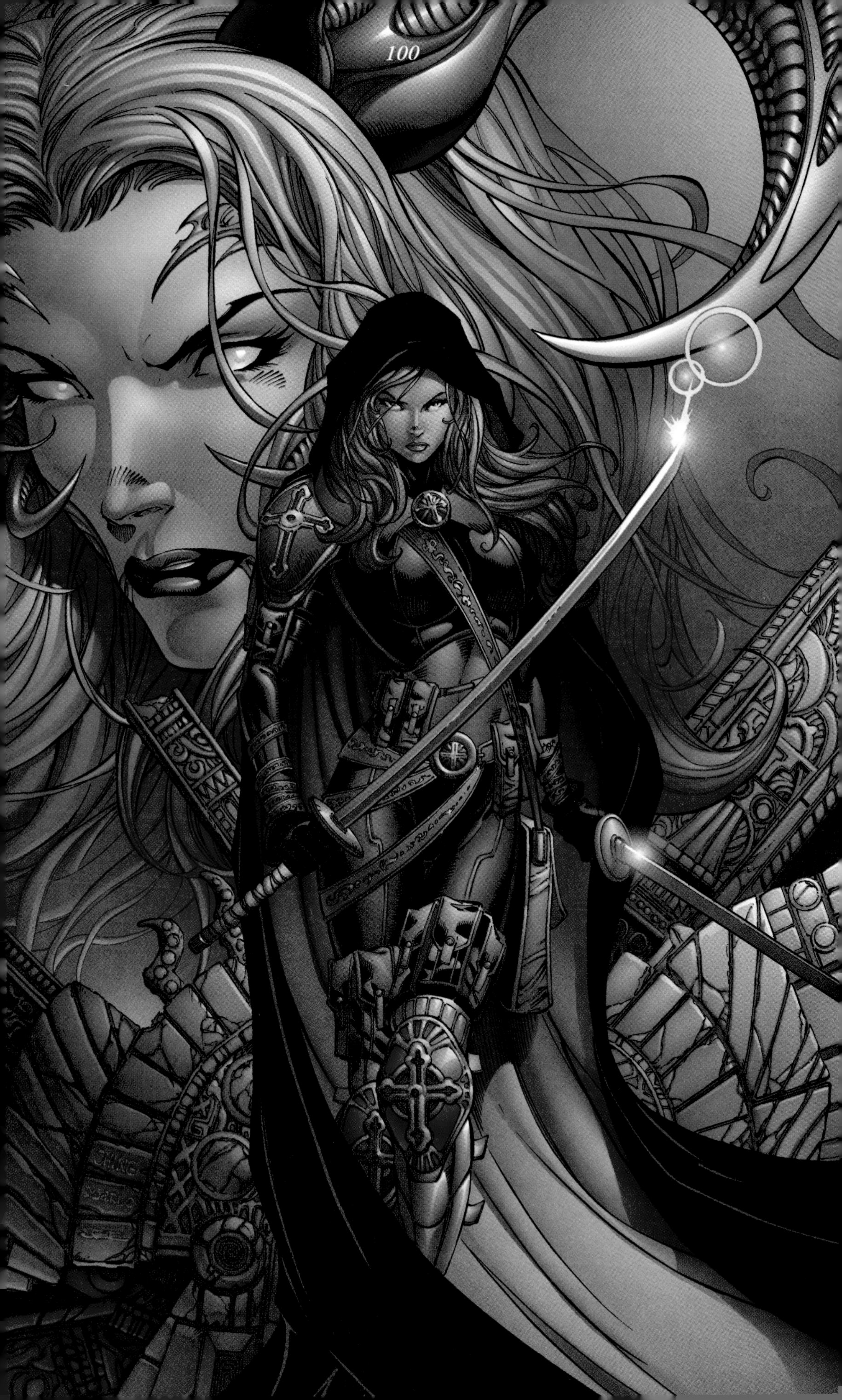

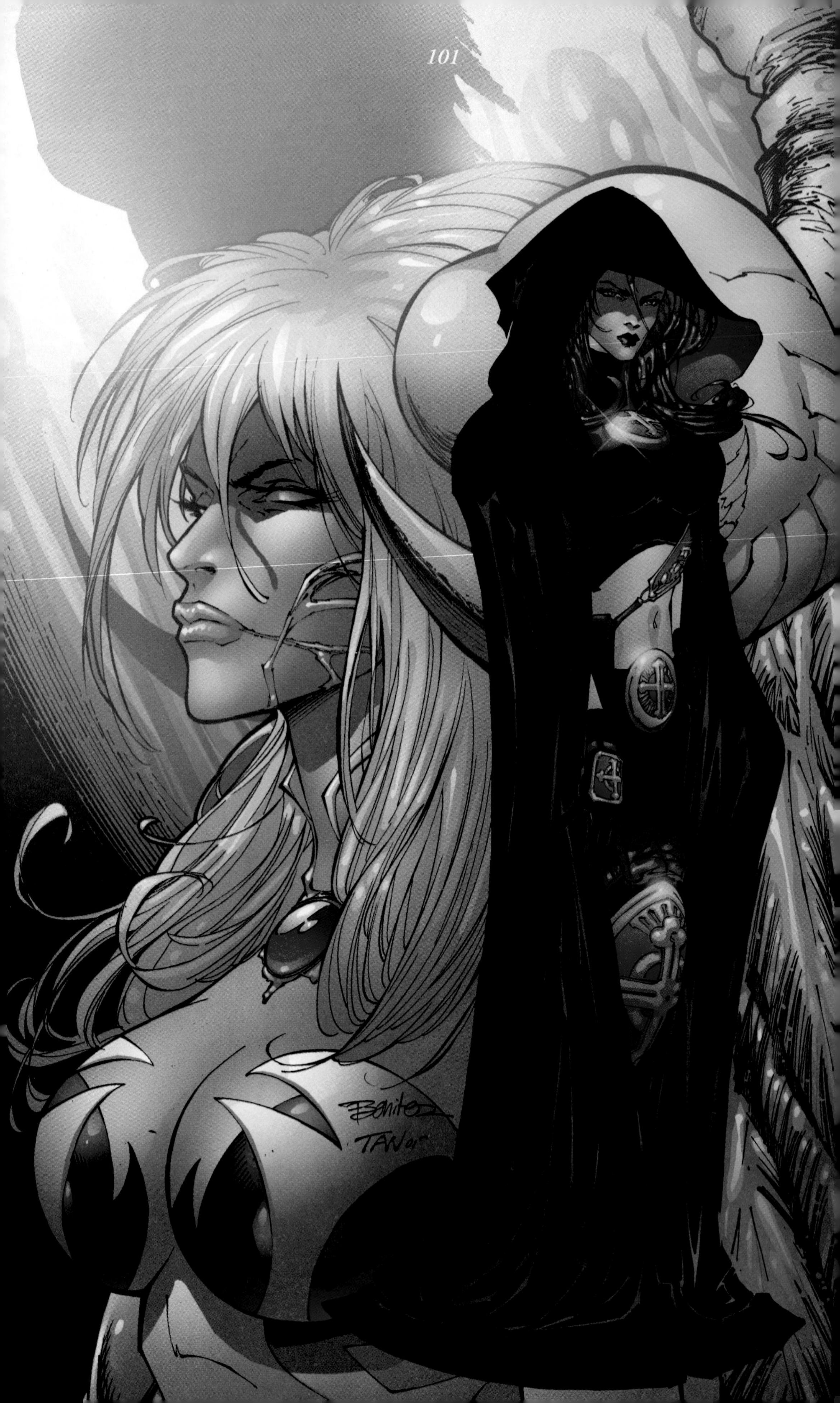

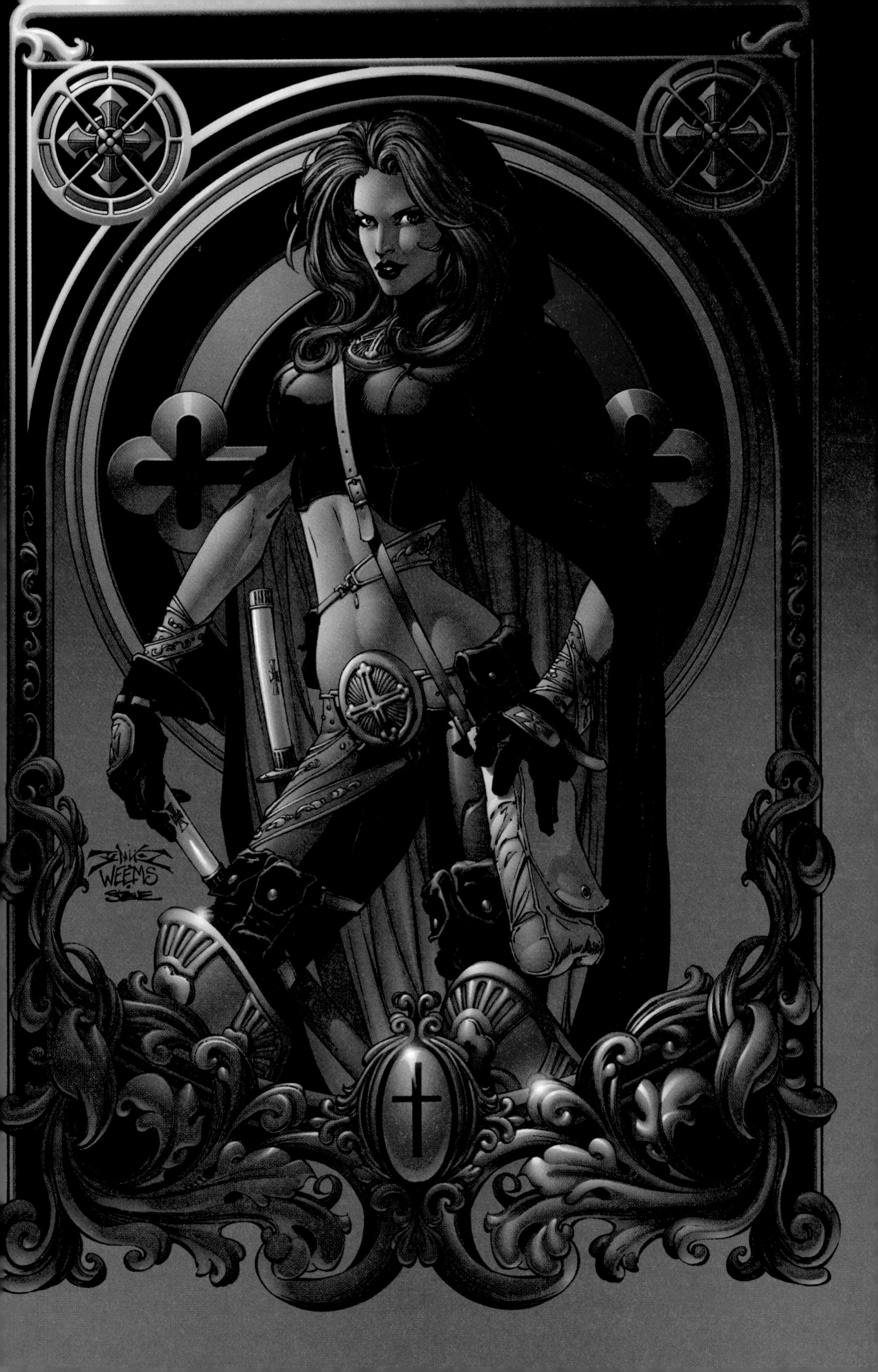
WEEMS

By a stroke of luck, a friend of a friend of a friend helped get me my first job in comics, working the trenches as an assistant inker at Top Cow. Many years and tears later (including co-writing some Darkness issues and finishing up the Ascension storyline), I'm writing my own book! Pretty cool, huh? I'm still a fangirl and continue haunting my local comic book shop every Wednesday, eagerly awaiting my weekly fix (I'm sure you know what I mean). My faves right now are Witching Hour and Crimson, but my favorite character will always be Catwoman, the old animated version, and of course Michelle Pfeiffer in Batman Returns. Nothing says "Mreow!" like shiny black vinyl!

ABOUT THE PENCILER (of Chapters 1-3)—Joe Benitez

Joe Benitez was born at an undisclosed location on May 21, 1971. He grew up in East Los Angeles and spends his free time collecting action figures [Translation: dressing up his G.I. Joe's and other dollies]. He was discovered at the San Diego con by Marc Silvestri in 1993 and has been at Top Cow since. His first ever published work was a 3 page Weapon Zero story. Cyblade Origins and Strykeforce 8 followed before he helped with the creation of Weapon Zero which he drew for it's entire run (T-4 thru issue 15). After the the Weapon Zero finale Joe moved onto The Darkness before passing the mantle to Clarence Lansang after issue 25. While on The Darkness, Joe developed the Magdalena character with Malachy Coney. The Magdalena character's popularity and Joe's passion for it has spawned this book. Joe is currently working on new projects at his home in Los Angeles. He drops by Top Cow once and a while to remind us he's better than we are.

ABOUT THE INKER (of Chapters 1-3)—Joe Weems V

Born at the Singing River Hospital in 1973, Joe Weems has always had a love for art. Originally wanting to become a penciler, he took his art to the world of comics. Although, penciling was his first choice, he soon learned that his inking talent was winning him accolades and praise. His first professional work was on a XXX book named Black Pearl #2 for Eros Comics. With some experience now behind him, he took his samples to the San Diego International Comic Con where he impressed the people over at Harris Comics who offered him the inking duties on Vengeance of Vampirella #2. Other Harris titles soon followed including Chains of Chaos and The Rook. While gaining this experience, he met Marc Silvestri and Brian Haberlin and was offered a job at Top Cow on his first book Ripclaw #1/2. Since then he has inked over many of Top Cow's premiere artists including Keu Cha, Marc Silvestri, Joe Benitez, and Michael Turner. The last of which he has inked for on the best selling comic book series of 1998, Fathom. And now re-united with Joe Benitez, The Magdalena.

ABOUT THE COLORIST (of Chapter 1)—Tyson Wengler

Mr. Tyson Wengler was born on the 4th day of the 11th month in the year 1972. When not coloring such hit books as Creech and Magdalena, Tyson fills his time with numerous side projects and as many forms of recreation as he can put his body through. He currently lives in Nevada close to the desert and mountains where he spends much time on bike, foot or board. Enjoying everything.

ABOUT THE COLORIST (of Chapter 2 & 3)—Jonathan D. Smith

Jonathan D. Smith began his comic career in 1993 with the release of a fully painted graphic novel from Dark Horse Comics entitled Universal Monsters: Dracula.

After that auspicious beginning he did cover work on various projects for Malibu and Now Comics. In late 1994 he landed on Top Cow's doorstep and began working there doing color guides for books such as Cyblade, Weapon Zero, Cyberforce and Codename: Strykeforce.

Soon in 1995 he was introduced to the computer by Brian Haberlin and began his career as a digital colorist for titles such as the Ballistic mini-series, Killrazor, Medieval Spawn-Witchblade and an assortment of other titles including Witchblade.

Currently, he is coloring Universe, Tomb Raider and Tomb Raider Journeys for Top Cow.

ABOUT THE LETTERERS—Dreamer Design's Robin Spehar & Dennis Heisler

Robin Spehar, Dreamer Design's Creative Director, started lettering comic books in College because he was tired of spinning pizzas. He spent a few years hand lettering Vampirella and CyberFrog for Harris Comics all night and studying theater all day at the University of California, Irvine. After graduating, Robin toured Europe, performed at the Edinburgh Festival, and got some much needed sleep.

Robin began his journey into the digital realm under the wing of Dennis Heisler, Dreamer's senior letterer. After years of defending his computerless existence, Robin finally broke down and purchased his first Macintosh Computer. He began creating fonts and digital tools at an alarming rate. Now he works day and night, creating beautiful designs, stupendous lettering and keeping his vast library of digital tools sharpened and oiled.

Robin was recently awarded the prestigious TDC2 2002 Certificate of Excellence in Type Design from the Type Director's Club.

Dennis Heisler, Dreamer Design's Senior Letterer, has been lettering comic books since Cyberforce #3 in 1994 with Top Cow Productions. He has been steadily lettering comic books since then. His lettering credits include nearly all of Top Cow's books since that fateful issue as well as: Shi, Tomoe, The Maxx, Stone, Aria. And this was all before he joined Dreamer Design in 2000!

Dennis now lives in Northern Idaho with his wife, Sharene, his daughters Shinnn and Zoe, and his faith-

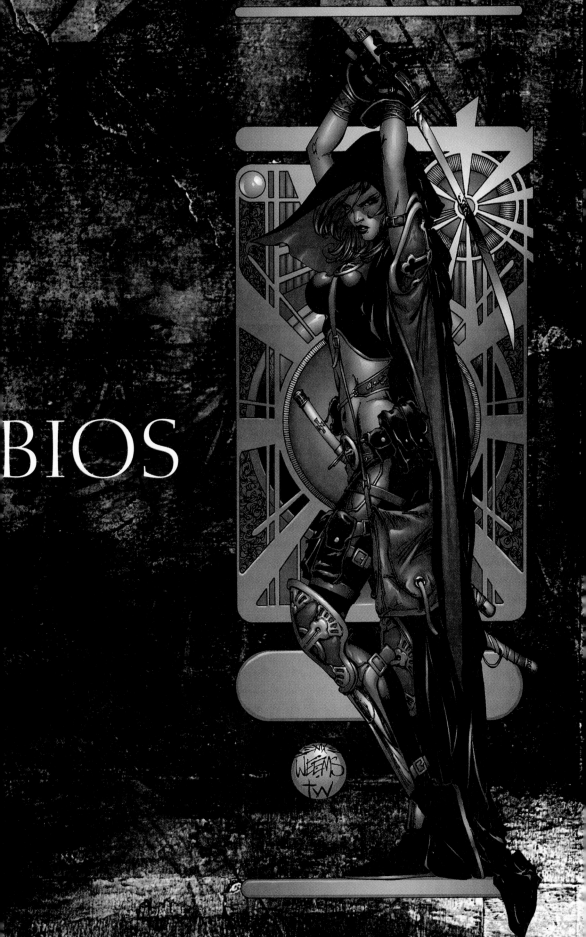

BIOS

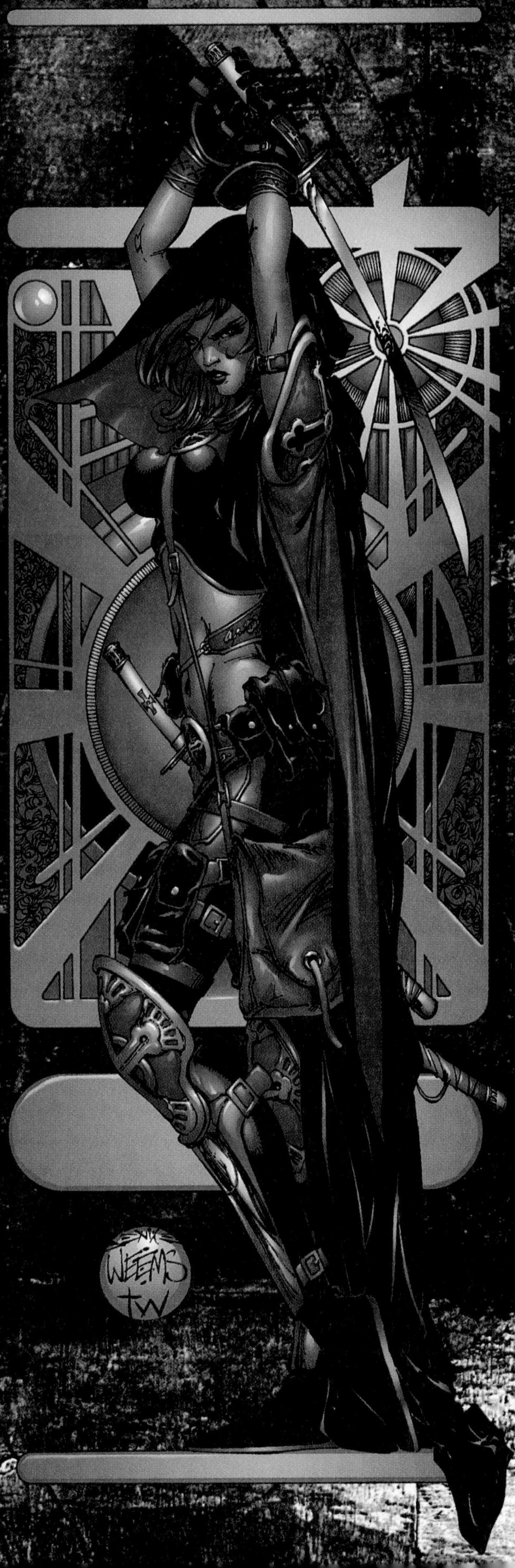